Couples in Treatment, Second Edition

COUPLES IN TREATMENT

Techniques and Approaches for Effective Practice

Second Edition

Gerald R. Weeks
Stephen R. Treat

BRUNNER-ROUTLEDGE
ALERE FLAMMAM
Taylor & Francis Group

Published by
Brunner-Routledge
29 West 35th Street
New York, NY 10001

Published in Great Britain
Brunner-Routledge
11 New Fetter Lane
London EC4P 4EE

Brunner-Routledge is an imprint of the Taylor & Francis Group

Brunner-Routledge

Couples in Treatment, 2e: Techniques and Approaches for Effective Practice

5   6   7   8   9   0

Printed by Edwards Brothers, Ann Arbor, MI, 2001.
Cover design by Ellen Seguin.

A CIP catalog record for this book is available from the British Library.
∞ The paper in this publication meets the requirements of the ANSI Standard Z39.48-1984 (Permanence of Paper).

Library of Congress Cataloging-in-Publication Data
Weeks, Gerald R., 1948–
    Couples in treatment : techniques and approaches for effective practice / Gerald R. Weeks, Stephen Treat.
        p. cm
    Includes bibliographical references and index.
    ISBN 1-58391–038–7 (alk. paper)
    1. Marital psychotherapy. I. Treat, Stephen, 1951 - II. Title.
RC488.5 . W44 2001
616.89'156--dc21   00-049805

ISBN 1-58391-038-7 (case)

Additional titles by Gerald Weeks available from Brunner-Routledge:

Paradoxical Psychotherapy (with Luciano L'Abate, Ph.D.)
Integrating Sex and Marital Therapy (with Larry Hof, M.Div.)
Treating Couples
Promoting Change Through Paradoxial Therapy
Marital-Relationship Therapy Casebook (with Larry Hof, M. Div.)
Integrative Solutions (with Larry Hof, M. Div.)

Dedicated to

KATHY WEEKS
and
ELIZABETH TREAT

to whom we are committed
in marriage with all of its
problems, promises, and pleasures

CONTENTS

PART II:
BASIC APPROACHES AND TECHNIQUES

ACKNOWLEDGMENTS

In the early 1980s, Mr. Bernie Mazel, then President of Brunner/Mazel Publishers, asked if we would be interested in writing a book on couples therapy. He was familiar with the fact that we had been teaching one of only a few year-long courses in couples therapy, which was widely acclaimed.

Inspired by Mr. Mazel's suggestion, we later wrote *Couples in Treatment: Techniques and Approaches for Effective Practice*. Writing this volume has led us to appreciate how much our students have taught us about what is usable, and often used, by the beginning therapist. We not only teach, but also supervise students, and it is they who have helped us recognize what the beginning couples therapist needs to learn in the long trek to becoming an effective therapist.

We want to thank several colleagues for their careful editing, helpful suggestions, and constant support for the original edition and this revised edition. Joellyn Ross, Rick Mack, Bea Hollander, Shirley Jacoby, Larry Hof, Dawn Reilly, Laura Tsang, and Jack Choi were always there when we needed them. Dr. Frank Dattilio was helpful in updating the chapter on cognitive therapy with couples and Dr. Nancy Gambescia helped in developing the chapter on the treatment of extramarital affairs. The senior author would also like to thank Dean Martha Watson for her support in this project.

Finally, Sherrie Buchanan did much of the retyping, organizational work, and editing in putting together this revised edition. We appreciate her good humor and wish her good health.

PREFACE

When this book was released in first edition in 1992, we did not anticipate that it would become so widely used and positively reviewed in professional journals. In spite of our intent to write a book for the professional, we found the book was being adopted as a text in many marriage and family therapy courses. The reason we think it was so widely adopted was because we tried to avoid the use of jargon and to present clinically useful and effective techniques in a simple and straightforward way.

The purpose of this second volume is still to present the basic techniques, methods, and strategies needed by the couples therapist. In a previous volume, Weeks (1989, 1994) presented his theoretical approach to couples therapy and provided an overview of the structure and process of treatment. This text takes the next step, that of providing the "how to." In this book only enough theory is given to make sense of the techniques that follow. The current revision will be familiar to those who used the first edition. We have maintained the same basic structure and content and updated the text where appropriate. Some chapters required little updating, as the last decade did not produce much new literature. Other chapters required significant updating of material to reflect the newer literature. We have also added two additional chapters, on treating the narcissistically wounded couple and treating extramarital affairs.

The authors of this book both have extensive teaching, supervisory, and clinical experience in working with couples. This experience has taught us the need to provide clinicians with skills that have broad applicability and can be readily used. The skills described in this book are simple, straightforward, and foundational for couples work. Advanced skills, unorthodox techniques, and techniques with limited applicability have been purposely excluded. For this reason, the text is ideal for the beginning couples therapist and as a review volume for the seasoned couples therapist. Over the years, we have refined these methods in order to make them teachable and usable, and, unlike other texts, we discuss in detail the implementation of the techniques.

Another unique feature of this book is the emphasis on couples' growth and not just problem resolution. Many couples therapists assume that by eliminating problems, they will enhance the intimacy of the couple. Our approach is to focus on both goals simultaneously—problem resolution with enhanced intimacy. By adding this dimension to couples therapy, the process is enriched for both the therapist and the couple.

☐ Chapter Overview

Chapter 1, Assessment and Case Formulation, describes the comprehensive assessment and treatment of the couple using the Intersystem Model. This assessment enables the clinician to formulate a multileveled treatment plan. The chapter also discusses some of the common mistakes made during the evaluation phase and provides suggestions for avoiding these pitfalls.

Chapter 2, Orienting Couples to Therapy, discusses principles that will enhance the ability of a couple to use the therapeutic process effectively. General topic areas are: expectations and myths; boundary issues such as lateness, fees, and missed appointments; and instructions on how to help a couple take responsibility for their growth.

Chapter 3, Balanced Intervention, covers the importance of balance in systemic therapies. Several techniques for a balanced approach to individual partners in dyadic therapy are discussed. Included are: client understanding of balance; inclusive language; intensity and balance; and seating arrangements to promote balance. Understanding psychopharmacology and balance; determining whether balance has been established; and loss of balance as an important area for personal insight conclude the chapter.

Chapter 4, Systemic Intervention, contrasts linear thinking and interventions with a systemic perspective. The difficulties many beginning therapists have in learning to think systemically are elaborated through the descriptions of a number of systemic interventions.

Chapter 5, Moving from Content to Process, covers the challenges of learning to listen to the *content* of a client communication while understanding and being sensitive to the *process*. Content and process are defined and contrasted. Methods of understanding the process of a therapeutic session are enumerated.

Chapter 6, Building and Managing Intensity, orients the reader to skills of building intensity and relatedness within a therapeutic session. Approaches to building intensity and emotional expression, as well as learning to manage them for the couple are discussed. The use of images and analogies, a description of specific interventions to raise emotion, use of repetition, and the importance of focus on primary themes and material are the main topic areas.

Chapter 7, Individual Therapy and Systemic Intervention, discusses the use of systemic intervention when counseling an individual member of a marital dyad or committed relationship. Issues of balance, empathy, self-responsibility, and the development of personal power are emphasized.

Chapter 8, Working with Highly Reactive and Narcissistically Wounded Couples, is an entirely new and deals specifically with the narcissistically wounded couple. These couples are very difficult to work with and often fail to respond to traditional approaches to couples therapy. The dynamics of this couple are described and a step-by-step process is laid out for their treatment.

Chapter 9, Enhancing Intimacy in Relationships, provides a growth-oriented model for the clinician based on a clinically useful theory of love. Techniques to enhance intimacy are suggested for the couple that wants to move beyond a problem-focused therapy. The underlying fears of intimacy, which generate many problems, are also discussed.

Chapter 10, Reframing, covers one of the most generic of all therapeutic techniques used with couples. *Reframing* is a cognitive technique used in our work to change the meaning of symptomatic behavior from negative to positive, and to help couples move from seeing their problem as individual, to one of relationship.

Chapter 11, Communication Techniques, offers a framework for teaching couples how to communicate more effectively. A general framework is used to teach couples different levels of communication, specific techniques are reviewed; and communication problems are elucidated.

Chapter 12, Conflict Resolution, addresses the issues of anger and conflict as inevitable in all relationships. This chapter examines anger as a constructive emotion which has many underlying emotional components. A teachable conflict resolution model is outlined.

Chapter 13, Cognitive Techniques, reviews a largely ignored area of couples therapy. How and what partners think—their cognitions—are examined with an emphasis on common cognitive distortions. A systemic model for using cognitive therapy is described.

Chapter 14, Techniques of Marital Contracting, focuses on three methods of contracting that couples may use to help renegotiate their relationship. Ways of implementing and maintaining contracts are also discussed.

Chapter 15, Feelings, follows the cognitive and behavioral chapters with a discussion of feelings. The authors describe techniques to help identify and express emotions as well as to manage feelings in the session.

Chapter 16, Extending Techniques from the Office to Home Using Homework, covers the subject of between-session work. All of the techniques in the volume may be extended to such practice at home. This chapter discusses how to give homework, identifies the structural elements of a homework assignment, and offers suggestions to increase the compliance to doing homework.

Chapter 17, Treating the Extramarital Affair, was added to this book because readers kept asking about the treatment of marital infidelity. Little literature exists on treating this common issue in couples therapy. The chapter offers an integrative approach to treating extramarital affairs.

INTRODUCTION

The development of the systems theories and therapies has represented a major paradigmatic shift in psychotherapy. These new therapies all represent a shift away from the individualistic and intrapsychic theories developed and employed by Freud and the psychoanalytic/dynamic therapists. The systems theories all share the concept of the individual-as-part-of-a-system and they focus on interpersonal variables.

The past thirty years have been the "systems era" in the history of psychotherapy. In this short period of time, eight major schools have developed, which Kaslow (1981) has grouped under the following headings: (a) psychodynamic–psychoanalytic; (b) Bowenian; (c) relational or contextual; (d) experiential; (e) structural; (f) communication-interaction; (g) strategic-systemic; and (h) behavioral.

These schools of thought all share some basic assumptions about the nature of dysfunction and treatment, but they are clearly different in content. In fact, these schools of therapy were originally presented as if each was to be used exclusively, without "cross-fertilization" from others (see Gurman & Kniskern, 1981a). However, most practitioners of systems therapy and others who are not systems oriented do not operate from such a purist basis. They recognize the implicit need to fit the theories to their clients rather than fitting the client to a single theoretical approach.

This clinical need for integration has led to a new effort within the systems approaches. The latest development, one which spans approximately the last twenty years, is toward the integration of intrapsychically and interpersonally oriented theories and the integration of the various systems theories. A number of papers have been published advocating the synthesis or integration of various theories. Many of these papers have moved thinking within the field towards developing models demonstrating how different, sometimes apparently mutually exclusive, theories and therapies can be combined. For example, Kaslow (1981) published one of the earliest papers advocating an integrative approach to family therapy, in which practitioners can draw "selectively and eclectically" from various theories.

Duhl and Duhl (1981) presented one of the first clinically integrated models that they called "integrative family therapy." They looked at all the levels of the system, for example, developmental level, individual processes, and transactional patterns. Their approach was focused primarily on how the therapist thinks and intervenes and was less concerned with theoretical discussion regarding how theories could be integrated. Berman, Lief, and Williams (1981) also published a chapter on marital interaction, in which they described principles of marital interaction and also discussed how several theories could be integrated therapeutically. In this paper, they succeeded in presenting a coherent way of combining contract theory, object-relations theory, multigenerational theory, systems theory, and behavioral analysis all within a developmental and therapeutic model.

In addition, a number of other articles and books have appeared which address the issue of integration in systems therapy. These include: Hatcher (1978) on blending Gestalt and family therapy; Abroms (1981) on the interface between medical psychiatry and family therapy; Stanton (1981) on how to integrate the structural and strategic school; Green and Kolevzon (1982) on convergence and divergence in family therapy; Levant (1984) on a classification scheme for different theories; Lebow (1984) on the advantages of integrative approaches; a series of articles on the integration of structural-strategic therapy edited by Fraser (1984); Doherty, Colangelo, Green, and Hoffman (1985) on ways of reconceptualizing structure and distance in integration; Wachtel and Wachtel (1986) on designing intervention strategies based on family dynamics in individual therapy; Weeks and Hof (1987) on integrating sex therapy and marital therapy; and Weeks (1989a, 1989b) on integrating individual, interactional, and intergenerational approaches.

In revising our text, we were disappointed that more efforts toward integration have not taken place since our original publication of *Couples in Treatment* in 1992. Unfortunately, the field of psychotherapy in general appears to be making greater strides in this area. Some of the more recent efforts in the field of couples therapy include: Christensen, Jacobson, and Babcock, 1995; Jacobson and Christensen, 1996; Lawrence, Eldridge, Christensen, and Jacobson, 1999; Clark-Stager, 1999; Gurman, 1992; and Dattilio, 1990. The majority of the new efforts toward integration involve behavioral approaches, and stress cognitive/behavioral/systems integration. The major book to come out of this effort, *Integrative Couple Therapy: Promoting Acceptance and Change* (Jacobson & Christensen, 1996) is an acceptable book on couples therapy, but does little to advance any systematic effort toward integration. They stress what we call an eclectic rather than integrative approach due to the lack of a coherent theory.

Johnson and Lebow (2000) recently published an article in which they proclaimed that marital therapy had "come of age." Although marital therapy began formally in the 1950s and has received consistent, yet sparse, attention since that time, we do not believe it has "come of age."

There are relatively few texts on marital/couples therapy when compared to the number of books devoted to family therapy. Most training programs offer one course in marital therapy even though they are called marriage and family therapy programs. Clinicians and some faculty still believe anyone trained in family therapy can automatically do couples therapy. The fact is, these two approaches require different skill sets although they sharing many of the same basic assumptions. Our experience in training literally hundreds of therapists is that family therapists know little about couples therapy.

The field of couples therapy has also been one that is overlooked and under-funded by governmental bodies such as NIMH. Thus, empirical studies are scattered and those that are conducted are usually done with no funds or with small university grants, have small sample sizes, and are sometimes poorly designed. Couples therapy simply is not viewed as fundable research, which has meant university faculty fail to investigate important questions about couples therapy.

Given the lack of funding for empirical research and a lack of scientific rigor, the field has attracted its share of self-proclaimed experts who are really expert self-promoters. Some of the more charismatic figures have managed to capture the attention of many of the newer, more naive members of our field. As an example, in the Johnson and LeBow (2000) article some of these figures are mentioned without due criticism of their work. The clinician that is unfamiliar with this field would assume a John Gottman and a John Gray are of equal significance and value to our field. In addition, both fields of marital therapy and family therapy are highly political. Certain groups are "in" and others are "out" depending on the source.

In particular, the Johnson and Lebow article mentioned above, which purports to be a comprehensive review of the field, does not mention the several volumes the current authors have produced. In spite of the fact that the senior author has published more professional texts on couples therapy than anyone in the U.S., not one citation is made to his work while several are made to the articles of the review article's authors.

The therapist who is new to this field is urged to have a critical attitude and maintain a healthy degree of scientific skepticism, objectivity, and scholarship. Unfortunately these values are under-emphasized in Master's-level training programs, partly due to the fact that clinical practice tends to run ahead of empirical validation, and faculty do not stress the connection between research and practice. The clinician must learn to balance his or her clinical experience with empirically-based research.

☐ The Intersystem Model

The approach we have developed to treating couples is known as the Intersystem Model. This approach is a comprehensive, integrative, and contextual approach, originally conceived by Gerald Weeks, and published in 1977 in a paper on dialectics in psychotherapy. The concept was further refined for couples in the 1989 edited book *Treating Couples: The Intersystem Model of the Marriage Council of Philadelphia* (Weeks, 1989). The theory was completed in 1994 in *The Marital-Relationship Therapy Casebook: Theory and Application of the Intersystem Model* (Weeks & Hof, 1994). According to this theory, whenever a couple is being treated, three systems or subsystems must be simultaneously considered: the individual, the interactional, and the intergenerational. Most other approaches to marital and family therapy focus only on one or two of these systems, whereas we have found an integrative approach requires focus on all three. Perhaps our most striking departure from other systems approaches is our focus on the couple as a system consisting of two individuals. Other systems approaches have for the most part been anti-individual and antidiagnostic in the traditional sense. Unfortunately, systems thinkers have been so intent on separating or differentiating themselves from individual approaches that they have totally discarded the value of seeing the individual as an individual. In our approach, the individual's coping mechanisms, defense mechanisms, life cycles, ethnicity, intrapsychic dynamics, and individual psychopathology are assessed and treated within this context, rather than denying that individuals exist in such contexts.

Obviously, the couple's interactional system must also be assessed and treated, because a couple is more than the sum of its parts. Couples develop spoken and unspoken contracts, communication styles, patterns of dealing with or avoiding conflict, and so on, and the interactional system is usually the first experience a therapist has with a couple. This system is always present and the easiest to observe. The third part of the couple is the intergenerational system. Each member of the couple has a unique history rooted in his or her family of origin. These experiences, historical and current, influence the current relationship. In many cases, couples recreate unresolved issues with their own parents or previous relationships using their partner or children as a substitute. Consequently, intergenerational influences are often hidden until an exploratory process uncovers them.

The purpose of this book is to help the reader conceptualize and treat the couple from multiple perspectives and with a multitude of techniques. We do not advocate any single approach to couples therapy. The therapy should be crafted for the couple *and* their problem(s). Techniques can be sequenced and blended in order to tackle different problems and problems at different depths. The techniques described in this volume are not advanced or complex. They are basic techniques with wide-ranging applicability and power to effect change.

BASIC PRINCIPLES
AND PROCESSES
OF COUPLES THERAPY

CHAPTER 1

Assessment and Case Formulation

In order to use the techniques presented in this book effectively, it is necessary to conduct an assessment of the couple and develop a formulation of the case. The assessment phase consists of the initial interview and four to five more sessions. This chapter will not focus on the details of how to conduct these initial sessions because this aspect of treatment has been adequately covered elsewhere (Friedlander & Heatherington, 1998; Heller, 1987; Odell & Quinn, 1998; Young & Long, 1998). Heller is a colleague of ours, and thus her article is especially representative of our approach.

Our ideas for case formulation stem directly from the Intersystem Approach developed by Weeks and colleagues (DeMaria, Weeks, & Hof, 1999; Weeks, 1977, 1986, 1989; Weeks & Hof, 1994; Weeks & Hof, 1995). The senior author advocated an assessment approach that is comprehensive, multidimensional, and multilayered, which will allow for comprehensive, multidimensional, and multilayered treatment. A case formulation is a method of summarizing the data provided by the clients into a theoretically consistent framework that includes the couple dynamics and a treatment plan based on those dynamics and the goals of therapy. Many case formulations in our field are based on a single theory, which means the couple is conceptualized and treated within narrow parameters. This fact exists because many practitioners tend to adhere to just one model of intervention. As we have indicated, the field is becoming more theoretically and technically integrated. In previous books, Weeks (1989a; 1994) stressed theoretical integration. This volume stresses technical integration or the use of techniques from different approaches.

Before describing how to develop this type of case formulation, we would like to give the reader some guidelines on how to get started with the assessment phase of treatment. These guidelines are framed in terms of "don'ts and do's" and are designed to help the clinician avoid some of the common mistakes which are made.

☐ Common Mistakes Made in the Evaluation Phase

The evaluation phase of couples therapy usually requires two to four meetings. During these meetings the therapist's task is to join with the couple, collect information needed to develop a case formulation, and avoid mistakes that would disrupt development of a therapeutic relationship. The first two tasks mentioned above have been discussed widely in the literature. With the exception of Haley (1976), little attention has been given to describing the typical mistakes a couples therapist might make which can abruptly end treatment. The purpose of this section is to list some of the don'ts and do's which are so important during this phase. Many of these ideas apply throughout treatment, but it is probably more important to adhere to these ideas during the first few sessions than later sessions. Once the therapist has established a rapport with a couple, a mistake does not have as much potential to result in premature termination. The couple is more likely to be forgiving and discuss mistakes openly with the therapist. Although we call this list don'ts and do's, the reader should view them as useful guidelines and not as dogma.

Don'ts and Do's

1. *Don't take sides.* It is easy to get seduced into taking one partner's side, especially when that partner's pathology or contribution to the problem is not as clearly evident. The therapist must keep a systemic perspective. Otherwise, the partner being sided against is unlikely to return and the accusing partner has his or her linear view of the situation reinforced. The therapist should shift back and forth trying to understand each partner's perspective. The way the therapist uses language during this phase is important. The therapist needs to use reflective listening and use phrases such as "It is your perception . . . " (belief, opinion, idea, thinking, and so on). For example, the therapist should say, "It is your perception that your wife is controlling" rather than "Your wife controls much of your behavior." The latter statement implies that the therapist agrees with the validity of the statement being made.

2. *Don't intervene too quickly.* The therapist may feel obligated to start changing the system before understanding it. Premature intervention may destabilize the couple in such a way that it is too threatening for them. It is best to go slowly and intervene in ways that appear safe or nonthreatening to the couple. The task is to join, and to collect information early in treatment. The couple can be told the first few sessions will be devoted to conducting the evaluation and then to developing a treatment plan with their collaboration.

3. *Don't answer questions from the couple until ready.* In some cases, a question from a partner is designed to show how the other person is wrong, sick, or crazy. Questions need to be viewed with skepticism. The therapist needs to quickly assess whether the question has a hidden purpose or is designed to get the therapist to take sides. The therapist may respond to problematic questions by saying she or he does not know the answer yet or by deflecting the question, asking the questioner what she or he thinks, and getting the partner to offer an opinion. Legitimate questions about the therapeutic process, though, such as how long, should be answered openly and honestly.

4. *Don't proceed until the problem(s) and goal(s) have been clarified.* Couples usually present with a number of different problems. In the initial session, it is useful to get an overview and then come back to discuss the problem in some depth. Part of the process is deciding which problems to work on first, whether the presented problem is the real problem, and whether the partners desire the same resolution of the problem. The couple need to share a definition of the problem and the goals. Their ideas should be agreeable with the therapist and then interventions may be made.

5. *Don't discuss problems abstractly and nonconcretely.* Couples will sometimes begin therapy stating their difficulties in abstract, nonspecific, nonbehavioral language (e.g., "We have communication problems"). This type of language does not lead to any understanding of the problem, particularly the sequence of behaviors involved in their reciprocal interactions. The therapist can quickly move from the abstract to the concrete by asking *who, when, what,* and *how* questions. By focusing the couple in this way, they will usually see what the therapist is asking of them and alter their description of the problems.

6. *Don't discount problems, even small problems.* When partners come in together, they are sometimes reluctant to discuss complaints openly, honestly, and with the intensity they actually feel about the problem. This tendency results in problems being understated or minimized. In some cases, the real problem is not brought up at all in the initial session because of the level of sensitivity, embarrassment, or shame associated with it. The therapist must listen with a "third ear"

to what is being presented and, as the relationship develops, go back to those problems, which may fall into this category. Problems that are often understated include alcohol and drug abuse, spouse abuse, and sexual difficulties.

In addition, the therapist could inadvertently fall into collusion with one partner by agreeing that the other partner's problem is not that distressing. For example, a wife may complain that her husband is not attentive enough. The husband may then discount her statement by giving numerous examples of having been attentive. If the therapist summarily dismisses her complaint, then she or he has colluded with the husband. In order to effectively join, the therapist must take each partner's concerns seriously.

7. *Don't allow differences to escalate.* Couples come to treatment when they are unable to resolve their differences. In all probability they have struggled over these differences for some time, and with some intensity, at home. During the assessment phase, the therapist does not want to escalate these differences. She or he wants to understand them. When the level of emotional intensity begins to escalate, the therapist can ask cognitively-oriented questions (e.g., who, where, what, how) or shift to another topic, stating that it is clear the partners are very much at odds on the issue at hand and that it will be discussed later.

8. *Don't assume the partners in the couple will perceive the problem in the same way.* The reason the couple is coming to treatment is because they see things differently. The therapist should communicate this idea to the couple and not push for a similarity of perception. At this stage, it is useful to normalize differences stating that it will take time to work through the problem. When the therapist communicates this attitude she or he is giving the couple permission to express their differences.

9. *Don't unbalance the system.* This guideline has two meanings. The first was discussed above in terms of not intervening until the therapist understands the problem(s), goal(s), and consequences of change. The second meaning deals with siding with one partner or accepting one partner's definition of the problem over the other's. Although it may be useful to conduct separate interviews during the evaluation phase, one of the greatest risks is that of appearing to be or actually siding with one partner. Each partner may be very convincing about the pathology in the other. The therapist should reserve judgment, stay neutral, and keep a systemic perspective unless all the data suggest otherwise.

10. *Don't make premature interpretations.* One of the fundamental techniques in psychotherapy is interpretation. In individual therapy, early and/or

premature interpretations are often forgiven, overlooked, or constructively challenged. When an interpretation is made about one partner in the context of a couples session, the therapist may be seen as blaming or siding with one partner against the other. It is best to contain interpretation until enough information has been gathered for the therapist to feel confident of its validity and only after the joining process has been completed. The safest interpretations early in the treatment process are systemic (e.g., "the two of you . . .") or bilateral (e.g., "when one of you does _____, the other of you does ____").

11. *Don't get hooked in the past.* When couples begin treatment, it is easy for them to begin rehashing the past all over again. The therapist may see the 50th or 100th replay of an argument. The therapist's task is to enable the couple to talk about the past and how the past is currently affecting them, not to allow the couple to regress. The therapist may need to intervene actively and directly in cutting off this type of cycle. Questions designed to unravel the argument, get at individual meanings, and understand current feelings are helpful.

12. *Don't get hooked on the partners' theories or explanations.* It is useful to ask, if the partners don't volunteer, how they each explain the problem. One way to keep their theories from getting put forth as the truth is to ask simply, "What is your theory about the problem?" The question communicates that whatever answer is given is not going to be given the status of absolute truth. This information is useful in beginning to reframe or to redefine the problem. If the therapist's reframe is too incongruent with that of the couple, it will be rejected. Incorporating aspects of the couple's frame is more likely to meet with acceptance by the couple.

13. *Don't allow the couple to tell stories.* Some couples believe they have to tell stories in order to exemplify their problem. The stories may recount every detail, require a great deal of time to fully tell, and is not a productive use of time. The therapist should attempt to get to the point that is being made by taking charge of the session. Otherwise, the therapist may be waiting 30 minutes while the full rendition is given. The therapist can begin by asking focused questions in order to obtain information that is clinically useful.

14. *Don't allow emotion to take charge of the session.* One or both partners may become emotionally distressed to the point of ruling the session. The therapist's task is to manage affect. In later sessions, the therapist may want to intensify and escalate affect. However, in order for the couple to feel safe and secure with the therapist early on, they must know the therapist is not frightened by their emotions and is able to keep them under control. In some relationships, one partner is controlled by the emotions of the other. If the therapist allows this pro-

cess to be repeated, the controlled partner will not see how the therapist can be helpful. Techniques to control affect are discussed later, in Chapter 15, Exploring and Expressing Feelings.

15. *Don't allow the couple to take charge of the session.* One of the most difficult tasks for the beginning couples therapist, and for any therapist at the beginning of treatment, is learning how to take charge of what happens in the session. The therapist does not want to appear rigid or controlling, yet some partners/couples can be very controlling. In order to deal with these situations, the therapist can stick to the evaluation procedures outlined in this chapter in a businesslike fashion. Of course, if the couple are in crisis, the evaluation procedures are put on hold while the therapist takes charge of dealing with the crisis situation.

☐ Case Formulation

The case formulation proposed here is comprehensive and theory based (see Weeks, 1994). It requires the therapist to have a general and broad understanding of personality theory, psychotherapy, psychodiagnosis, and the major approaches to marital/family therapy. This approach to case formulation has been used since 1984 in training student clinicians. Currently, students in our program at the University of Nevada Las Vegas find this form of case formulation to be challenging and time consuming, but also providing them with more insight than any other method they have employed. To develop the formulation, we use a form that our students must complete prior to supervision and during the initiation of treatment. The remainder of this chapter will be devoted to reviewing this form item by item. Each section or question is numbered. These numbers will serve as reference points for the item-by-item description provided later in this chapter.

Item Descriptions

The first section of the form asks for is general background information such as age, occupations, names of family members, and so on. It is also useful to know by whom and why the couple was referred. Permission should be obtained to talk with the referring therapist, often the therapist of one partner. The reason they were referred or referred themselves is very useful. Of all the reasons they might have for coming to treatment, most important is *what was the precipitating event that motivated them at this particular time.* Unless this question is asked, the therapist may not be told this critical event.

☐ **Case Formulation Form**

FAMILY NAME: _____   DATE OF 1st INTERVIEW: _____

Partner's name: _____   Age: _____ Occupation: _____

Partner's name: _____   Age: _____ Occupation: _____

Children and other family in home:

_____   _____   _____

_____   _____   _____

ETHNIC GROUP: _____   YRS. MARRIED/IN RELATIONSHIP: _____

REFERRED BY: _____   REASON FOR REFERRAL: _____

1. Initial impressions and reactions:

_____
_____
_____
_____
_____

2. Presenting problem(s)—Give a concrete description, including the who, where, what, how. What is each member's view of the problem? How is the problem maintained in the system?

_____
_____
_____
_____
_____

3. History of the problem—abbreviated form of No. 2, above:

_____
_____
_____
_____
_____

4. Solutions attempted—including previous therapy:

_____

_____

_____

_____

_____

5. Changes sought by client(s):

_____

_____

_____

_____

_____

6. Recent significant changes—stressors and life-cycle changes (e.g., new job, move, death, divorce, child leaving home, etc.):

_____

_____

_____

_____

_____

Intersystem Assessment Questions

7. *Individual system(s)* (Intrapsychic components; i.e., cognitive distortions and irrational thinking, defense mechanisms such as denial, projection; definitions, predictions, and interpretations; also include Axis I, II, and III: DSM-IV diagnoses):

_____

_____

_____

_____

_____

8. *Interactional system* (e.g., emotional contracts, styles of communication, patterns of dyadic interaction, linear attributional strategies, such as debilitation, justification, vilification, rationalization, conflict-resolution skills):

_____

_____

_____

_____

_____

9. *Intergenerational system* (e.g., anniversary reactions, scripts, boundaries, cutoffs, triangles, closeness-distance issues):

_____

_____

_____

_____

_____

Treatment Plan Questions

10. Hypothesis Regarding the Client(s):

_____

_____

_____

_____

_____

11. Treatment Plan & Strategies   (Individual, Interactional, Inter-generational):

_____

_____

_____

_____

_____

INDIVIDUAL PROBLEMS	CHANGE STRATEGY OR TECHNIQUES
_____	_____
_____	_____
_____	_____
_____	_____
_____	_____

COUPLE PROBLEMS	CHANGE STRATEGY OR TECHNIQUES
_____	_____
_____	_____
_____	_____
_____	_____
_____	_____

FAMILY-OF-ORIGIN PROBLEMS   CHANGE STRATEGY
                                   OR TECHNIQUES

_____   _____
_____   _____
_____   _____
_____   _____
_____   _____

12. Prognosis and expected length of therapy (provisional):

_____
_____
_____
_____
_____

13. What are your strengths and weaknesses in dealing with this client system?

_____
_____
_____
_____
_____

Item 1 deals with the therapist's initial impressions and reactions. It is the therapist's first, intuitive response to the couple. Clearly, this item is impressionistic and idiosyncratic. It consists of intuitions about the couple, strong emotional reactions observed and felt, and projections (counter-transference) the therapist may experience. This item helps the clinician better understand the context in which the case is being formulated. For example, if the major initial reaction is one of extreme tension, fear, and suspicion in the couple, then all the data about the couple are filtered through this emotional environment. If the couple are open and relaxed and both partners take some responsibility for the problem, the therapist may believe what is being said is open, honest, and direct. The degree of probing and listening with a "third ear" would be needed less.

Item 2 has to do with obtaining a picture of the presenting problem(s). The therapist needs to get a clear and complete picture of all the problems. Each partner is permitted to express his or her perception of the problem. After each one has a turn, they may be asked to comment on the other person's perception of the problem. An essential part of asking about the presenting problem(s) is to get a sense of each problem from an interactional or circular perspective. The therapist is always searching for the contribution the other person makes to the problem. By exploring the sequence of behaviors through a complete cycle, the therapist may begin to discover the role of the other partner. What appears to be a problem in only one partner is actually part of an interlocking system of behavior.

Item 3 asks about the history of the problem(s). Once the current problem(s) is/are understood, it is useful to go back in time to find out whether the pattern has been the same or different. In some cases, the therapist may see the same pattern with reversals in roles. The problem(s) may predate the current relationship, having been present in all intimate relationships. If the problem has a beginning time that can be identified, it is useful to know what precipitated it. Perhaps the problem began the day after marriage, after the discovery of an affair, or with the birth of a child.

Item 4 is aimed at getting some information about the solutions the couple have tried in order to solve the problem. In some cases, the couple will have an unsuccessful history of therapy. The current therapist will want to know how or whether their previous therapy ended. Some couples jump from therapist to therapist prematurely with no therapist ever having been given a chance to help. Knowing what happened in the previous therapy lets the present therapist in on the problems discussed earlier and the efforts made to solve those problems. Because the previous therapy may have been unsuccessful or incomplete, the present therapist wants to avoid the mistakes made earlier.

Item 5 gives the therapist the opportunity to find out the couple's goals. After the couple have described their problem(s) and it is clear to the therapist what the problem is/are, the therapist should not make any assumptions about what kinds of changes are desired. Each partner should be asked what he or she wants changed. The therapist must seek to help the couple jointly agree on the changes they want and collaboratively decide on the order in which the work should be done.

Item 6 recognizes the importance of stressful events in precipitating and/ or creating problems. The therapist may simply ask what changes and stresses have occurred during the last two years, especially the last six months. Many couples will not connect the level of change/stress in their lives to their problems. The number of changes in some couples is truly remarkable, and they should be helped to understand the consequences of these events.

The first six items of the case formulation are data-based, with subjective and objective information gathered. The therapist sticks close to the data without drawing many inferences. *Items 7, 8,* and *9* are more inferential. The data in the items is organized according to different levels and theoretical systems.

Item 7, which assesses individual systems, may strike the couples therapist as odd within the context of a systemic approach. Marital and family therapy started as a reaction against individual psychopathology and therapy. For many years individual concepts have been viewed as antithetical to systems thinking. Yet, couples are composed of individuals. Each individual has his or her own set of dynamics and pathology. To deny this fact for the sake of taking a pure systems perspective would be unnecessarily dogmatic and also limiting. Consequently, we suggest an assessment of each individual's intrapsychic dynamics. This includes, but is not limited to, the individual's use of defense mechanisms, cognitive distortions, and the concepts of definitions, predictions, and interpretations mentioned earlier in the introductory chapter.

The issue of individual psychopathology requires the therapist to consider the interlocking nature of psychopathology. In our companion text, Goldberg (1987) discussed how to view individual pathology from a systems perspective. An assumption in systems theories is that partners are equally healthy or unhealthy, and that the severity of individual pathology is often quite similar. That notwithstanding, an area of diagnosis that has been neglected with couples is that of personality disorders. We see numerous cases in which partners present with personality disorders or traits of personality disorders. Some common combinations are the narcissistic/dependent or inadequate; pair the obsessive–compulsive/histrionic—borderline pair; and the aggressive/dependent pair. Millon (1999) has written extensively about these personality types in his book *Personality Guided Therapy*.

Individual diagnoses help the therapist understand and treat the interlocking parts of the pathology. The couple may also need concurrent individual therapy that is coordinated with the couples therapist. In general, individual diagnoses should not be shared with the couple, as they may be used by one partner to project more blame or craziness onto the other. Obviously, some individual pathologies require attention prior to the onset of couples therapy. Severe psychopathology is a clear contraindication for couples therapy. Cases involving psychosis, severe depression, suicide, and drug/alcohol abuse all require individual attention first.

Item 8 is the one most directly concerned with the couple's functioning. This item involves assessing the interactional problems of the couple in accord with any number of marital therapies and concepts. Some of the common concepts in this category deal with deficits in communication and conflict-resolution skills, emotional contracts, interlocking cognitive distortions, and inappropriate and blocked emotions. Special emphasis should be given to understanding how the couple uses attributional strategies which are designed to externalize personal responsibility and blame the other partner for the marital problems. In couples, the spouse bearing the symptom (e.g., depression) may simply blame the other partner for the dysfunctional mood. The linear attributional tactics seen in couples is, however, more varied than simple projection.

Four methods of destructive linear attribution have been identified by Strong and Claiborn (1982):

1. *Justification* is the practice of assigning the negative or harmful effects of one's behavior onto external causes (e.g., "I cannot help the way I act because of my crazy family");
2. *Rationalization* is the practice of denying that one's internally controlled behavior was intended to be harmful (e.g., "I just did it [*it* is being overcontrolling] to help you");
3. Debilitation involves assigning hurtful behavior to causes inside of one but beyond one's control (e.g., "I cannot help it, when you do that, I go off . . . you should know that and stop what you are doing"); and
4. *Vilification*, in which the other person is made a villain by attributing negative intent to him or her. Consequently, the partner's behavior is justified as a response to hurtful behavior (e.g., "You just have to put me down in front of your family so you can feel superior").

The therapist may note whether these tactics are being used and then, with the couple, work toward eliminating them.

Item 9 is concerned with how family-of-origin issues may play a role in the marital dynamics. Patterns learned in the family-of-origin tend to be repeated in later relationships. It is beyond the scope of this section to describe all of these patterns. Readers should be familiar with the major concepts of Bowen's theory (see Kerr, 1981) and the genogram assessments in *Focused Genograms: Intergenerational Assessment of Individuals, Couples, and Families* by DeMaria et al. (1999). In addition to the concepts found in these books, there are questions or issues that deserve mention. They are:

1. What were the roles you observed in your parents' marriage?
2. What did your parents appear to expect from each other?
3. What did you learn about being a husband/wife?
4. How much closeness/distance did you see in your parents' marriage?
5. How did your parents handle their anger and conflict?
6. Did your parents show their affection/intimacy openly?
7. How did your parents order their priorities among self, marriage, children, and work?
8. What emotions were encouraged, allowed, not allowed, denied, said to be bad?

9. Were there any traumas in your parents' marriage such as affairs, incest, unresolved grief, or psychological and medical problems?
10. What did you learn about intimacy from your parents?

In cases where the couple are also presenting with a sexual problem, another series of questions is useful. Larry Hof and colleagues (DeMaria, Weeks, & Hof, 1999; Weeks, 1987; Weeks & Hof, 1987) have found that some sexual problems are rooted in family history. Weeks and Hof published a set of questions to help obtain information pertinent in these cases (pp. 48–49). His outline of the sexual genogram process, along with these questions are listed below:

The Sexual Genogram Process
1. Introduction - Explain and discuss the role of early learning and intergenerational processes in the development of individual, couple, and family systems. "Life Scripts," "Family Scripts," "Family Loyalties."
2. Creation and Exploration of a Genogram - Graphic depictions of three or four generations of each partner's family (if couple-oriented) or of the individual's family, emphasizing facts, feelings, alliances, boundaries, coalitions, closeness, distance, emotional cutoffs, conflicts, connectedness, and so on.
3. Creation and Exploration of a Sexual Genogram - Reconsideration of the multigenerational system with a specific focus on pointed questions relating to sexuality and intimacy.

   a) What are the overt/covert messages in this family regarding sexuality/intimacy? Regarding masculinity/femininity?
   b) Who said/did what? Who was conspicuously silent/absent in the area of sexuality/intimacy?
   c) Who was the most open sexually? Intimately? In what ways?
   d) How was sexuality/intimacy encouraged? Discouraged? Controlled? Within a generation? Between generations?
   e) What questions have you had regarding sexuality/intimacy in your "family tree" that you have been reluctant to ask? Who might have the answers? How could you discover the answers?
   f) What were the "secrets" in your family regarding sexuality/intimacy (e.g., incest, unwanted pregnancies, extramarital affairs, etc.)?
   g) What do the other "players on the stage" have to say regarding the above questions? How did these issues, events, and experiences impact upon him/her? Within a generation? Between generations? With whom have you talked about this? With whom would you like to talk about this? How could you do it?

h) How does your partner perceive your family tree/genogram regarding the aforementioned issues? How do you perceive his/hers?

i) How would you change this genogram (including Who and What) to meet what you wish would have occurred regarding messages and experiences of sexuality/intimacy?

4. Exploration and Discussion of Genogram Material/Issues with Extended Family Members - Review of the total process and integration within the treatment plan for sexual dysfunction.

Genogram assessment may be done early on, later on, or scattered throughout the assessment and treatment phase. The use of these questions depends on the extent to which the problem appears to have an historical versus current basis. More information on how to collect historical (genogram) information can be found in DeMaria et al. (1999).

Item 10 consists of the therapist's hypotheses based on all the data. To begin treatment involves making some basic hypotheses about the nature and causes of the problem. The major hypotheses are listed in this section. For example, the therapist might hypothesize that the basic problem is one of closeness and distance based on the husband's experience of having a rejecting mother and the wife's experience of incest with her stepfather.

Hypotheses are "tested" as treatment proceeds. If the hypotheses produce the desired outcome for everyone, the hypotheses are probably valid. If not, it might be time to reconsider the hypotheses.

Item 11 is the treatment plan and change strategies. Marital therapists have not stressed this aspect of treatment enough in their work. For each category of assessment, a treatment goal and strategy may be formulated. For an individual with severe depression, a referral to a psychiatrist would be an appropriate strategy. In the same case, the denial of depression in the other partner might require a reframe of the depression so that the "unaffected" partner sees his/her role in the depression in the system. There also might be an intergenerational pattern of depressed women in the family, requiring some family-of-origin work, accompanied by sessions involving mother and grandmother. The treatment plan can involve any combination of techniques, approaches, or strategies. The plan needs to be developed with an awareness of which changes to make first, the couple's readiness for work in different problem areas, and how to sequentially build on successes.

Item 12 is the therapist's prognosis and estimated length of treatment. It is useful for the therapist to be realistic about the outcome of therapy and to share the most probable outcome with the couple following the evaluation phase. In so doing, the couple will not be operating on their assumptions about what to expect. Couples often ask about the length of treatment. Being realistic means starting with a valid contract. If a couple will need at least six months and they are unwilling to go more than six weeks, there is no basis for a working relationship. When the therapist has followed the procedures outlined above, she or he can explain which problems will be treated, how, with what probable success, and for roughly how long. The couple can then make an informed decision about continuing treatment.

Item 13 is designed to help the therapist recognize the strengths he or she brings to the case and potential countertransference issues. One therapist may find he or she has significant experience in working with conflict in couples, while another is intimidated by anger in men because of personal history. The therapist who experiences a countertransference reaction from the outset should seek supervision and/or therapy to resolve this problem. If the therapist is unwilling to be responsible for the countertransference reaction, the case should be referred. Treating a case when there is a countertransference reaction is at best likely to be unsuccessful and at worst damaging to the couple.

The 13 items covered in this approach to case formulation are by no means exhaustive or unique. It is the combination of items that makes this approach stand out as more comprehensive than others. As the marital therapist becomes more knowledgeable and practiced in this approach, this series of questions will become second nature. To reach this point will require time and persistence.

☐ Conclusion

The purpose of this chapter was to discuss two topics. First, guidelines for conducting the first few sessions were offered. These guidelines are designed to help the couples therapist avoid some of the more common difficulties in getting started with the couple. The guidelines are just that; they are not hard-and-fast rules that must be adhered to strictly. The therapist should use her or his own judgment in deciding when these guidelines do not fit. Following the assessment/engagement phase of treatment, it is much less important to follow these guidelines. In fact, they may be counterindicated in some circumstances. For example, the therapist may later want to unbalance the system by temporarily taking sides. This procedure would be done for therapeutic, not diagnostic, reasons.

The second issue covered in this chapter was assessment. Assessment and treatment are usually blended in doing couples work. The difference is in the emphasis paid to one or the other. The approach described reveals a procedure for collecting a tremendous amount of information in a systematic way. Some of the information may be collected much later in treatment as the need arises and as the need to further develop the treatment plan emerges. During the assessment phase, at least enough information should be collected to permit the development of our initial case formulation. The case formulation is the basic road map that enables the therapist to begin the course of treatment.

Orienting Couples to Therapy

A couple's myths about the nature of marital therapy and unrealistic expectations concerning the therapist's role can get the therapeutic process off to a difficult start. One of the therapist's tasks is to teach couples about realistic and unrealistic expectations. Appropriate expectations can set a positive tone for the entire therapy and for the couple's relationship with the therapist.

Important tasks for the marital therapist are: 1) to inquire about general couple expectations for the therapy and to educate where necessary; 2) to teach couples about specific boundary issues pertaining to length of appointments, lateness, use of telephone, fees, missed appointments, and so on; 3) to discuss general expectations of the therapeutic process, for example, instructing a couple on how to take responsibility for a session; discussing who speaks to whom and the importance of balance; and advising the couple not to quote *or triangulate* the therapist in a negative fashion during arguments or discussions at home. When these issues are clear, the clients can benefit more from the therapy hour. This chapter will elaborate on each of these tasks.

☐ Unrealistic Expectations

The therapist needs to inquire about the reasons a couple has initiated therapy and to educate them about any misconceptions. The following misconceptions are often held by clients during a beginning session.

"We are going to the therapist so that she or he will tell us what to do."

In most cases, instructing clients how to behave or what to do next is not a therapist's role. A systemically trained therapist is not seeking regressive behavior or dependency from a couple. Instead, encouraging active couple participation and insight into areas of difficulty, as well as facilitating behavioral changes, are desired. A therapist could share several images depicting appropriate relationships between the couple and therapist, with the therapist being *a guide* to help the couple reflect on key or historical dynamics, *a teacher* with whom to explore interpersonal relationships, *a confronter* of possible cognitive distortions or dysfunctional behavior, *a referee* to maintain some balance and fairness in the couple's communication, or *an empathetic person* to talk with during times of stress and depression. Many images and roles are applicable for the marital therapist. There are also some roles that are generally not appropriate. In most cases a marital therapist should not be: a mother or father leading and instructing dependent children, an all-knowing person who does not respect the intelligence of the couple, or the sole interpreter of truth concerning a client's relationship. The therapist should not claim to possess a monopoly on what is right or wrong for a client, shame a client to take a specific ethical position, or be a friend who relates or develops a dual role to couples outside of the therapeutic setting.

"I'm afraid we will be doing all of the talking and the marital therapist won't be saying anything at all."

Systemic therapists are most often *interactive and assertive*, not passive. If clients come to therapy feeling angry about certain issues and an argument ensues, they are probably reenacting a communication pattern repeated many times in private. Such a couple may be seeking therapy in the hope of breaking this repetitive communication cycle and exploring feelings of discouragement or rejection. The passivity of the marital therapist can and probably will lead to more couple conflict and feelings of despair. *Passivity will rarely break the destructive couple process issues.*

Lack of interaction between the therapist and clients is one of the primary reasons couples leave therapy. Often, a couple is searching for someone who will institute some control, structure, fairness, boundaries, and the confidence that their relationship could be different in the future. To accomplish these goals the therapist's primary tools are sharing insight, structuring behaviors, changing process, assigning homework, and creatively using his or her personality to effect change. The marital therapist needs to demonstrate an active stance during the initial stages of therapy to raise the hope that interactions could be less dysfunctional and more nurturing and healing in the future.

"I did not think that a marital and family therapist would work with an individual."

Systemic issues can be approached in the context of an entire family, a couple, or an individual coming to therapy. In the systemic framework, change in an individual's behavior can affect the interaction of a couple or a family as directly as change in the couple or family can affect an individual.

One mistake that many therapists make is to turn away an individual coming to work on his or her marriage when the other partner refuses to participate. A partner who can understand how different patterns have developed within a relationship can begin to realize the part she or he might play in perpetuating or altering those patterns, and eventually considerably affect the quality of his or her marriage. In other words, the partner can begin to understand the circular nature of his or her relationship—that is, how the communications of one partner elicit a response in the other partner and vice versa. On the other hand, if the partner who comes to therapy insists on spending the therapeutic time projecting onto his or her absent partner all of the responsibility for the problems in the relationship, the therapy will probably not be very fruitful. These clients see their problems in linear terms, and blame their partners for the conflict, in spite of the therapist pointing out how such a view is counterproductive. Linear terms are blame and projection when responsibility for a problem is seen as one person's fault. For example, a husband might say that his wife does not want him to drink and have a good time, so he leaves home whenever she returns home to find him "hanging" out with his friends. He blames her for having to leave because he can see she is angry. He is unable to see his part in her being angry.

A frequent mistake a therapist can make is to alienate the presenting individual client by having him or her "beg" the absent partner to come into therapy. The more a reluctant or outright resistant spouse is pressed to participate in therapy, the more power the presenting individual may lose in the marital relationship. This is because the most power in a relationship is held by the person with the least investment in whatever is being pursued. If the reluctant partner finally agrees to come in, his or her attitude is often expressed thusly: "I have no need to be here" or "How can I help you change, because I don't have a problem?" Such placing of responsibility onto the partner, and lack of desire to be in therapy, will probably undermine the process.

"The success of the therapeutic process is based on the skill of the therapist."

The insight and skill of the therapist are certainly key components to the success of the therapy. However, a seasoned therapist will realize and accept his or her limitations when clients are highly resistant to working productively on the relationship. A client needs to be taught that responsibility for movement in therapy depends on every participant. The inexperienced therapist who is overly anxious or insecure can assume too much responsibility for change. For example, he or she could lecture or be more invested in client growth than the couple. In so doing, she or he can inadvertently teach the couple not to be self-responsible, and take more responsibility for client movement or growth than the clients. Getting both partners to accept responsibility for the problem is a goal of the systemic therapist. Then, if change occurs, the clients can attribute the change to themselves and not to the therapist. The therapist who claims responsibility for client growth and movement infantilizes the couple and diminishes the effectiveness of therapy.

"A male (or female) therapist will be more sensitive to my needs."

A competent therapist of either sex will be able to maintain balance and be just and fair to both partners. Maintaining balance involves confronting, sharing empathy, and talking to each partner in an equal and fair manner (refer to Chapter 3). The therapist who continually ends up siding with one sex or the other is in need of personal therapy before continuing to practice *conjoint* therapy. Continual siding suggests transference or countertransference issues that the therapist may not have worked through from his or her experiences in the family of origin. Sometimes it is helpful for the therapist, especially if she or he senses one client is fearful of being sided against, to verbalize how every attempt will be made to keep a balanced perspective and to look at mutual responsibility. For instance, saying to a client, "Do you think that because I am male/female I may be more likely to side with one of you?" Direct questioning and processing these balance issues out loud to a couple might calm anxieties about issues of fairness in terms of gender and make the clients aware that the therapist recognizes and understands such concerns. The therapist may also ask the couple to voice their concerns during conjoint therapy if they believe the therapist is siding on the basis of gender.

If a client maintains the bias that a therapist of one sex or another will be more sensitive to specific issues, and is resistant to the therapy, referral should be offered. It is probably better client care, and more productive for the therapeutic process, to help such a client begin therapy with a minimal amount of bias or prejudice.

"Once the therapeutic process begins, it will never end."

Clients sometimes fear entering a therapeutic process without knowing how to terminate and leave. It is often helpful for the therapist to explain that this process is to help them, that it was their initiation that determined when they entered, and that *they* will determine how much each invests in the process and when they are ready to terminate. A therapist who needs a particular client for ego gratification or financial security should not be doing therapy. Such needs can override sound therapeutic judgment. Clients entering marital therapy can be taught that the duration of marital and family therapy averages anywhere from several sessions to several years. If members of a couple feel they have the power to determine the length and frequency of therapy, they are more likely to invest in the process. A therapist might say to a client, "I'm not sure how long the therapeutic process should last. In general, therapy continues until your goals are achieved. Many variables can contribute to that decision. First let's see if it is helpful, and if not, we can decide on other directions or I can refer you to another therapist."

☐ General Boundary Issues

Most couples come to therapy with some difficulty in establishing *effective interpersonal or structural boundaries*. Many couples are enmeshed or disengaged due in part to boundary problems in their respective families-of-origin. If the therapy and the therapeutic relationship between client and therapist *do not* model healthy boundaries (i.e., flexible rather than rigid or chaotic), the client's dysfunctional boundary problems can be reenacted in the therapist–client relationship and in the overall therapeutic process. The therapist needs to maintain appropriate boundaries in both the content and process of therapy. *The health and welfare of both therapist and client is at stake.* The following discussion will illustrate and explain five kinds of boundary issues.

Length of Sessions

Most therapists work on a 50-minute hour. Clients need to be told this limit directly and, if possible, to have their check written out before the session begins. The process of finding the checkbook, writing the check, figuring out the correct date, and recording the correct check number, while often talking to the therapist at the same time, can be an awkward and cumbersome period of time. A client has the right to a full session and the therapist has the right to take a break before the next therapeutic hour begins.

The reasons a therapist might not boundary time appropriately are quite diverse and most often indicative of unresolved personal issues or insufficient structuring skills. Possibly, the therapist is taking too much responsibility for the movement or growth of the couple and believes that one more intervention will make the difference. One of the worst effects of not placing boundaries on the length of a session is that clients' resistance to dealing with significant material sooner in the therapeutic hour is reinforced. A client who knows that the therapist is going to start and stop on time is much more likely to be prompt and invest in substantive material early in the session. It is a myth to think that because some movement and insight were achieved in one hour, twice as much can be accomplished in two hours.

Lateness

In general, if a couple is late for a session and the therapist accommodates by exceeding the allotted hour, they will be reinforced to not worry about being prompt. The therapist can unwittingly collude in a couple's resistance and manipulation by not setting limits. Lack of personal limit-setting can result in a therapist feeling disrespected and abused. A therapist should explain to the couple that if they are late, the time cannot be made up; however, if the therapist is late, the full 50-minute session will take place.

In marital therapy, one protection against triangulation of the therapist is to not visit with the one partner of a couple who comes on time. A therapy session begins when both partners arrive. Waiting for both partners to be present before therapy begins is a *dynamic* that should be explained to the clients. The issue of always starting sessions together becomes less important when considerable trust and a balance of perspectives has been established between couple and therapist.

Missed Appointments

In the first session, it is helpful to lay down the ground rules concerning missed appointments. If the therapist makes a mistake and schedules two clients at the same time, *hopefully* a rare occurrence, it is important that he or she makes up the session for the couple who is turned away, and does not charge them for that session. The client has made the trip to therapy twice and has been seen only once. If the client misses an appointment, especially more than once, the therapist in most cases should charge the client and set up another time to meet. The therapist who communicates clearly to a couple or family that at least 24 hours notice is needed for a cancellation, or the therapy hour will be charged, demonstrates appropriate boundaries and self-respect. Therapists who do not set up these kind of parameters will find themselves feeling abused by the whims of clients who are too tired to come to therapy or who found, due to resistance or desire, something more "fun" to do.

Phones, Knocking, and General Disturbance

Many couples come to therapy because they have been unable to establish effective boundaries regarding their children, parents, work, or personal lives to allow for strengthening and protecting their marital relationship. The therapy must model the appropriate boundaries that are needed for a couple to develop definition, security, stability, and intimate communication. The therapist can inform clients that, in general, during a session they will not be disturbed. The therapist will not answer the phone, go to the door, or do anything that would take away from the primary therapist–client relationship. In turn, the therapist does not want to have a client knock on a closed door, but to wait in the appointed waiting area.

With some possible exceptions, a client should be taught to honor the boundaries of the therapist and not call him or her at home. Clients with few boundaries can intrude upon the therapist's private time and undermine the therapy by having private conversations that exclude one partner. An exception might be a therapist giving his or her telephone number, and permission to use it, as a demonstration of caring and concern. Sometimes it is easier for a therapist to request that a client call during certain hours to change appointments or express concerns that cannot wait until the next session, instead of playing telephone tag. In general, the more a therapist feels that a client will honor the therapist's boundaries and personal time, the freer the therapist might be to give out his or her telephone number. If the therapist misjudges and ends up getting interrupted unnecessarily, she or he needs to be able to effectively boundary the client from use of the phone and further intrusion.

Payment

Therapists who are confident about the services they provide feel appropriately entitled to directly receive payment for their services at the conclusion of each session. Therapists who do not *directly* receive payment from a client do the therapeutic process an injustice. A client who pays a receptionist might devalue the therapy or therapist. Couples who do not pay may resist working, prolong the length of therapy, or in a passive-aggressive manner elicit anger from the therapist. Furthermore, a therapist who does not insist on payment can establish client indebtedness and a subsequent imbalance of power. When a client feels that he or she owes a therapist for sacrificing his/her time and energy, the dynamics of guilt and obligation can be manipulated. For instance, a couple may not leave therapy when they feel it is appropriate because the therapist has been so generous with his or her personal time, or a therapist might manipulate a couple to stay in therapy by sharing feelings of self-sacrifice. A practical matter is that when a therapist is not paid directly, unpaid client bills are almost always higher. *Clients find it easier to not pay a receptionist or cashier than to pay a therapist directly.*

If the therapist charges on a sliding scale, the negotiation of a fee for services gives the therapist a great deal of information about the client and the client gains insight into the therapist. The therapist can learn how resistant a couple might be when comments by the couple in the negotiation suggest that therapy might not be a priority. Early patterns of manipulation might appear at this time when a couple hedges on the actual amount of their income. Cries of poverty, combined with elaborate vacation plans on a later date, can create angry feelings in the therapist.

Conversely, a couple who negotiates in good faith for a lower fee or agrees to the fee presented by the therapist can communicate a respect for the therapy, personal motivation, and the value of the therapist's time. A client learns a great deal about the therapist who lowers every fee and doesn't insist on payment. Perhaps the therapist does not value his or her time or have a high regard for his or her competence. The way a therapist negotiates fees, the degree of flexibility, the tone of voice, and the level of anxiety can raise hope and respect or, conversely, erode confidence in the therapist.

In general, negotiation of the fee is a good way for the therapist to learn about client's investment, resistance, control needs, and assertiveness, while the client can learn about a therapist's professional identity and confidence. At best, the dynamics surrounding the setting of fees and timely payment teach effective boundaries and self-respect. At worst, it becomes a dysfunctional aspect of the client-therapist relationship.

☐ General Expectations of the Therapeutic Process

Issues of Personal Responsibility

"Tell me what to do." Many couples make this statement directly, while others indirectly attempt to get the therapist to claim or to take responsibility for change. The therapist who takes responsibility for the content and emotional energy of a session might find himself or herself working very hard, often exhausted at the end of the session. Furthermore, a client who does not accept enough responsibility can have the luxury of sitting back in a resistance mode, wondering why the therapist is not more effective.

Enabling the Client to Begin the Session

In between sessions, the couple should be working on their relationship and planning to bring to therapy communication difficulties, insights, and issues that stymie or confuse them. If clients know that their session will begin with a directive or structure chosen or imposed by the therapist, they will most likely be passive and defer responsibility to the therapist. If the direction and content of the therapeutic hour is left to the initiation of the clients, they are more likely to have talked and processed material between sessions and will arrive at therapy with issues and concerns upon which to focus.

A therapist who gives growth responsibility to clients will begin a session with silence or with an open-ended question. Open-ended questions do not guide the content of the answer or the direction of the session. Therapy, in general, is grounded in an individual's ability to explore himself/herself from the inside-out. When the client begins the session, it forces the client into self-confrontation and helps to reveal hidden resistances. Therapists who initiate the content of a session can thwart the sharing of a client's most important insights and fears.

Examples of open-ended questions are:

- Where would you like to begin?
- What should we talk about today?
- How would you like to use this time?

Therapists mistakenly believe they are giving responsibility to the clients when they ask closed-ended questions, but in fact they are controlling the content and process almost entirely.

Examples of closed-ended questions are:

- Have you been feeling angry? (A client then talks about feeling angry instead of anything else.)
- Did you do your homework last week? (The client does not begin with the feeling or idea that he or she wanted or intended to share or discuss.)
- Would you like to begin with what you said last week? (Clearly, the therapist is setting the agenda. This information can be requested at a later time in the session, but hopefully not at the expense of the couple's agenda.)

Another type of interaction that results in transferring responsibility from the clients to the therapist is when clients' passivity is demonstrated in the "question and answer game." An example of this kind of very exhausting and difficult interaction is given below:

Therapist: How are you today?

Couple: Fine.

Therapist: What would you like to talk about?

Couple: We aren't sure.

Therapist: How about discussing the intimacy in the relationship?

Couple: What about?

This type of question-and-answer sequence can be endless. In such a process, the client takes little responsibility for exploration into personal issues or difficulties, and the therapist continually tries to guess what would be meaningful content. A therapist will know that this dynamic is occurring when he or she is spending all of his or her mental energy in the session trying to figure out the next question. By worrying about how to frame the next question during an interactive process, the therapist will be distracted and will not be able to listen effectively to the clients. When a couple take responsibility for the content and process of a therapeutic hour, a therapist can monitor and guide the process instead of remaining responsible for the content of the interaction.

Another difficulty with a question-and-answer process, when used during initial sessions, is that of setting a standard and/or expectation for the couple about what the process of therapy is going to entail. Once this mental set has been established, it is difficult for couples to make the shift from the therapist asking questions to taking responsibility for the content of the session. An intake should not only include therapist inquiry, but also give to the couple a sense of their central role through their initiation and exploration. Couples begin to learn that they have the larger portion of responsibility from the very first session.

A therapist might encourage client responsibility and investment by saying something like, "I could ask you many questions that I may deem important, but I would rather focus on your ideas, perceptions, and questions and have you talk about them together. I won't be silent for long and will ask for clarification and insight into your understanding of the strengths and weaknesses of your relationship." The skill in this process *for the therapist* is to explore the relationship with the couple through the specific themes and emotions that may surface as the clients take responsibility for sharing the presenting problem(s). This approach is in contrast to asking unrelated or *discontinuous* questions about the couple relationship and family of origin as if the therapist were reading off a list. For example, if a couple state that they feel the relationship has grown very distant, the therapist can orient the discussion about the relationship and the family of origin around the idea of distance. The history, feelings, origins, and behaviors of the couple can all be explored using distance as a theme. If a wife states that she feels very abandoned and the husband retorts that he feels smothered, the feelings of abandonment and smothering can be focused upon and explored as the therapist gets to know the couple through their concerns and feelings and not the unrelated "packaged" questions of the therapist. Using the themes and feelings presented by the clients places responsibility for the presentation of material with the clients and not on the questions of the therapist.

Facilitating Communication Between Spouses as Central to the Process of Marital Therapy

The marital therapist often creates the expectation that the couple will come to therapy after having talked at home, and will be prepared to discuss significant issues both between themselves and with the therapist. To establish the above expectations, part of the initial session should include the couple spending time talking to each other while the therapist observes. This dialogue helps in the assessment of reciprocal patterns of communication, which then can begin to be processed in the session.

The most natural way to introduce the idea that the therapist would like the couple to talk to each other, is to redirect the conversation away from the therapist to between the partners. Most often, each partner, *due to some fear of being intimate,* will be intent on sharing directly with the therapist her or his specific version of the couple's difficulties. While it is important for the therapist to hear and respond to each individual to facilitate joining, ultimately it will be positive couple communication that will create some healing and reconciliation. With repeated therapist insistence on partner communication, the couple will soon realize that the therapist will not fill up therapeutic time with lectures and advice, but is far more interested in the couple's communication patterns in and out of therapy.

Confronting Blame and Judgment and Inspiring Self-Responsibility

The most common presentation in therapy by each spouse is to place blame and responsibility for the marital difficulties on the other partner. As both are sure that the other is the primary cause of the difficulty, each attempts to align the therapist to his or her perception. As the marital therapist stays balanced and fair, she or he attempts to empower the clients by helping them to see their specific contributions and to begin the process of accepting responsibility. Central to all systemic thinking is the idea that clients have a great deal of power to change themselves and very minimal power to change their partners. Communication patterns are most often characterized by blaming. These patterns can be broken through the client's acceptance of individual responsibility and behavioral change.

Warning the Client Against Quoting the Therapist or Using the Therapist's Name at Home in a Destructive Manner

It is sometimes helpful to ask that the therapist's name not be used negatively in order to support one person's perception over the other in the couple's communication at home. "Dr. _____ said . . . "—especially when attached to a misquoted or badly communicated "fact"—can create anger and dissatisfaction over the therapy. If the conversation gets heated enough, both partners might become angry with and attribute blame to the therapist. If clients do repeat information, feelings, or ideas about a session, they most often should communicate them as their own subjective experience. "I believe" instead of "the therapist said" will lead to a healthier communication, without putting the therapist in the middle of every conversation.

The use of the therapist's name can be useful in specific couple interaction if each individual has a positive regard for the therapist and a desire to share sensitively and reflectively with his or her partner. "Dr. _____ said that we should be talking amongst ourselves, how about tonight?" is an example of a couple using the name of the therapist positively in order to strengthen their resolve and initiate more intimate communication.

☐ Conclusion

In summary, many couples come to therapy with apprehension, unrealistic expectations, and a lack of information about the roles and boundaries of client, therapist, and therapeutic process. Educating clients on some of the above mentioned issues, and making what might seem obvious to the therapist explicit to the couple, can prevent a great deal of misunderstanding and help the therapy begin in a healthier, more productive manner.

Balanced Intervention

The concept of balance is central to systemic thought and the process of marital therapy. When the therapist thinks systemically, she or he believes that both partners of a relational dyad contribute to the intimacies and difficulties they might be experiencing. The marital therapist who is balanced in approach asks both partners to be accountable, confronts both with relatively equal intensity, and finds ways to be supportive and nurturing to each person. In such an approach, the marital therapist does not align with one partner or form a coalition against the other, but consistently addresses the influence and contribution of both spouses. If the therapist loses balance, the therapy is often destructive to one or both marital partners. Judgment and fault can take the place of personal responsibility and the establishment of a climate of fairness and trust. The clients' perception that the therapist is not balanced or fair is one of the main reasons for early termination.

This chapter will discuss several techniques for a balanced approach to individual partners in dyadic therapy. These techniques involve the therapist joining with clients in an impartial manner, educating couples about the importance of the therapist's balanced approach, and structuring therapy in a balanced way. Also discussed will be considerations of the clients' understanding of balance, the use of inclusive language, intensity and balance, and using seating arrangement to promote balance. Understanding psychopharmacology and not attributing blame when one partner needs medication, determining therapeutic balance, and examining the potential for the loss of balance as a vital area for personal insight and growth are topics that will conclude the chapter.

☐ Joining with Clients

It is most important to establish balance during the process of joining and getting to know a couple in the initial session. New clients will be especially sensitive to the balancing skills and objectivity of the therapist. Such sensitivity is dualistic. On one hand, clients will join and commit to therapy on the basis of a therapist's ability to implement balance, and on the other hand, a client might be angry that his or her attempt to seduce the therapist into his or her way of thinking did not work. Despite the possible negativity, the therapist's mandate is to be systemic and impartial.

The following are some commonsense ideas for the therapist to use in order to join with the couple and establish a balanced approach.

1. Shake the hands of *both* husband and wife.
2. If small talk prevails for the opening minutes, make sure you are as invested in the conversation with the husband as with the wife, and vice versa.
3. When asking for the presenting problem, try not to allow one partner to monopolize the conversation for too long. While the verbosity of one spouse and the quiet of the other is "grist for the mill" in assessing marital dynamics, letting one person dominate in the opening session could create destructive coalitions. To be fair, the therapist might have to stop one partner in the middle of his or her discourse, or to look to the other partner and simply ask for his or her perspective or response.
4. A first session would include the therapist seeking to understand the perceptions of both partners to let each know that what he or she has to say is important.
5. Opening attempts at assessment should be very balanced and fair in terms of responsibility; never confront only one partner. For example, saying to the couple, "I can see how you elicit this from him and how you elicit this from her."

☐ Educating Clients

It is often difficult for the therapist to approach a dyad in a balanced way. Many clients will attempt to persuade the therapist that their own particular view of the marital relationship is correct (usually that the partner is at fault). In the initial stages of therapy, there is frequently a battle for the loyalty of the therapist. In addition, the couple often enters the therapeutic process already experiencing the advice and counsel of individually aligned friends and family members.

Educating clients about the importance of the therapist being balanced is crucial. When such education is done well, time that otherwise would have been spent justifying individual positions and perspectives is frequently saved. At the beginning or end of the initial session, the marital therapist can discuss the following balance and process issues with the couple by stating the following:

- I am going to work hard to understand both of your perspectives. Both of you are key to making effective change.
- I am going to try to be very balanced in my approach. What this means is that I assume that both of you have some responsibility for the problems and the solutions, and that each of your contributions to the problems will be addressed.
- I am going to try not to take sides. I can feel each of you trying to convince me of the rightness of your perspective, but if I do my job well, I will remain fairly neutral.
- If you feel unfairly sided against or judged by me, please let me know. It is not my intent, and I want to talk about it right away when you feel it happening.
- In order for the marriage to become more nurturing, both of you must begin to think more systemically. We will talk about this often, but briefly it means that behavior does not happen in a vacuum, and that the ways you are both treating each other are circular in nature. Your behavior influences the responses of the other. Each of you needs to take some responsibility for creating and continuing the circular and negative interactions.

The above are examples of how to educate clients about the systemic and balanced approach. When the education is explicit, trust can develop and the healing process will often proceed at a quicker pace.

☐ Overall Structure of Therapy: Who Participates?

There are many views about who should participate in the therapeutic process. Many individual psychotherapists believe that in-depth work can be done only during the course of an individual session. Some marital and family therapists conceptualize therapy as needing to include every member of the family. Others believe couple work includes only partners. Whatever the perspective, several key considerations are important for the maintenance of a balanced approach.

1. If the therapist sees the wife for an individual session in the beginning of couples therapy, the husband should also be seen separately.
2. If individual sessions are deemed necessary to break up emotional blocks

or enmeshment, the number of individual sessions should be approximately equal for the partners.

3. If one individual appears for a session when both partners were supposed to be present, it is a judgment call on whether the therapist should see the individual client. If the individual client is seen, the next session might be an individual one for the other partner in order to maintain balance.

4. Often individual therapy will evolve into couples therapy. If the individual has been in therapy for a long time, it is problematic as to whether the current therapist ought to do the conjoint work. In many cases, this can be counterproductive because loyalties, real or perceived, have been established with one individual. If it is decided that the same therapist should do both the individual and the conjoint therapy, several techniques to balance loyalties and alignments are important. The longstanding individual client must be educated about what feelings he or she might anticipate when the partner is included in the therapy. The education might include saying the following:

Therapist to Couple: When your partner is included in the therapy, you might very well experience some feelings of loss or of being judged. I will attempt to be very balanced in my approach and will try to understand your spouse's perspectives as well as yours. Because you have felt my loyalty, you might feel this as a betrayal. If you do, let's process this in the conjoint session.

In terms of structuring the session, an effective approach to try to establish a sense of balance might be to see the partner who is joining the therapy in several individual sessions. During this time, the therapist can listen to his or her perspectives and show some empathy for his or her perspectives. It may be helpful to make clear that the transition from individual therapy to couples therapy is provisional, and if it is not helpful, other alternatives will be sought. What is crucial to process directly with the spouse entering therapy is the following:

Therapist to Couple: I am concerned that you will feel that my approach to both of you is not fair. There is a danger in what we are about to do in that you might feel aligned or "ganged up" against. I am going to try to be very balanced. However, if you feel otherwise, please let me know immediately.

☐ Clients' Understanding of Balance

A primary fear of the individual spouse in a couples session is that the therapist will blame, focus upon, or confront one partner more intensely than the other. In a balanced approach, the timing of confrontation is very important. When the marital therapist decides to confront one individual at a time, it is crucial that the partner who is first being confronted or asked probing questions about his or her complicity in a certain dynamic, trusts that the partner will also be confronted in a similar manner. To establish balance and build trust, before asking one partner a question, the marital therapist can make statements such as:

- I am going to ask you both the same question.
- I will want you both to take a turn.
- What is your responsibility? And, in a minute, what is yours?
- I will ask you both to respond to what your understanding is."

The importance of timing is that the spouse who is first confronted needs to understand prior to making a response that his or her partner will be next asked a question or comment of similar intensity. Consider the following interaction in which the promise of a balanced approach is not adequately established prior to the confrontation.

Therapist to Wife: Can you see what you were doing in that last interaction?

Wife: I was just trying to express myself.

Therapist: You were expressing yourself in a very judgmental way.

Wife: But he never listens to me and just walks away.

Therapist: Your judgment pushes your husband away.

Note what each of the three parties present in the therapy session could be thinking while this particular interaction is taking place. The wife might be feeling unfairly judged and confronted by the therapist. She cannot understand why the therapist does not confront her husband. Consequently, in response to the therapist's intervention she spends most of the time being defensive and trying to convince the therapist of the husband's role. The therapist might be thinking in a systemic manner, but is not functioning in one. It may be in his or her mind to confront the husband next; however, she or he has not communicated this fact to the wife and ends up fielding her defensiveness. The husband is thinking that the therapist understands how his wife's critical nature is the crux of the problem and is forming a coalition with the therapist as he or she confronts his wife. The husband was able to communicate non-verbally with a nod, suggesting agreement with the therapist's assessment of the wife's "problems" and became a "co-therapist."

Each partner of a dyad needs the a priori trust and understanding of the therapist's intent and ability to balance interventions, especially before being confronted in an individual way. Such trust is needed whether the confrontation is nurturing and supportive or points out cognitive distortion or dysfunctional behavior. By providing adequate preparation and education about having a balanced and fair approach, the therapist can confront the individual in couples therapy with a very positive result. For example:

Therapist to Wife: Can you see what you were doing in that last interaction? (The therapist then looks at the husband before an answer is given and says, "I will ask you the same question next".)

Wife: I know I get very angry and critical.

Therapist to Husband: And what do you contribute?

Husband: I guess I do something to annoy her.

Because the wife understood that the therapist was going to ask the husband also, she was able to reflect more on her own functioning and be less defensive. The client's perception of balance is essential for allowing him or her to share deeply and vulnerably.

However, balance can be lost in an intervention such as the one given above. While the therapist asked fair and just questions to both parties, the husband did not respond at the same level of insight and reflection as his wife. He did not share the same level of vulnerability or take personal responsibility for his part of the negative communication. The therapist needs to recognize that the vulnerability of the wife is being exposed and not that of the husband. Direct and supportive confrontation of the husband is necessary to establish balance. If and when the husband is reflective, the therapist might return to confront the wife. As the therapist moves back and forth between clients, she or he constantly assesses the balance of intensity, the depth of responsibility being asked of and responded with by both partners, and the partners' perception of balance. Of course, as discussed later, the easiest balance technique is to confront or inquire of the couple and not an individual. An example of balanced intensity and personal responsibility would be:

Wife: I know I have been very angry and critical over the last few days. I feel very alone and am afraid of losing you.

Husband: I understand. I keep withdrawing and going into myself, in part because I have felt so rejected and hurt. I just couldn't communicate my feelings directly.

Both partners are sharing their vulnerable feelings and insights into how their behavior has influenced their partner. When such balance is achieved, deeper meanings and feelings can be explored.

☐ Inclusive Language

If the process of therapy consists mainly of the therapist talking to each partner with little couple interaction, the therapist is probably more oriented toward individual psychotherapy. Such an orientation might lead to a loss of balance, with the therapist speaking to only one spouse at a time and failing to structure couple dialogue and conflict resolution. Also, significant time might be spent confronting one partner or the other and striving for insight, but in an unbalanced way. When the therapist asks questions such as, "Can you both see what is happening?" and asks this of both partners, a sense of fairness can be established. Inclusive language such as "both," "the two of you," and "similar," used to suggest mutual responsibility will often decrease the competition for who is more "right" and contribute to a systemic understanding in the couple. This kind of inclusive language helps to set the tone of mutuality in the session.

Consider the following balanced interventions, which could be used by the marital therapist to heighten the awareness of the couple.

> *Therapist to Couple:* Can you see how you both contribute to the problem? Can you understand what you both did to nurture each other? The two of you are being very hurtful to each other. Do you understand that you are both really saying, "I miss you?" You are both very similar in the way you handle stress. You are both competing to be heard. Let's examine this interaction. Can you see what each of you is eliciting from the other?

Such interventions *addressed to the couple* attempt to make both partners accountable. They are not made to an individual, but to both partners at the same time, thereby enhancing a balanced approach and perspective. Often such balanced interventions are used to stop negative and destructive interaction by insisting that each individual reflects on his or her own behavior.

Therapist interaction with one spouse and not the other is fraught with opportunities for miscommunication. Issues of fairness, therapist objectivity, and individual responsibility become the focus when there are beliefs that the therapist is aligning with one spouse and not with both. For example, in a therapy session both members of a couple might feel frustrated and begin to argue about how each feels ignored. If the therapist loses balance and points out that the husband is not listening and is being judgmental, the husband might become frustrated because he feels judged. He may then become more enraged or possibly never return to a session. However, if the therapist says, "Please stop; you both are right. Neither of you is hearing the other person and you both are feeling judged." The destructive interaction is much more likely to be slowed down or reframed into a more constructive conversation. The therapist who demonstrates a balanced and impartial approach to a couple calms down the fear each spouse holds of not being heard.

For the purpose of maintaining balance, whenever possible, it is helpful for the marital therapist to intervene in such a way that both partners of the dyad will simultaneously look at his or her own functioning in either a destructive and unhealthy interaction or a positive, nurturing one. However, interventions addressed to one partner and not to the other can be important and effective also. Some ideas about how to maintain balance when working with individuals are discussed in the following section, Intensity and Balance.

☐ Intensity and Balance

Applying balance in the questioning of clients, and managing the timing of interventions are essential skills for the marital therapist to learn. Assessing balance in terms of the intensity and depth of questions and confrontations is a more difficult, higher-level skill to develop. The following interaction is unbalanced because the intensity of intervention with the wife is at a very different level from the one with the husband.

Husband: I'm trying as hard as I can!

Wife: But it just is not good enough. You aren't thinking through anything you are doing prior to doing it.

Husband: Well if you would help me once in a while, I wouldn't get into these predicaments.

Wife: But I don't want to help you. I want you to take the initiative.

Therapist to Wife: Do you see that you are communicating in an unfair way!

Therapist to Husband: Try and communicate what you need without blaming.

The therapist has the concept of balance in mind but is confronting in quite an unbalanced way. The word "unfair" said to the wife differs significantly in power from "Try . . . without blaming," said to the husband. Understandably, the wife could feel blamed by the therapist, while her husband might feel the therapist to be quite reasonable. A possible intervention to the husband to balance the somewhat harsh response to the wife might be one of the following:

Therapist to Husband: Do you see how you are also communicating unfairly? Do you understand how you could be perceived as unfair to your wife?

The intensity of an intervention needs to be balanced both in terms of the power of the confrontation and the request for vulnerability and insight. It is important that the marital therapist when asking for significant revelation from one spouse also asks the other spouse. Even when the therapist feels balanced in approach, she or he never truly knows the entire impact of an individual intervention. In fact, the partners themselves might not perceive the power of an intervention until much later. Therefore, the therapist must constantly assess a client's verbal and nonverbal responses and reactions. If defensiveness occurs in one partner, it might be the consequence of a perception that the therapist is unfair or unjust.

The immediacy of balanced intervention is also very important. In the above dialogue, if the therapist stated that she or he would like to deal with the husband's issues in the present session and the wife's difficulties in the session the following week, a number of problems could occur. The husband's vulnerabilities and responsibility for the dysfunctional couple patterns would be exposed for an entire week before the wife might have to deal with her complementary role in the couple dynamic. In that time, the husband could feel sided against and the wife could feel justified. Coalitions might be formed with friends or family that would need to be processed. The wife's responsibility in the couple's circular patterns might never be examined as the sessions become more imbalanced toward confrontation of the husband.

Balance techniques should be demonstrated within each therapeutic session, not week to week. In heated confrontation, the most effective balance might occur every several minutes. This means that the therapist orients the conversation back and forth between two partners while trying to keep the length of discussion and the depth of intervention and intensity balanced and fair.

☐ Using Room Setting to Promote a Balanced Session

One of the simplest balancing concepts to understand, and one of the most violated, pertains to the room setting and the couple and therapist seating positions. Assessment of alignments and coalitions among any group of people can be readily ascertained by watching nonverbal cues such as who faces whom and physical proximity (Minuchin, Lee, & Simon, 1996).

The positioning of the chairs and the posture of the marital therapist can affect therapist balance and client perceptions of fairness and the therapeutic process. For example, suppose the therapy room is set up with the two clients directly facing the therapist, as if in a classroom, and not at all towards each other. This structure suggests that the therapist will be the leader or instructor. Implicit is the idea that the therapist's insight and direction are the important dynamic in the couple's therapy. By making it difficult for the couple to face or to speak to each other, the therapist reinforces clients' dependency on the therapist and inhibits the use of couple interaction to explore issues. This is a reason the use of couches often makes it difficult to promote real interaction.

By making the therapist central to the therapeutic process, there is more chance to stop the reactiveness of the couple than if the couple were to continue to look directly at each other. Of course, the eventual goal is to move the therapist out of the center and to increase the effectiveness of the couple interaction, while encouraging the couple to face more towards each other.

A structure in which the couple directly faces one another could, in a negative way, increase the likelihood that the clients will be enmeshed and conflictual and, in a positive way, structure an intimate communication amongst themselves with the therapist as an observer. Clients who are conflictual might independently move their chair; to face the therapist and away from each other to create more safety and less couple intimacy. The couple who has been working hard at their intimate communication might not need the buffer or the safety that the therapist provides and move their chairs towards each other. In cases in which couple intimacy is sought, the therapist might want to take himself or herself out of the middle of the couple interaction and encourage the partners to speak directly to each other. The active therapist should certainly be able to intervene no matter the seating arrangement.

In an initial session it is suggested that each chair be positioned equally to face the two other chairs, somewhat like the three sides of a triangle. With equal ease of conversation among clients and therapist, there is the greatest likelihood for balancing the input of the therapist with enactments and couple interaction. From this position the therapist and clients can turn their heads to make the therapist more or less central to the couple conversation.

Relative height between client and therapist is also important to consider. If the therapist sits in a professional chair and the clients on a soft couch, the height difference could be one or two feet. Looking down at someone can definitely affect the process of conjoint therapy. Understanding the relationship of body language and concepts of fairness and balance is crucial for every marital therapist. When the therapist positions herself or himself towards the couple and not towards an individual, a sense of balance and fairness is created. By facing one partner and not the other, feelings can emerge in the clients of being picked on or sided against or, conversely, being aligned with and being the favorite. The general body position of the therapist when not making a specific interaction should be towards the middle of the space between the clients or equally towards both partners.

Balance of eye contact is important. Looking straight at one partner by the therapist will probably engage that partner. If continually done in an unbalanced way, the therapist is communicating a number of possible things. Perhaps she or he is aligned with or against that person or is reacting in some way to the personality of the client. Whatever the reason, the most difficult effect of maintaining eye contact with one client and not the other is that the individual being stared at will find it hard to look away and could be pulled out of an interaction with his or her partner.

Eye contact should be balanced in intensity and duration with each client as much as possible. When an enactment, an opportunity for the couple to interact with each other, is being structured by the therapist, the therapist might look down. By the therapist avoiding any eye contact with either partner at those times, the clients will find it more difficult to resist intimate communication with each other by engaging the attention and eyes of the therapist. Unconsciously, a therapist who fears intimate emotional conversation can disrupt the depth of couple conversation by looking only at one partner.

Touch, if perceived to be appropriate by the therapist, should be of the same quality and nature with both partners. For instance, if the therapist shakes the hand of the husband, she or he should do the same with the wife. A hug offered to one partner and not to the other can create issues of injustice and feelings of alienation. Touch, in general, should emerge out of the feelings of the session and the needs of the client. When done as a habit, touch can communicate a superficial intimacy. For example, a hug after a difficult session has a very different meaning than a hug after every session.

☐ Psychopharmacology and Balance

Perhaps one of the most difficult couple interventions for therapist to make in a balanced way is the suggestion of medication for one partner and not for the other. Medication is *often* prescribed for the purpose of alleviating anxiety or depression, which affects both the individual and the health of his or her marital relationship. The client needing medication can be tempted to view himself or herself as the "sick one," or the spouse not needing medication may feel vindicated of personal responsibility. Every marital therapist should be versed in the effective use of medication to enhance the health of an individual, and to alter a negative circular pattern of couple interaction. For accurate psychopharmacology, a psychiatric referral is needed. Framing such an intervention for the couple, in a balanced way, takes considerable thought. Possible frames to suggest medication are:

1. "You both are contributing to the problems in ways we have discovered over the last number of sessions. (To one partner) Some of the difficulties you are having with depression and your consequent negative feelings, I believe, could be helped with the use of medication. (To the other partner) On the other hand, your issues won't respond to medication and have more to do with learning and family-of-origin issues. You will have to work hard to positively influence these tendencies and personality traits. With the use of medication for you, and with both of you working on issues of family of origin, the quality of your relationship could be enhanced."

2. "I believe that medication can help you to function better and to feel less down on yourself. If that is the case, and one of you begins medication, you both will have to look at the relationship differently. (To the partner in need of medication) When not depressed, you might look at the actions of your spouse very differently, with less hurt or rejection. As this stops, you (looking at the partner not in need of medication) may have to examine some of the fears you might feel when intimacy is more of a possibility."

3. "The issues you both describe are certainly workable. I believe that about 10 to 20 percent of the difficulty has to do with the anxiety that seems to have control of you. I would like you to try medication to determine whether it can alleviate some of the symptoms. I can refer you to a psychiatrist, whom I know and respect, who can assess for the possible use of medication. I will continue to see both of you in therapy. The three of us will focus on the other 80 or 90 percent of the difficulty that the medication will not affect."

By balancing the responsibility for progress *in the therapy* and not making it impinge on the effectiveness of the medication, the individual member of a couple will be more likely to accept the referral for a psychiatric assessment. In the last example, if the importance of medication is put in perspective, the referred spouse is less likely to feel like a patient.

☐ Techniques Used to Determine Balance

There are three objective means for the therapist to assess balance and level of bias. These include monitoring time, counting interchanges as to who speaks to whom, and making inquiries to the client couple.

Monitoring Time

While there are always exceptions to any rule, a therapist unknowingly spending considerably more time with one partner versus another is often a reliable indication of transference or countertransference issues or alignment and coalitions between therapist and one or both partners. A good exercise is for a marital therapist to assess how much time is spent with each client. If 45 minutes is spent in discussion with one partner and 5 minutes is spent with the other, this might be a warning sign to the therapist that the therapy is losing its systemic foundation.

Length of time spent can also be measured for the *amount of time the therapist talks*, the amount of conversation between the two partners, and the length of silences. If the marital therapist is doing the majority of the talking, there is probably little *in depth* therapy taking place. Instead, the therapist is giving *a lecture* or, at best, offering some psychoeducational process. The verbose therapist, one who does not let the clients speak, probably has little sense of the process of marital therapy. The therapist spending time both talking to the individual spouses and helping both partners engage in conversation with each other is probably facilitating a more effective marital process.

If, especially in later sessions, all conversation is channeled through the therapist, she or he is probably either anxious and fears losing control or has been inducted into the resistance of the couple. Client interaction in enactments, structured by the couple and the therapist, is central to marital work. The presence of some silence in a session can be a positive indication that the therapist is asking probing questions for thought and insight or perhaps is allowing for a more profound level of feeling. Sessions filled with a constant flow of words are probably indicative of high levels of anxiety.

Counting Interchanges

Another helpful tool for determining balance is the counting of interchanges between the various participants. An excellent exercise to determine the nature of the process of a session is to listen to an audio- or videotape and count how many times each person speaks to every other person. If all dialogue is between therapist and one individual of a couple, the therapist might actually be doing individual therapy in a conjoint setting. At certain times, such as when exploring family-of-origin issues or eliciting affect, such individual therapy with both partners present might be preferable.

However, in most cases when the dialogue is predominately between an individual and therapist, the therapist does not have a clear enough understanding of the use *or the importance* of enactments in marital therapy. The marital therapist who is central to all conversation might have a need for control or have an overresponsible attitude for the movement and content of the session. Most often, a constructive and dynamic process of marital therapy will include significant couple dialogue, therapist's comments and interventions to each individual, and process comments directed towards the couple.

Making Inquiries

Perhaps the most obvious technique for adequately assessing the balance of the therapist's approach is to ask a client couple, "How have I been balanced or unbalanced in my approach to both of you?" or "What is your perception of the responsibility you both are being asked to take in the marital difficulties?" Clients will often feel safer with a therapist who can ask such questions because they know the therapist is thinking about issues of fairness, and can recognize that she or he is fallible in terms of a offering balanced approach and welcomes constructive feedback. If balance is lost and these questions are asked, there is a greater likelihood that the clients will verbalize their feelings before trust and confidence in the effectiveness of the therapy are undermined.

☐ The Meaning of Loss of Balance

When a client feels unfairly confronted, when siding and coalitions are created that alienate one of the spouses, or when the marital therapist diagnoses a couple in cause-and-effect rather than systemic terms, there are a number of possibilities for the therapist to consider.

1. The therapist might lack the skill and ability to think systemically.
2. The therapist might have unresolved issues from family-of-origin that are being tapped by the client's content or process.
3. The therapist might be in a countertransference as a reaction to projections from the client, or in a transference, in which the therapist is projecting his or her own material onto the client.
4. The clients are not free of responsibility and might be working to get the therapist to be unbalanced so that they can exit therapy or fail to change a homeostatic pattern.

Whatever the reasons, violations of fairness, justice, and balance should prompt a therapist to discuss them with his or her supervisor. The therapist should reflect in order to understand the etiology of the imbalance of approach, and then do what needs to be done to correct the imbalance.

☐ Conclusion

In conclusion, balance is a central systemic concept. It is necessary for the marital therapist to develop skills to maintain a balanced and fair approach so that both individuals of a couple can examine their responsibility in the marital difficulty.

Systemic Intervention

In systems theory, addressing the individual, as well as the context in which the individual relates, is important. Systems theory delineates the interrelatedness of the family members to each other (Bowen, 1972). An ability central to systemic thinking is to differentiate linear interventions from systemic ones. Many marital therapists have never made the conceptual transition from a more linear and individual approach to one more circular and systemic. So much education is designed around an almost exclusively linear way of thinking that it is virtually impossible for some therapists to reorient their conceptual perspectives to include learning to assess and question clients in a circular *systemic* manner as well. Circular epistemology is a view of reality that one event does not directly cause another as in linear epistemology. Such a circular model of causality is multicausal and multidetermined.

Linear thinking is based on the ability to probe for cause and effect. Such cognitive processing looks at why people act the way they do. *In the interchange below, each of the questions asked without the other is quite linear. However, combinations of linear questions can develop a circular understanding of the nature of a couple's interaction.*

For example:

Therapist to Wife: Why do you get so angry?

Wife: Because he always withdraws from me.

Therapist to Husband: Why do you withdraw?

Husband: Because she is always so angry.

Withdrawal and anger contribute to a circular and reciprocal pattern. Singular linear questions that do not probe the interrelatedness of behavior can result in a therapist or client attributing blame by focusing the responsibility for a problem or conflict upon a single person or event. Using the above example, the wife justifies her anger on the basis of her husband's withdrawal. The linear-oriented therapist may think the same way and attempt to help the husband not to withdraw without also examining the effect of the wife's anger on the pattern of withdrawal.

Linear thinking could be diagrammed as A → B. Therefore, fix A, and B will be fine. However, it is equally valid that the wife's anger is contributing to the husband's withdrawal. Consideration of the interaction of anger and withdrawal brings the therapist from a more linear perspective to a more circular one. Linear thinking does not take into account the more complex and circular nature of human behavior and interrelationships because it focuses responsibility in only one direction.

Systemic thinking includes cause and effect, but extends the concepts to include identification of circular and reciprocal patterns. The diagramming of such patterns would be A → B → A → B ad infinitum (Penn, 1982). In systemic thinking, discovering who is at fault or who began the problem is secondary to exploring how each partner, family member, influences of family-of-origin, societal values, and so on contribute to the reciprocal patterns. If the client says, "I am happy because my husband is so attentive," the therapist who thinks in a systemic way will discover that the husband is attentive, in part, because the wife is happy. The feeling of happiness and resulting intimacy experienced by both partners form a positive reciprocal and circular pattern.

The therapist who thinks linearly tends to stay focused on the individual, while the systemic therapist tends to look at the relationships and processes between partners, families, and social contexts. Systemic thinking reinforces the idea that even an illness such as depression, with its "cause" perhaps rooted in psychobiology, *still* has enormous ramifications for spouses and family members. The role and function of the depression and how two partners and family members respond to them are always significant factors in marital dynamics and the depth of the depression itself.

The relationship of any behavior, emotion, or thoughtful expression to the personality of the individual, marital relationship, family, or society is always key (Pierce, Nichols & DuBrin, 1983). It is the function and purpose of behavior that can be elaborated more fully in systemic thinking. What was the behavior for? How does the behavior fit into the relational patterns? Where does the behavior come from? How was it influenced by family of origin? This chapter will illustrate linear and circular or systemic questions and techniques for the marital therapist seeking to intervene in diverse ways.

☐ Circular Questions Deepen the Meaning of Linear Questions

The information elicited by circular questions extends beyond linear inquiry. For example, if the client says, "I feel depressed," linear questions might be:

1. What caused the depression?
2. What event began the depressed feelings?
3. When did your mother or father first comment on the depression?

Questions that seek a more systemic understanding might be:

1. Is anyone else in your family depressed?
2. How does your spouse respond to your depression?
3. What role does depression play in your marital intimacy?

If the client says, "I am furious!" linear questions might be:

1. What causes you to be furious?
2. When did you get so furious?
3. Who causes you to be so angry?

Circular, systemic questions might be:

1. What does your spouse do when you are furious?
2. What is the relationship between your anger and your ability to be intimate and vulnerable?
3. Were either of your parents angry in a similar manner?

Both sets of questions are important. However, the circular questions are going to enrich the therapist's understanding of how an individual issue is part of a couple or family pattern in ways that linear questions will not. Linear questions will give the therapist a more single-minded approach to the etiology and understandings of an individual's or couple's behavior. While finding cause can be enlightening, looking at cause as part of a more complicated set of circumstances and relationships will give the therapist more opportunity to intervene and change couple patterns. The question "Who caused you to be so angry?" will possibly lead to the identification of one person as the cause. Asking the question "Were either of your parents angry in a similar manner?" begins the process of a client looking at family-of-origin introjected patterns, and developing insight into how anger has affected his or her past and current relational patterns.

☐ Circular Questions and Balanced Intervention

One of the primary roles of the marital therapist is to remain balanced and to demonstrate fairness by relating to both individuals of a couple. "There are two sides to every coin" and "It takes two to tango" are colloquialisms that suggest the importance of looking for shared responsibility in any marital issue or problem. When the therapist thinks linearly, it is often quite difficult to remain balanced and fair because blame can more easily be attributed to one partner. The therapist can be easily inducted into a couple's dysfunctional pattern by listening and agreeing with one spouse's description of the other's faults. By looking at the circular patterns of behavior, the actions of both spouses are taken into consideration. By extending the understanding of systemic thinking beyond the couple, the therapist seeks to encourage both partners to look at patterns of relating in family-of-origin and social contexts. The systemic assumption that nothing happens in a vacuum and that both partners should be held accountable makes balance and fairness easier to establish.

☐ Learning to Think in a Systemic Manner

How does a therapist learn to think in a systemic way? Part of the answer is to look for the meaning of any behavior outside of, as well as inside of, the person exhibiting the behavior. Consider the following examples:

1. A woman client begins to cry during a conjoint therapy session. Linear thinking will lead the therapist to ask who or what caused her to cry and probably limit the inquiry to that understanding. A more systemic thinker will attempt to ascertain the function and purpose of the crying for both the individual and the system in which she relates. For instance, the therapist will notice how the spouse or partner responds to the crying. If the partner becomes angry in response to the crying, perhaps it means more than a sharing of a sad feeling. Crying may be used to manipulate or to elicit guilt. The partner's anger may be a safer way of expressing feelings of fear or incompetence. In such a manner, the couple might create distance from each other. There are many possibilities for the meaning of crying and the response of anger within a dyad.

2. A husband grows very hostile towards his wife. Before the therapist responds or intervenes, it is crucial that she or he look over at the wife to determine her response. The nature of the response will provide the therapist with an increased understanding of the meaning and pur-

pose for the hostility. If the woman withdraws, maybe the husband is trying to *create* rejection and withdrawal. If the wife yells back in a hostile way, perhaps this is the only way that the couple stay out of depression or know how to be intimate. *Many couples find anger and hostility as their primary way of creating "closeness" and avoiding feelings of abandonment.* The man's hostility may be grounded in feelings of powerlessness. Once expressed, it may serve some personal and systemic function. The therapist can examine each partner's reaction in order to better determine the meaning of the hostility from multiple perspectives.

3. A man states, "I really feel sad." On the surface this statement seems to be assertive and quite revealing. Because the therapist thinks in a systemic way, she or he looks to the partner to see the response. To the therapist's surprise, the woman is disinterested. When asked about her disinterest, the woman states that whenever her husband wants sex later in the day, he starts to express his sadness and vulnerability early in the morning. He has a circuitous and passive way of asking for intimacy and care. The therapist discovers that the wife is angry about her husband's indirectness. The husband asks circuitously in part because he fears his wife's anger. The couple's sadness and anger then organize in a circular fashion. Systemic interpretations can aid in the therapist's understanding of the function of an individual's specific behavior. In the above example, "I really feel sad," was not a catharsis or an attempt to share an emotion to establish intimacy, but an indirect request for sex, which was then perceived as a manipulation by the partner. *The therapist, however, will not know this if he/she immediately intervenes with linear questions.*

4. A husband states, "Every night when I come home from work I approach my wife and want to be very affectionate." The therapist who concludes, without inquiry, that this statement is sensitive and caring is not necessarily thinking in a systemic way. A systemic question is, "When the husband is affectionate, what does the wife do in response?" Upon further inquiry, the therapist finds that every night just before the husband comes home, his wife becomes agitated and withdrawn. When the husband approaches, his wife wants to pull back. The affection now takes on a new meaning. The husband may be unconsciously distancing his wife because he knows that she will withdraw upon his approach. He then can criticize her unavailability and justify his own behavior. This example of one partner reaching out in a seemingly affectionate way for the purpose of distancing his partner is a common marital dynamic (Napier, 1978; Nichols & Napier, 1996). The systemic therapist must be able to sit back and be enough of an observer of the

couple's process to determine how a singular comment by one partner is received by the other.

5. A woman states, "I really understand how I have let you down. Please give me another chance." The man receiving this message remains unforgiving and rigid in his response. The therapist can confront the man for not being more open by saying, "This was a *sensitive*, reasonable, and assertive statement by your wife." But what the therapist may not understand is that the woman's statement is part of a dance that the couple does together (Lerner, 1989; 1997). After the woman asks for forgiveness several times, the man finally softens and becomes more giving. As soon as this occurs, the woman disappoints the man again and he becomes enraged and rigid as the cycle repeats itself. Both spouses feel abused and rejected, which are old repetitive feelings derived from their families-of-origin.

Once the message is sent and the answer received are understood and their interrelationship is noted, the function of a behavior can be examined as it relates to one's family of origin, to levels of differentiation with parents, to individual personality, and to self-concept. The partner who recognizes systemic patterns, their origins, and the effects on personality can take some personal responsibility to change him- or herself, the couple patterns, and other relationships in which the patterns are manifested.

☐ Systemic Thinking Leads to Wider Interpretation and Intervention

Systemic thinking leads to other types of interventions that assist the therapist in his or her understanding of the intricacies of a couple's relationship and their extended family relationships. A therapist who thinks systemically assumes that behaviors of a couple are not random but rather intricately connected. What one partner receives from another is not by mistake and often there are some, or many, covert or overt dynamics creating patterns and responses that, positively or negatively, are of service to each individual.

In the frequently observed reciprocal patterns of anger in response to withdrawal and vice versa, one systemic intervention is to probe whether the person who is angry is unconsciously asking his or her partner to withdraw (Napier, 1990). Is the person who withdraws for some reason asking for anger or abuse? Part of the answer to such questions may be found in the early introjected feelings from the husband's or wife's family background. Early introjects, if strongly negative and hurtful, can result

in repetitive patterns later in life, which are unconsciously repeated with a spouse (Scharff & Scharff, 1987, 1991, 1995). Unresolved childhood feelings often find expression in the intimacy and commitment of a marital relationship. *Other areas for insight exploration are the repetitions of negative entitlements, negative self-concepts, and unconscious contracts between couples.*
For example:

1. Bob is an adult child of an alcoholic mother. He experienced a great deal of verbal abuse and inconsistent parenting. Overall, he felt abandoned and rejected as a child. Feelings of abandonment and hurt were introjected and, once he was married, *projected onto his wife* and transformed into issues of abandonment within the marriage. Bob picked a woman who was also hurt in her upbringing. By being emotionally unavailable to his wife, he elicited a great deal of criticism and rejection from her. By blaming her for being emotionally distant, he repeated an old pattern and lacked understanding about his own repetitive creation. Bob did not understand the function of his critical behavior *as that of creating distance*. A systemic intervention, done with good timing and with sensitivity, is to inquire about how being abandoned is predictable and perhaps keeps him safe. After gaining some understanding, the patterns of eliciting rejection in a repetitive way can be directly confronted and worked through. This is discussed further in Chapter 9.

2. Joan married a man who was completely unaware of his feelings. She spent a long time in the marriage trying to elicit feelings and closeness from her partner, but the more she pushed, the more he resisted. The couple came to therapy with the goal of decreasing the tension. Joan had the unspoken goal of trying to get her husband to express his feelings. Linear thinking by a therapist might encourage him or her to attempt to elicit the husband's feelings. Such change is one crucial aspect of altering the couple interaction. A systemic thinker will also ask what investment Joan has in being married to someone so quiet and unemotional, and how she overfunctions in an effort to maintain his silence and lack of intimacy.

3. A client comes to a therapist saying, "My wife left me for another man." The therapist is immediately empathic and sides with the husband's view of the distressed relationship. Systemically, however, the therapist needs to think at least in terms of what part the husband played in his wife's leaving or, at the very minimum, how he was distancing his spouse. Does this recent abandonment fulfill some old loyalty or legacy in the husband's background? Thinking systemically stimulates different ways of thinking and of conceptualizing the dynamics of the couple's interaction.

In systemic thinking, family-of-origin issues reconstituted in current relationships are a key focus. A tendency exists, called homeostasis, to maintain the status quo and to organize these reconstituted patterns by keeping everything the same in a marital dyad and the family, as well as between generations. Within such repetitive patterns, another type of systemic intervention and series of questions might invite insight and allow for movement. Everyone has some resistance to change. Thus, the recognition of reciprocal and systemic patterns can be very frightening for one or both partners. For instance, a wife might constantly complain that her husband is never around or is never emotionally available. If the systemic assumption that she has some investment in the distance is true, then the following interventions, either directly asked of the client or elicited through client insight, might make sense. For instance:

- Would you be scared if your husband turned to you and was emotional?
- How do you contribute to the undermining of your husband's attempts to be affectionate?
- Would you be able to feel or to see if your husband was being emotional? You seem very sure that he can't be.

A general systemic assumption is that one spouse will generally resist the movement of the other if the couple's established homeostatic patterns are challenged. Even though one partner is finally giving the other exactly what is being asked for, change can be frightening and unpredictable. Change of behavior might increase the possibility of vulnerability and intimacy. Systemic questions can point out the lack of reinforcement given to change, make clients aware of the different levels of resistance, and increase the likelihood of movement. For instance, "Would you be frightened if you received what you asked for?" "If you felt loved by your spouse, think about how you would have to change the way you think about yourself." It is part of the marital therapist's task to anticipate that what a husband and wife might want most could be what they most vehemently resist and at deeper levels fear. As small movements of change are not reinforced, and given insight, significant couple growth is thwarted.

Systemic thinking, when modeled and taught to a client couple, begins the process of the couple having some power over enhancing the quality of their relationship. Replacing the linear processes of blame and judgment with personal understanding and insight into the interrelationships of different behaviors gives the spouses the opportunity to take personal responsibility for changing the patterns in the relationship. If a husband or wife understands that withdrawal elicits anger from a wife or husband, she or he can work on the withdrawal to effect change. One definition of personal power is the ability to take responsibility for one's own functioning without projecting blame onto another. Insight into the function of behavior and the expression of thought or feeling gives an individual the tools to relate in a more powerful and effective manner.

☐ Conclusion

In conclusion, it is important to understand the relationship of linear and systemic thinking and intervention. Linear thinking examines cause and effect and systemic approaches seek to discover the meaning and function of symptoms in reciprocal and repetitive patterns of relationships. Basic to a systemic approach is the assumption that both partners of a couple or every member of a family are at least somewhat invested in every conflict and issue. If an individual can understand his or her contribution to a dysfunctional communication or reciprocal pattern, then he or she can be empowered towards change and growth. Within the systemic approach, circular questioning deepens understanding, helps to maintain a therapist's balance, and leads to wider interpretations and interventions than linear questions alone.

CHAPTER 5

Moving from Content to Process

Content consists of what is being said—the data and information. Process is the manner and intent by which the content is shared. The systemic therapist needs to be skilled in eliciting and hearing the content as well as understanding the function and meaning of the communication—the process. This chapter will discuss how to explore for and interpret the deeper meanings underlying content.

To become skilled in identifying process, the therapist needs to concentrate on developing more effective listening skills so as to uncover the "between the lines" meanings of clients' language. Concurrent with tracking the content, the marital therapist can listen for the meaning behind a certain tone of voice, the "why" of a specific word choice, and the overall intent of a message that is not fully expressed in words.

This chapter will provide some suggestions on how to become a more perceptive listener of client process. Tone of voice will be discussed as a way to control relationship intimacy and as an expression of assertiveness, aggressiveness, submissiveness, or passive-aggressive behavior. Word choice and meaning will be emphasized as focuses of therapist intervention. The goal is for the therapist to track the content while simultaneously understanding the process of the communication on a number of different levels. A discussion of common language patterns between partners will conclude the chapter.

☐ Tone of Voice

Clearly, tone of voice suggests to the therapist a great deal about the intent and meaning of a communication. A difficulty for many marital therapists is that they do not confront *the way* something is being said, but instead respond to and elaborate upon the *content* of a message. However, the marital partner who is listening will often respond *more* to tone of voice *than* to the content of his or her partner's communication. A negative tone of voice can be aggressive and invasive, creating defensiveness in the listener. Invasive language violates the ego boundaries and identity of an individual. It is language that is aggressive and often controlling and manipulative. For example, one spouse might say to the other,

> "You never are affectionate, you are selfish and uncaring and only think about yourself. Are you listening to me?"

These types of phrases said in an angry, aggressive tone will probably feel like an attack. They are difficult for the listener to simultaneously hear and respond to without becoming defensive. In general, invasive language and tone of voice, no matter how accurate the content, will not be heard and will produce a defensive response. The content of such discussions is often misunderstood and misinterpreted. In other words, the couple can talk about many content areas in the same defensive manner and aggressive tone of voice and have the same negative result: *No one is listening and destructive patterns are maintained.*

The marital therapist needs to confront both the tone of voice and the invasiveness of the language; the defensive and aggressive attitude that probably masks deeper feelings of fear or pain, and the response or reaction of the listening spouse, before discussing the content of a message. The confrontation could be in the form of a request: "Could you say the same thing and change your tone of voice?" or "Your tone of voice is aggressive; try and say the same thing assertively." Or to the listener: "How are you hearing what your partner is saying?" Other possibilities include asking why the communication was verbalized aggressively, or inquiring about what the aggression elicits from the partner. The intention of such interventions is to develop a process that is less reactive and more cognitive, thoughtful, and sharing of the *vulnerability and feelings* on the part of the sender.

Another form of language that creates difficulty for the process of effective communication is, paradoxically, a tone that is soft and carries very little intensity. Passive and unassertive language is so difficult because the listener strains to hear and interpret what the communicator is trying to say. Often the result is a listener who might give up trying to understand the communicator. In this way, a couple might be colluding to resist more intimate sharing.

To establish a healthy process of communication, the therapist might ask the communicator to speak louder, to intensify his or her speech, to become more assertive; or ask the listener to respond in a more assertive, less reactive manner. Inquiry into the meaning of speaking with little intensity and the way the partner reacts to it may bring insight into deeper personal feelings and thoughts about a couple's dynamic.

Effective communication is characterized by a tone of voice that is assertive, not aggressive, and is sensitive to the emotional boundaries of others. Often, there will be a reflective quality to the tone. For instance, a spouse might say,

"I understand that I . . . "
"I feel sad about . . . "
"I realize that I . . . "

Clarity without force or coercion and listening with an intent to understand and not to defend are characteristics of effective communication.

☐ Word Choice and Meaning

Client word choice and meaning constitute another area of concentration for the marital therapist. The specific words used by clients are major clues to innermost feelings and thoughts. Words that carry emotional weight or cognitive significance may well be the focus of an entire session, as deeper and more significant interpretations and feelings to increase couple intimacy are sought. Such significance is evident with a client who expresses emotions in unqualified terms such as, "I am sad" instead of "I am sad today about . . . " or "I am stupid" instead of "I do not understand this." Feelings expressed in absolutes often have direct historical roots from the client's early experiences and relationships.

"I am *always* rejected by him/her."
"He/she has *never* loved me.
"Why do I *always* have to take care of you?"
"He/she abandons me *all* of the time."

When feelings are communicated in the absolute, without qualification, a therapist should delve for deeper historical significance than what is apparent in the current relationship.

The therapist must make inquiries and pursue definitions actively to clarify a client's intent and to specify meaning between speaker and listener. *The same pursuit of meaning needs to be encouraged for both individuals of a couple.* It is important not to assume that the partners understand each other. For example, there are many ways a therapist could respond to the client who expresses these feelings:

I feel down.
I feel sad.
I feel happy.
I am scared there is no floor.

Many therapists think they understand the meaning of these feelings without obtaining more specific explanations and descriptions for increased insight and emotional expression. Although it may seem that the content of a message is clear, the meanings behind and hidden within a communication affect the process a great deal. Much miscommunication occurs when the communicator is inadequately clear or the listener is hearing from a specific set of preconceived ideas. After the therapist shares empathy and understanding regarding how the partner is feeling, the next step could be to ask about the words "down," "sad," "happy," "scared," and "no floor" to determine the deletions, distortions, and generalizations, which can help to characterize, expand, and further interpret the above expressions (Bandler & Grinder, 1975, 1990; Milliner, Grinder, & Bretto, 2000). The following illustrates this kind of inquiry:

Client: I feel down.

Therapist: Down about what?

Down about whom?

Can you describe down?

How far down?

Do you feel down some of the time or all of the time?

Client: I feel sad.

Therapist: Sad about what?

Sad towards or about whom?

What kind of sad?

How deep is the sadness?

Are you sad all of the time?

Are you sad about everything?

Client: I feel happy.

Therapist: Happy about what?

Happy about whom?

How happy are you?

Are you happy all of the time?

Client: I feel scared all of the time.

Therapist: Scared about what?

Scared about whom?

At what time do you feel scared?

How scared are you?

Are you truly scared every day?

The attentive and realistic therapist will not assume understanding of a client's specific meaning, but will ask questions and share feelings to understand more deeply the intention, conscious or unconscious, of a word choice. *Of course, the skilled systemic therapist will teach each spouse to inquire and seek deeper meaning from each other in the same manner he or she might with each individual. It is of far more value to teach client couples this exploration skill and sensitivity than to simply model it in therapy.*

Because language is sufficiently inexact, the therapist or individual partner of a couple has to inquire as to meanings that are deleted, distortions that are present, and generalizations that exaggerate the true intention of the expressor and the response of the listener. Consider the family characterized below:

The Stewart family presented in therapy with their 12-year-old son, John, as the identified patient. John's brother Paul and his mother and father all described John as being rebellious and a troublemaker. The therapist decided to orient part of the session around the meaning of the words "rebellious" and "troublemaker." The therapist realized that both words were packed with deletions, distortions, and generalizations, which if left hidden, would prevent the family from seeing how they had constructed a view of itself based on language and the lack of shared meaning.

Each family member was asked what these words meant. The father discounted the seriousness of his son's behavior and attributed his actions to those of a normal teenager; rebelliousness was a part of growing up. The mother interpreted "troublemaker" to mean John was heading down a path toward juvenile delinquency. Paul was jealous of the rebelliousness. For him, it meant that John could get away with so much more than he could at that age. He believed John was receiving preferential treatment. John thought that "rebelliousness" was fine and normal, especially in comparison to the actions of his peers.

The alignments and coalitions within the family structure became quite clear as the meanings of the words were elicited from the family. The therapist watched as the mother said in an angry, anxious way, "John is so rebellious and a real troublemaker," while the father laughed in a condescending fashion and as brother Paul sat in an angry sulk.

Words communicate meaning, but never reveal the complete meaning. Further elaboration and intention of the communication needs to be sought by the therapist and/or a spouse who is actively listening.

☐ Common Language Patterns in Couples

Couples develop language patterns that are important for the therapist to identify and understand. Five general patterns will be discussed: Language as a Manager of Distance; Assertive, Aggressive, Submissive, and Passive-Aggressive Communication; Reactive and Responsive Listening; Reciprocal Language Patterns; and Hierarchical Intimacy Patterns.

Language as a Manager of Distance

Language is a powerful tool that can be used to determine the amount of closeness and distance in a relationship. The therapist must listen not only to the content, but also to the intent of a specific communication by focusing on the response it elicits. This will help the therapist determine whether the communication brings a couple closer or moves them farther apart, condescends or puts down, or the opposite direction, places one of the partners on a pedestal and the other one-down.

Assertive language often brings two people closer. "I" followed by a feeling and said in a reflective or sensitive tone of voice will frequently elicit a positive response. Even a message such as "I feel angry," which could be heard defensively, said with the intention of opening communication could be received positively and increase understanding between two partners. In order to communicate assertively, the sender must feel entitled to have feelings and thoughts, to speak, to be heard, and to feel that what he or she has to say is important. There needs to be a history of feelings of safety, trust, and respect within a couple's relationship for assertive communication to occur.

Language that distances a partner is often characterized by *judgment* or *blame*. Such language *often* starts with the word "you," and the intention is to project or attribute blame and responsibility onto another person. A spouse who says "You never hug me!" or "You aren't very sensitive or caring!" is ostensibly communicating a wish for closeness, but the defensive response it provokes creates distance. Separation and alienation are common outcomes in communication that unconsciously repeats early destructive patterns from one's family of origin. By harboring feelings of rejection or abandonment from the past, the spouse believes that he or she is asking for closeness but in truth is establishing distance, perhaps to protect against further pain.

The following comparison of statements illustrates how the same basic content can be used in a healing, intimate way, or in a more regressive, alienating manner to push a partner away. The first statements can increase intimacy and are congruent with a wish to be nurtured and understood. The second set will probably establish distance and are incongruent in that the spouse is starving for closeness and struggling to be heard but uses words to alienate those around him or her.

Statements probably said to establish intimacy:
- "I need you."
- "I need a hug."
- "I really want to spend some time with you."
- "I am really hurting inside."
- "I feel angry with you and want to talk."

Statements probably said to establish distance:
- "Why aren't you ever there for me?"
- "You never hug me.
- "You never spend any time with me."
- "You always hurt me."
- "Why did you do this to me?"

The therapist needs to encourage and confront clients who use distancing language and help them recognize the underlying meanings of their communications. Perhaps a client's fear or pain contributes to the trepidation of being too vulnerable with a spouse. Feelings of rejection or abandonment from family-of-origin or originating in the marital relationship might have helped this person to develop a defensive posture. Or perhaps the couple might be colluding to establish distance because of their internalized fears. *The goal in most effective communication is to be congruent in process and content. What is being said and the manner in which it is said all in agreement. "I need a hug" is congruent. "Why don't you ever hug me?" is incongruent because the request for a hug is masked in aggression.*

Language also can be used by a partner in an arrogant, condescending, and/or self-denigrating way. All three suggest underlying feelings of low self-worth in the communicator and perhaps, if believed, in the listener. Consider this dyadic communication between a husband and wife:

Husband: Why don't you ever do it the right way?

Wife: I tried, I really tried.

Husband: I've taught you before, I don't know how many times I have to repeat myself.

Wife: I'll try and do better next time.

Husband: I hope so.

The arrogance of the husband and the self-denigration of the wife create distance and diminish feelings of safety in the dyad. Such language can indicate a parent-to-child dynamic in a marital relationship. In such roles, there may be little intimacy and an absence of sexual relations. *Parent-child relationship dynamics often destroy feelings of wanting to be sexually intimate.*

The process-oriented marital therapist needs to be attuned to listening for arrogant or self-denigrating behavior. Usually, one spouse will take an arrogant position and the other will take a complementary role of being angry, undermined, and hurt. Fearful of intimacy, the couple might work on this destructive communication in a collusive manner so that each person's behavior reinforces the other. If the therapist simply listens to the content of the message, she or he might very well side with the underdog against the condescending partner, without taking into account the one-down partner's passive-aggressiveness and distancing behavior. If the therapist remains objective, she or he will recognize the patterns of distancing as they are collusively established by both partners and will confront them to encourage change and to increase understanding. It is the nature of the communication and not only the specific content of that communication that should demand a therapist's attention and confrontation. It is the role of the therapist to teach the same sensitivity to both partners so that they can discuss their relationship process without intervention by a third party.

Assertive, Aggressive, Submissive, and Passive-Aggressive Language

Assertive language is direct, differentiated, subjective, and without judgment. Examples of assertive language usually begin with "I" and are followed by a clear statement of feeling, thought, need, or wish: "I feel very sad," or "I need you to hold me." *Aggressive* language is invasive to the ego of the listener, often characterized by projection, blame, and *anger*. Examples often begin with "you" and have an attacking tone of voice. "You are never there for me!" A *submissive* communication uses tentative language and is spoken by someone from a one-down position. Examples might include a diminutive statement such as "I never can do it correctly." *Passive-aggressive* messages might at first sound quite assertive, but the passive-aggressive person hides the fact that she or he shares the opposite feelings from those expressed directly. Although "I like you" sounds assertive, the statement can be interpreted as passive-aggressive when the listener leaves the room and the communicator says, "I really don't like him or her at all."

Assertive styles often facilitate the listener/spouse responding in an assertive manner. If the spouse does not, the message probably was not perceived as assertive in the first place. Aggression in one spouse often inspires aggression from the other. However, the partner might respond submissively and fearfully, passive-aggressively, or passive-resistantly. It takes a very insightful and differentiated spouse to be able to respond in an assertive, emotionally present way to a spouse who is aggressive. A submissive partner often elicits aggression. Passive-aggressiveness almost always elicits aggression or passive-aggressiveness at first and can eventually lead to frustration, so that eventually the listener/spouse does not try to relate anymore.

Submissive, aggressive, and passive-aggressive styles of communication by a husband or wife could suggest that childhood dysfunctional relationships, characterized by rejection, abandonment, or low self-worth, remain unresolved and are being repeated in the dynamics of the marital communication. The therapist who is sensitive to these patterns is able to intervene in a balanced and profound way. The therapist can confront each spouse on what she or he is actually trying to elicit from his or her partner to increase client awareness. Asking questions such as, "Can you understand what you are asking for?" or "Do you see what you are creating?" can lead to systemic understandings. The responses of both partners offer insight into the circular communication patterns of the couple.

The following process questions and statements might help improve couple communication and position clients to be more assertive.

> Try and say it without the aggression.
> Can you get out of the submissive position?
> You aren't saying what you really mean and are being passive-aggressive.

After gaining insight into the meaning and effect of a communication, a couple, with the help of the therapist, must alter aggressive, submissive, and passive-aggressive language to make messages congruent with the healthier intentions and needs of the communicator and listener. *The therapist must teach each client to maintain assertiveness even amidst aggressive behavior. Assertive inquiry for meaning in responding to a partner's aggressiveness can often break down the aggression and turn it into more vulnerability.*

Reactive and Responsive Listening

A person who consistently reacts tends to feel attacked, insecure, and on the defensive. *Reaction* is defined in the Random House College Dictionary as "the action caused by the resistance to another action, or force; counter tendency." A reactive retort answers to the statements of the communicator in primarily an emotional, not thought-out, and defensive way.

The responsive individual has more ability to listen and seek further clarification. *Response*, on the other hand, defined as "an answer or reply," has elements of both emotion and thought and is intended to further the depth and meaning of the conversation.

> *A wife states:* "You did a very poor job."
> > *A reaction . . .*
> > > "I did not."
> > > "You did just as bad a job."
> > > "I don't care what you think."
> > *A response . . .*
> > > "What was poor about it?"
> > > "What do you mean by poor?"
> *A husband states:* "I don't like you."
> > *A reaction . . .*
> > > "Who cares?"
> > > "I don't like you either."
> > *A response . . .*
> > > "What about me don't you like?"
> > > "What do you mean?"
> > > "Could we talk about it?"

A person who is reactive perceives attack in most direct communications. She or he defensively assumes knowing the meaning of the words used by the communicator. A responder will assume that meaning is person-specific and that inquiry is important before an adequate response can be made. With a primary attitude of respect and interest, the responder seeks to build communication. In terms of reciprocal patterns, reaction breeds more aggression, while response often calms down what was originally an aggressive communication and moves it toward assertion and deeper understandings.

The therapist who listens accurately will understand that if a spouse reacts to a statement made by the other spouse, there *probably* was a perceived attack or sensitive area touched. In reactive communication, the couple can get quickly enmeshed. A responsive communication, however, suggests a high level of differentiation and desire to understand the meaning of the husband's or wife's messages. Healing, forgiveness, and couple intimacy are built on the foundation of responsive, nonreactive, partners.

The marital therapist needs to interrupt the reactive communications of clients. Intervention can take many forms: for instance, (a) inviting an awareness of the origins of the reactive patterns; (b) providing insight into the emotions behind the aggression; (c) examining the attributions of each partner, that is, what each partner thinks of the other; (d) restructuring the seating and redirecting the focus of conversation so that the therapist is more central; and (e) directly educating the clients about the difference between reaction and response.

One direct technique is an experiential exercise to teach clients just how reactive they are and how difficult and rewarding *responding* instead of *reacting* to one another can be. For example, amidst the couple's reactive argument, the therapist can say to both clients, "You know I don't like either of you!" This will probably stop their reactive communication and surprise the couple. Before they respond, the therapist can challenge them to respond to the statement and not to react. Often clients will think this so strange that they will laugh and parlay back a reaction such as, "I don't like you either!" The therapist can tell them it is a reaction and confront them until they begin to respond. A response would be for either partner to ask something like, "What don't you like about me?" thereby going after the deletions which were left out of the original expression (Bandler & Grinder, 1975, 1990; Milliner et al., 2000).

A positive and direct challenge is to ask a couple to respond to each other at home, especially in communications in which reactions are commonplace. Another exercise, seemingly the opposite but often achieving the same result, is to send them home with the task of seeing if they can get the other to react, and to keep score. Paradoxically, this task can encourage the couple to respond, even during overt aggression. This exercise often sensitizes clients to their reactive instincts and begins the process of more responsive communication. However, this exercise should not be used with volatile or overtly aggressive couples. It is more appropriate for couples that are able to reflect and maintain some differentiation.

Reciprocal Language Patterns

The process-oriented therapist needs to be knowledgeable and sensitive to reciprocal patterns in couple communication. With such awareness, the therapist is able to anticipate and confront dysfunctional communication before it becomes too intense and hurtful. Several of the frequently observed patterns in communication are attack and defense, anger and withdrawal, and thought followed by feeling or vice versa.

Attack and a subsequent defense by marital partners represents a common breakdown of communication. The mistake of many therapists is to wait quietly and passively, without intervening, while the couple intensify this dysfunctional pattern.

Wife: You are never affectionate to me!

Husband: I am too. Last night I reached out to you.

This pattern of attack and defense creates distance and prevents the couple from feeling too vulnerable. The therapist who can intervene after an attack and ask the communicator to share the feeling behind the attack, or ask the listener to try to respond without defending, can begin to break into this process and aid the couple's discovery of more functional communication. For example:

Wife: You are never affectionate to me!

Therapist: Can you share the feeling behind what you just said?

Wife: I am feeling lonely and unloved! You are never affectionate to me!

Therapist: (To Husband) Try not to react or defend, but respond.

Husband: Let's talk about what you mean.

Such interventions by the therapist provide the possibility for breaking the destructive communication and replacing it with one that is functional. It may require great persistence to change a spouse's attacks into the more primary feelings of hurt, rejection, or powerlessness. *Beneath most aggression and anger are vulnerable feelings which, if shared instead of the aggression, often elicit a different more intimate response and deeper understanding.* If the therapist intervenes in a couple's reciprocal pattern in order to change reactions into responses, she or he must not be passive, but rather forthright and determined.

Another circular pattern frequently demonstrated by couples in therapy is vulnerability in one partner creating a reluctance in the other to share negative feelings or thoughts, and the subsequent lack of sharing resulting in further vulnerability in the other partner. A husband and wife caught in a dysfunctional communication might justify their behavior by saying:

"Of course I feel vulnerable; he never shares anything with me."
"Of course I hold back; she is always emotional and acting vulnerably."

An inducted therapist is one who sides with one partner against the other and listens to or confronts the accusations of one spouse and not the other. In contrast, a *systemic* therapist tries several techniques to break the self-justification cycle. For instance, making a straightforward request that the clients take responsibility for their own behavior, and recognize how one behavior elicits the other, can begin to break the pattern. Another helpful technique is to model self-justification and blame so that clients can hear what these sound like. The therapist can say, "My husband/wife and I had a huge fight last night and it was entirely his/her fault. I was blameless. " If said in a lighthearted manner, the client often hears the one-sided nature of the accusation and begins to reflect.

The therapist who is sensitized to process issues will recognize that no behavior exists in a vacuum. When one partner expresses anger or withdrawal, the therapist needs to look for the response or reaction in the other and to determine the interrelationship.

Hierarchical Intimacy Patterns

There are hierarchies of intimacy which, when expressed, are experienced differently by people, often depending upon the depth and vulnerability of the relationship. Unfortunately, many couples relate to each other at the top of this hierarchy instead of in an in-depth intimate way. Consider the following set of greetings listed in a hierarchical fashion.

- Hi!
- How are you?
- It's nice to see you.
- I was thinking about you.
- I was really thinking about you.
- I missed you.
- I missed you terribly.
- I really love you.

Each intimate expression, intended to create some level of connection between two or more people, is appropriate depending on the depth and nature of the relationship. A marital couple could use each greeting listed. Distant acquaintances would probably use only the top three. The therapist's challenge is to assist clients in using more intimate language. Distant and emotionally estranged couples often only know how to use the top of the hierarchy and never express deeper words of affection and love to each other. The top part of the hierarchy is often used to maintain distance and individual safety and the bottom potentially can break through resistance.

☐ Conclusion

In conclusion, reciprocal patterns of communication are universal in couples. The therapist who recognizes these patterns and their circular nature can systemically intervene to isolate individual responsibility, reframe and deepen insights and feelings, and help couples break destructive patterns. Such intervention must be at the level of content and process. The content is important to give insight and orient the therapist to the correct topic areas. Attention to the process deepens the understanding of the feelings and thoughts behind the overt communication and helps the therapist gain a deeper knowledge and capacity to confront or inspire the couple's negative or positive systemic patterns.

CHAPTER 6

Building and Managing Intensity

In couples therapy, personal growth and integration are most enhanced by a dynamic *energetic* process in the treatment. Aspects of such a process include active interaction, feedback, humor, confrontation, empathy, a full range of emotions, and intellectual sharing. The systemically oriented therapist attempts to create appropriate emotional intensity among clients and between a couple and the therapist. Too much intensity can create an inability for a therapist to intervene in a constructive manner and for a couple to communicate effectively. Too little intensity can cause a therapeutic session to lack focus and prevent a couple from truly engaging each other in an intimate way. This chapter will discuss the management of intensity for the purpose of creating a dynamic therapeutic environment for clients. In addition, the often-observed phenomenon of therapist and client resistance to heightening emotional intensity will be reviewed.

The therapist working with couples needs to have skills to build intensity and relatedness within a session so that the couple will generalize the cognitive and emotional experience outside of therapy in their everyday relationship. Generating intensity within a couple's therapy session requires sensitivity to process issues and the ability to use cognitions and emotions creatively in the couple–therapist interaction.

The fundamental concept is that therapy is a dynamic process not to be reduced to an intellectual dissemination of information. When the session becomes limited to rational thought and the passive reception of information, an individual will have difficulty integrating what she or he feels and applying insight into personal experience. Emotion can be a strong motivator of change in behavior and interaction in marital therapy. However, the goal is not simply catharsis. Cognitive change will often follow emotional change, and emotional change, of necessity, involves change in cognition and action related to the emotion (Greenberg & Johnson, 1986a; 1988).

If a couple comes to therapy with little affect or intensity, what could be done? How does a marital therapist turn seemingly meaningless small talk at the beginning of a session into energized, focused conversation? How can the disorganized ideas frequently contained in a client's description of the presenting problem be transformed into insight, primary emotion, and behavioral change? Conversely, how does a marital therapist work with too much couple intensity that prevents any thoughtful communication?

Bugental's conceptualization of therapist skills into "four octaves" in responding to client sharing gives the reader a thorough description of how to manage intensity and facilitate joining, trust, depth, emotional and cognitive sharing, and structures for change (Bugental, 1987). These octaves consist of four major areas of therapist aptitude: 1) various listening skills; 2) guiding and focusing; 3) instructing and teaching; and 4) requiring or confronting.

The last point of the first octave is also the first point of the second octave. The listening skills outlined by Bugental include the use of silence, bridging statements such as "I see," restating, summarizing, encouraging talking, reflecting the obvious, inviting expansion, and asking open-ended questions. The second octave begins with open-ended questions, selecting a part on which to focus, sharing factual information, structuring information, pointing out alternatives, general structuring for how much focus a specific idea should take in a session, suggesting topics, and asking moderately-focused questions.

The third octave on instructing and teaching begins with asking moderately-focused questions, rational advising, supporting, reassuring, teaching, weighing alternatives, limiting direction, and narrowing the questions. The fourth octave on requiring or confronting discusses narrowing the questions, urging-on the client, approving, challenging, reinforcing or disapproving, superseding, commanding, and, only in rare cases, rejecting the client.

Four more strategies that further help to sharpen focus and create and manage intensity will be discussed: 1) specific uses of images and analogies; 2) description of emotional interventions; 3) use of repetition; and 4) the importance of the therapist focusing on primary material. The chapter will conclude with observations on the management of highly enmeshed clients who communicate with destructively high levels of emotional intensity.

☐ Using Images and Analogies

In most cases, superficial expression of emotion or intellectual discussion can be transformed into dynamic interaction through a client's or therapist's use of images and analogies. Although thought and the written word can certainly carry intensity, images and analogies usually increase the depth and the energy of an interaction. Napier (Nichols & Napier, 1996) wrote on metaphors, "It is in this way that our reality is transformed. A cluster of circumstances awakens in us feelings that become so charged and intense that they literally change what we are experiencing" (Napier, 1990, p. 2). A marital therapist can use images and analogies in several ways: for more accurate diagnosis, for disclosing deeper meanings and encouraging behavioral change, and for teaching different marital and family therapy concepts without the use of professional jargon.

Diagnostically, images and analogies are crucial for the assessment of the depth and seriousness of a disorder. If a female client states that she is feeling very depressed, description through analogy can be very elucidating. Besides asking the client to describe the depression in feelings and thoughts, the therapist might ask for specific analogies to further describe the depth of the depressive feelings or possible suicidal ideation. The following examples will describe less critical to more serious feelings of depression. In this example, the bottom of the hierarchy might very well prompt the therapist to consider hospitalization of the depressed individual. The client might state, "My depression is like . . .

- a mist that dulls all the colors around me.
- walking in mud; it takes so long to get anywhere.
- a huge hole in which I am holding on to the sides.
- a black cloud that is hovering over my head wherever I go.
- there is no floor beneath me and I am free-falling out of control.

The use of analogy is actually a projective device providing another view of innermost feelings and thoughts.

Diagnosis of the depth and intensity of anxiety and the possible need for medication are also improved by the use of images and analogies. After one male client stated that he felt very anxious, the therapist asked, "Can you tell me what the anxiety is like? What does it look like or feel like or sound like?" Consider the following hierarchy of responses, which, along with other corroborating data, might indicate the seriousness of the symptoms. "Anxiety is like . . .

- an uneasy feeling which comes and goes.
- having an unsettling feeling of danger all of the time.

- having uncontrollable negative thoughts.
- being part of a crowd trapped in a fire.

Differentiating the situational or more global character of the symptom will help the therapist determine the seriousness of a client's depression or anxiety. "I sometimes . . . " is different from "I am always . . . " Absolutes such as "always," "never," "constantly," "incessantly," and "consistently" are clearly of higher concern than more qualified words such as "rarely," "sometimes," "occasionally," and "sporadically."

Images and analogies are helpful in understanding deeper meanings. One of the greatest mistakes a therapist can make is to assume knowing what clients are trying to say and therefore not seeking further elaboration or clarification. The client's intellectual statement can be transformed into a more dynamic and meaningful expression when the therapist inquires about images or examples. (Further discussion in Chapter 5, Moving from Content to Process.)

The types of questions asked by the therapist are important for building intensity. If the client says, "I feel very hurt," the comment carries intensity and meaning, but may be a hint of deeper feeling only. The therapist needs to follow up on such a comment by inquiring further. "The surface structure the client has presented is incomplete, the next task is to help the client recover the deleted material. The most direct approach is to ask directly for what is missing" (Bandler & Grinder, 1975, p. 63). The questions below illustrate how the therapist might inquire:

- About whom or what are you hurt?
- Can you describe the depth of the hurt?
- What is the hurt like?
- Can you compare the hurt to an earlier experience?
- What kind of hurt?
- Give me an image that describes the feeling?

A client might state in an intellectual manner that she or he feels very angry. The therapist can inquire . . .

- About whom or what are you angry?
- What is the anger like?
- Does the feeling come and go, or is it always with you?
- In what part of your body does the anger live?
- Can you draw or describe a picture of the anger?
- How does the anger sound inside of you?

Such inquiries by the therapist or one client to another can help both clients understand that there is no universality of meaning in behavior, and that inquiry for further depth of understanding is a necessity. With the use of images and enhanced descriptions, the intensity of a session can increase and carry more meaning for clients and therapist.

Both meaning and intensity are enhanced when intellectual concepts can be translated into images and experiences. One task of the beginning therapist is to translate all of the concepts of the various schools of thought into everyday experience and example. For most clients, the use of marital and family therapy concepts and jargon during a session is not very helpful. Telling the client that she or he has been "triangulated" for years in a "fused relationship" where little "differentiation" has taken place probably will be misunderstood. To gain a better understanding of the richness and depth of marital and family therapy concepts, the therapist should work on creating images and analogies for the client. This language will raise the intensity and understanding of a particular couple's difficulty. Consider the following theories and concepts that have been transformed into insight and analogies more descriptive and applicable for use with clients.

Enmeshment or *fusion* is like . . .

- two people who hug in the diving area of a pool.
- two trains going in the same direction, on the same track; the speed of one is often determined by the speed of the other.
- two people shaking hands and not letting go.
- going scuba diving and sharing the same tank.

Being differentiated is like . . .

- being 30 years old and asked by your mother to get a haircut for the family picture and responding, "I do need one, I'd be glad to."
- holding onto yourself and your opinion when it seems that everyone around you wants to convince you of something else.

Lack of boundaries is like . . .

- contiguous backyards with no fences or markers; no one knows where to stop mowing his lawn.
- an inexperienced painter using watercolors.

Effective boundaries are like . . .

- fences with doors that are controlled from the inside.
- having the freedom to invite someone over and asking him to leave when you are tired.

Rigid boundaries are like . . .

- building a castle with a moat and no drawbridge.
- not letting new information cloud decisions of the past.

Intimacy is like . . .

- two swimmers, who swim together in a synchronized way for awhile, and then in an individual way swim apart.
- wanting to feel what the other feels as a fusing experience.

Positive entitlement is like . . .

- a father giving a child permission to go further in education than he did.
- a green light.

Negative entitlement is like . . .

- a red light.
- when the final paper of the final class for your degree cannot quite be finished.

Such examples are as numerous as a therapist's and client's experience and imagination. Through images and analogies the theories and concepts that organize, explain, and/or describe the clients' experience can be communicated in ways that increase understanding and meaning.

☐ Creating Intensity and Focus

When the beginning therapist is taught to track the content of a client's communication, she or he needs to learn to listen to the specific words and language used by the client. Inquiry and comment by the therapist should attempt to mimic and focus upon the language of the client. For instance, if the client states that she or he had a bad week, the therapist could ask, "What made the week bad?" By repeating the use of the word "bad" and not changing it to a word of the therapist's choice, a client can continue to elaborate with deeper personal explanation or meaning, without having to interpret the therapist's particular meaning placed on the word choice.

If the therapist were to ask, "Why was the week awful?" the meaning of the client's emotional word "bad" might be lost in trying to interpret or resist the therapist's use of "awful." By focusing on the client's language, the therapist can show respect for the client's view and interpretation of reality, instead of immediately superimposing another. Consider the following two dialogues, the first in which the couple's understandings are consistently translated into the therapist's word choice, and the second in which the couple's understandings were honored and enhanced.

Dialogue 1

Husband: We seem to be fighting all of the time.

Therapist: What are your arguments about?

Wife: We don't really argue. We just walk away from each other.

Therapist: Why do you both withdraw?

Husband: I feel very angry.

Wife: I don't withdraw. I just need a little time to gather myself.

Therapist: What do you think you are scared about?

Husband: I'm not really scared. I am just discouraged.

Dialogue 2

Husband: We seem to be fighting all of the time.

Therapist: Tell me about the fighting.

Wife: We both get very hurt and walk away.

Therapist: What kind of hurt? How do you walk away from each other?

Husband: For me it is a very deep hurt, a feeling of rejection.

Wife: While I do walk away, I feel more panicked and want to run.

By using the meaning and the language of the clients, a natural flow is created that increases the focus, intensity, and emotional depth of a session. If the therapist constantly transforms the client's language, the client has to work to interpret the therapist's particular meanings and the conversation becomes very disjointed.

Sharing of feeling in a natural and open way is another technique used to enhance the depth and intensity of a session. Consider the following feeling responses to a couple's pain:

Husband: We seem to be fighting all of the time.

Therapist: I'm sorry.

   or: That makes me sad.

   or: How discouraging.

Emotional expression followed by silence will often allow the client to continue the description of the fighting as she or he feels that the therapist is emotionally present. Such expressions from the therapist often have a greater likelihood of tapping into the feeling of the clients than does a more cognitive inquiry. *Most questions, including "How do you feel?" force a client to think about a response rather than express a feeling.*

> A client came to therapy depressed and very angry that his wife of 48 years had Alzheimer's disease. The session began with the typical question-and-answer format. Questions were asked such as:
>
> - How long has she been ill?
> - What has it been like for you?
> - How do you cope with the difficulties?
> - What did the doctor say is the prognosis?
>
> The client dutifully responded to each question, but became more depressed and angry about his situation as the session developed. What could the therapist offer? As the therapist stopped thinking about what question to ask next, he eventually expressed that he too was angry about the client's wife and that he was experiencing such pain. The session ended and the client made an appointment for the following week.
>
> At the next session, much to the surprise of the therapist, the man appeared considerably more at peace and less depressed. The therapist remained silent as the client said, "When I came in last week I felt alone and very angry. When I heard your anger *and feelings*, I realized that I was not alone and I felt better."

The therapist's sharing of his anger normalized the client's angry feelings. Through the therapist's normalization of the client's feelings, other emotions of loneliness, guilt, and fear were calmed and given expression.

Silence is perhaps one of the most effective techniques for enhancing the intensity of the client's statement. This is true especially when it is connected to a nonverbal indication that the therapist is present and emotionally available. For example:

Wife: I am really hurting!

Therapist: (leans forward, unfolds his or her arms, and says nothing)

Wife: He doesn't seem to care about me.

Therapist: (empathetic expression)

Wife: (tears) I feel all alone!

As the therapist was perceived to be quiet, and emotionally present, the client allowed herself to become more open and vulnerable. Silence and an engaged body posture by a therapist will probably do more to elicit the emotion of the client than any inquiry. Silence can create a vacuum and permission for the client to go deeper into hurt and pain.

☐ Using Repetition to Create Intensity

The therapist's use of repetition can provide focus and a conceptual orientation that clients have trouble resisting. Insights and questions intended to lead the client towards more depth of feeling and vulnerability can be very difficult for the client to hear. Resistances and defense mechanisms can interfere with listening. There is often a highly developed collusion process within the couple which results in their not understanding or responding to the therapist's attempts to facilitate change. Repetition can raise the intensity of the therapist's intervention. In the following communication, the marital therapist is making a systemic intervention that is difficult for the husband to hear.

Husband: My wife is never there for me; she avoids me constantly.

Therapist: Is it possible that you contribute to your wife's avoidance?

Husband: I don't. She is always off with her own friends.

Therapist: How do you help create the distance in the relationship?

Husband: It doesn't start with me. She leaves and then I react.

Therapist: You'll be better able to change the pattern if you can figure out how you help create the distance.

Husband: My wife says that I am angry all of the time.

Therapist: Is that how you contributed to the distance?

Husband: I know I push her away when I get very hurt.

This last statement by the husband was his first reflective one and it is the one that will begin the process of changing the circular patterns of the couple. Once the husband stops focusing on his partner and instead reflects on his own functioning and contribution to the problem, he begins to become individually powerful, that is, he can alter his behavior. It was the repetition that helped break through the husband's resistance.

In the next example, the repetition of the client's words creates a helpful confrontation to the client's distorted way of thinking.

Wife: I simply am not smart enough to take that job.

Therapist: You aren't smart enough?

Wife: I am sure I'm not.

Therapist: I didn't realize that you weren't very smart.

Wife: Well I am not stupid!

Therapist: However, you are probably correct that you need to have more intelligence to take that job.

Wife: I might be able to do it.

Therapist: I think that you will have to be smarter.

By the therapist repeating and exaggerating the cognitive distortions of the client, she was able to begin the process of altering her thinking.

Frequently, a beginning therapist does not trust him- or herself or have the personal confidence in his or her systemic interventions. When encountering client resistance, systemic interventions can be abandoned too quickly. Repetition can communicate that the therapist is focused and confident that another way of looking at things can be achieved. *Repetition often has the ability to break through successive walls of defense. Each defensive statement by a client is designed to stop the inquiry. However, when the therapist persists, sensitively, the vulnerability behind the defense can often be uncovered.*

☐ Focusing on Primary Material and Developing a Theme

Because the deeper issues of a couple are often painful and threatening, the real sources of their distress remain hidden behind a veil of repression and denial (Napier, 1990; Nichols & Napier, 1996). In order to protect the vulnerability associated with such distress, a couple can present many topics and issues to the therapist. The intensity of a therapeutic session is lost when the couple and/or the therapist allow for many issues or topics to be covered. Such avoidance can take two predominant forms: one is client-focused and one is initiated by the therapist.

As was mentioned above, marital patterns are resistant to change. One of the primary ways a couple has to resist and thwart movement is to bring up many topics, change the focus of the conversation when it becomes too intense, and generally detour the therapist away from the most meaningful material. As a client communicates the broader picture, intensity can be raised if the therapist focuses on a singular idea or feeling within that picture. Generally speaking, almost any focus is better than none at all. The easiest way for the therapist to know whether he or she is focused enough is to discuss the important aspects of a session to another therapist. If the therapist cannot summarize the essence of a therapeutic session in a couple of sentences, then there was probably not enough focus.

Consider the following communication by a couple:

Wife: You are never available to me. I have to keep begging for some affection.

Husband: I feel closed in. You are always on my back.

Wife: The children need you home, not off somewhere else all day. Last weekend you watched football.

Husband: I work very hard and deserve to spend time on my own.

This couple expressed variations of these themes many times, which further entrenches the negative feelings in their relationship. The therapist who is seeking to create a focus might initially say:

- Let us focus on . . .
- What you just said is very important.
- Let us spend the rest of the session on this topic.

Possible topics to focus on are . . .

- The distancing patterns of the couple.
- The meaning of the words "begging" and "closed in."
- Exploration of patterns in clients' families of origin.
- A discussion of time alone, time together.
- The understanding of intimacy dances.
- The role of entitlement.
- Issues of parenting.

The important factor is that the marital therapist or couple pick one topic and pursue it in depth. Deeper meanings explored in one area will almost always generalize to other important issues and concerns.

A lack of focus initiated by the therapist is reflective of the worst understanding and application of what a therapist might call an "eclectic approach." In such "eclecticism," a therapist knows a little about each school of thought, but not enough to actually orient his or her thinking and intervention. Without such focus the therapist will often confront superficially, be inducted into the resistance of the couple, and talk about ten different topics at a meaningless level.

An excellent exercise for the marital therapist is to listen to the content of what a couple present in therapy and to practice conceptualizing the material into a specific school and approach. Interventions can become more focused and purposeful once the therapist can conceptualize the clients' patterns. In the following examples, excerpts from client conversation are organized within different *conceptual* approaches. Each client statement can be organized into and understood from several theoretical perspectives.

1. *Client*: "My mother just walks into my house without even knocking."
   Conceptualization—This could be a boundary problem, best approached *structurally*.
2. *Client*: "My daughter wakes up every night and I bring her into my bed."

Conceptualization—This might be a reinforcement issue and might be approached *behaviorally*.

3. *Client*: "Every time we talk, we end up in a huge argument. We both get so defensive."

   Conceptualization—This couple might have few communication or conflict utilization skills and should work with *communication theory and practice*.

4. *Client*: "I am not very smart or competent in most things."

   Conceptualization—These could be "automatic thoughts" which need to be addressed from a *cognitive* perspective.

5. *Client*: "When I go home for the holidays, I seem to lose myself and get furious with my family."

   Conceptualization—This might be a differentiation issue that needs to be looked at from a *Bowenian* perspective.

6. *Client*: "I don't know why I have the attitudes I do."

   Conceptualization—This could be a loyalty or a legacy issue that needs to be approached *contextually* in the family of origin.

7. *Client*: "I don't know why I push away the people whom I most want to love me."

   Conceptualization—This could be a matter of early introjected patterns repeated compulsively which needs to be understood from an *object relations* perspective.

The list of examples is endless. The therapist needs to be able to organize the scattered information from the couple into concepts and theories that allow for both understanding and direction for change. If the therapist is conceptually focused, more energy for change and insight can be derived from specific intervention.

☐ Managing too much Intensity

Too little intensity is often boring for both client and therapist. A lack of intensity can be resistance-based and prevent movement from taking place. Too much intensity can be very intrusive, destructive, and counterproductive. Clients sometimes choose a marital therapist on the basis of their perception of the therapist's ability to manage their intensity and stop potentially destructive communications. The therapist needs to have the confidence to halt negative interactions. Without such confidence, the therapist's inclination might be to structure sessions with his or her ideas instead of allowing the couple's emotions to truly emerge. The less confidence the marital therapist has, the less likely she or he is going to enhance couple interaction and to let the couple discuss their issues with the accompanying emotions.

Four techniques for managing the intense interactions of a couple are: 1) asking process questions that demand the couple's reflection and insight; 2) using emotional interventions that seek the expression of primary feelings; 3) structuring a couple's conversation using stronger confrontation; and 4) changing the structure of the therapy. The following types of interventions are designed to manage the intense and judgmental communications of a couple:

1. *Process questions* are designed to help the couple observe and reflect upon their own communication by helping them to become more thoughtful, hence less emotional and reactive, and objective observers of themselves. The therapist might ask:
   - Is this what goes on at home?
   - What is the purpose of the arguing?
   - Do you want to get this out of control?
   - Can you see what you are both doing?
2. Certain *emotional interventions* take the focus off the anger and judgment of the couple interaction and redirect the discussion into more primary feelings of pain, hurt, or rejection. A therapist might say:
   - This is very painful to watch.
   - Please don't hurt each other like this.
   - I really feel the pain behind both your angers.
   - Talk about the underlying feeling.
3. *Stronger confrontations which structure the discussion* to lessen intensity might be:
   - Stop!
   - I'm not going to let you do this!
   - Don't speak!
   - I want one of you to share and the other to listen.
   - Start with "I" and try and leave out all of the attack.
4. Changing the structure of a session helps clients avoid becoming more enmeshed by stopping the interaction or moving the therapist into the center of the couple's interaction. The therapist might say:
   - I am going to end the session now. It is too destructive.
   - I am going to speak to one of you and then the other while insisting the other partner does not respond.
   - Would *one of you* please step out of the office for a minute?

The general rule is that the more destructively intense a couple are, the more central the marital therapist needs to be to the process. Such a couple need the therapist to actively take control and calm the system.

Anticipating the depth of intensity before it gets out of control is an important skill. One of the greatest blocks for many therapists to overcome is to *change perspectives* about what constitutes being polite. In a destructive communication between clients, it is not polite to wait until one of the partners is finished speaking. A five-minute husband/wife diatribe that keeps the therapist or partner waiting for his or her turn to speak or respond can set the tone for the entire session and derail efforts to be helpful. It is often effective for the marital therapist to interrupt, cut off, and prevent a client from finishing saying hurtful and destructive things. Below are two examples:

1. The "polite" therapist . . .

   Husband to Wife: I'm upset with what you did. You really are insensitive to my needs. You never once asked me for what I wanted . . . as a matter of fact, you never have and you are always selfish! You are a real bitch!

   Therapist: How are you feeling?

2. A "not polite" therapist who anticipates an evolving destructive interaction . . .

   Husband to Wife: I'm upset with what you did. You really are insensitive to my needs.

   Therapist: Your feelings are important, however, can you share them without attacking, and instead share what you want or need.

The therapist can then prevent expressions of aggression or judgment by intervening directly and quickly during an escalation of anger or hostility. *In general, inexperienced therapists process a couple interaction too slowly. To make the point, an extreme example would be that it is better to confront one partner as he or she is thinking about picking up a baseball bat to hit his or her partner than to ask a partner, "How do you feel?" after he or she has been hit.*

The levels of intensity and their management in a therapy session are usually determined by the therapist's confidence and ability to remain detached from the affect of the client so that she or he is aware of the subtle communications and process issues. As mentioned previously, the more self-respect the therapist has, the easier it is for him or her to trust interventions and follow through.

How anger is dealt with and processed in one's family of origin and the level of differentiation of the therapist are key issues. Differentiation includes the ability to separate the emotional and intellectual processes. Someone who is differentiated is flexible, adaptable, and independent of others. She or he can cope with the stresses of life (Bowen, 1976). If the therapist's family had the extremes of too little affect or too much intrusive arguing, the therapist might be greatly limited in his or her ability to manage intensity during a session. If anger was not allowed or punished or, conversely, if anger was rampant, a therapist could have a distorted reaction to client anger. Without adequate work on his or her own differentiation, a therapist will find it difficult to confront the collusion of an enmeshed couple's destructive communication and reframe it and remold it into something more positive.

☐ Conclusion

The management of intensity is an important part of marital therapy. Too much emotional energy can create destructive dynamics and enmeshment. Too little energy can prevent change, behavioral application of new ideas, and couple intimacy. Managing intensity is an essential skill for the marital therapist to develop.

Individual Therapy and Systemic Intervention

For a period of time in the 1970s and 1980s, many therapists in the field of marriage and family therapy insisted that for therapy to be effective, all members of the family should be present. Currently, working with subsystems (e.g., parental subsystems, marital dyads, and individuals as part of a family system) is more widely accepted. If a system consists of the interaction of a group of individuals, and theoretically every individual affects the system, then it follows that working in a systemic way with an individual can alter the destructive reciprocal patterns within the couple or family of which the individual is a member. A significant proportion of many marital and family therapists' caseloads are individual clients working on systemic issues. In many cases, spouses refuse to enter the therapeutic process or individuals report that they want to work in therapy by themselves.

The therapeutic task is to systemically address personal issues *of a relational nature*. If approached systemically, individual therapy can help the client *take responsibility for him- or herself* and become more constructively powerful and differentiated within his or her family, leaving open the possibility that a spouse or other family members might become involved in the therapeutic process at some future time.

This chapter will explore the difficulties and opportunities for the marital therapist working with an individual member of a marital dyad or with one person of a committed relationship. The ethical implications of aiding the growth of one partner without directly working with the other, combined with an understanding of the potential danger of the role of empathy when used to align with one partner against the other, will be discussed. In addition, specific consideration will be given to the therapist's role of encouraging client self responsibility and the development of personal power. Finally, the intermingling of individual and couples therapy will be discussed.

☐ Ethical Implications of Individual Therapy

Unwittingly, individual therapy may exacerbate couple conflict and contribute to divorce. By encouraging and enhancing one partner's growth without paying adequate attention to its effect on the partner, the therapist can unbalance and disrupt the homeostasis of the couple system (Gurman & Kniskern, 1981a, 1991). Clearly, this growth could be positive or negative depending on the many perspectives of the persons involved.

Every individual issue or concern has systemic and relational ramifications for an individual client who is part of a committed relationship. For instance, if a spouse is depressed, one systemic question that needs to be addressed is what role the depression plays in the couple's communication and overall relationship (Jessee & L'Abate, 1985). There are several possibilities. Through the process of overidentification, one partner might be experiencing depressive feelings similar to those found more severely in his or her partner. Perhaps the nondepressed partner colludes in deepening the feelings of depression in the other through criticism or withdrawal. For example, when one partner is depressed, there is little chance that the couple will be physically intimate or emotionally close. Often such collusion is derived from fears of intimacy and vulnerability.

Another possibility is that if one spouse is depressed, there is less likelihood that she or he will have the energy to leave the relationship. The less depressed partner, feeling fear of loss and a poor self-concept, knows this and unconsciously reinforces the depressive feelings. Whatever the presenting problem, whether it be anger, anxiety, weight, unemployment, self-punishment, or intimacy fears, each individual's behavior and subsequent dynamic has a multitude of systemic ramifications and possibilities.

The marital therapist working with the individual member of a dyad has an ethical responsibility to share the fact that personal growth and change, which may be enriching and constructive for him or her, might very well be debilitating or destructive for the marital or family relationships. When one spouse changes, the couple's reciprocal patterns will change and the spouse will eventually have to readjust or alienation might ensue. If the client understands the potential harm to the homeostatic balance of the marital dyad and still chooses to continue individual work, the therapy can continue. The marital therapist might say, "If you decide to work in therapy, you might grow or change perspectives *concerning your relationship*. If you examine these issues in the absence of your spouse, it might create tension, dissension, and/or general distance in your marriage."

Although being empathic is essential with the individual coming to therapy to work on marital issues, it can also be problematic because of its potential to create tension and chaos within the marital dyad. By not becoming emotionally involved in the dysfunctional interactions of the marriage, the therapist can often be perceived as being more patient, caring, and understanding than either of the spouses. "Why can't my husband be more like you?" "Why can't my wife be as sensitive as you are?" Such statements should prompt the therapist to explain that she or he is not perfect and has difficulties and successes in his or her own relationships.

The therapist might share some fallibility and personal history to decrease an exaggerated positive transference. The therapist might go on to say...

> One of the goals in my listening and caring for you is for you to learn that you are entitled to be treated well. You need to learn to ask for what you need in more effective ways within your marriage.

The therapist needs to be careful not to make unilateral interpretations, one-sided and linear, based on being empathetic to one partner's explanation of the difficulty. For example, a woman comes to therapy with marital issues, looking for support and understanding. The dialogue is as follows:

Wife: My husband is totally insensitive to my needs.

Therapist: What does he do?

Wife: He yells and swears at me. He comes home late and never helps around the house.

Therapist: It sounds awful.

Such empathy from the therapist, which sides with one partner against the other, can be very destructive for the future of the therapy and for the stability of the marital relationship. Because of this unilateral interpretation, the systemic framework is lost. What the wife's therapist did not know or predict is that the woman goes home after the therapy session and shares with her husband something like the following: "I talked with my therapist today and he thinks that what you do to me is really awful." The same week the husband went to *his* therapist and said:

Husband: I am very frustrated and alone.

Therapist: What is happening?

Husband: My wife refuses to get a babysitter and the baby is sleeping in the bed with us.

Therapist: It must be difficult. She is probably overattached to the children.

In this case, what the husband's therapist did not understand is that the husband went home to his wife and said: "The therapist thinks you are overly bonded with the children and you need to give me more attention. The therapist was very understanding of how I feel."

Through such examples of empathy and unilateral interpretations, the therapist can support each spouse to be more self-justified, less reflective, and less understanding of the other's feelings. Then each spouse might triangulate the therapist into a coalition against the other. In either therapy process, neither partner at this point is cognizant of the systemic issues of circular causality, self-responsibility, and fairness. Circular causality involves the feedback model of causality in which a circular process is involved. The so-called cause is really an effect of a prior cause. What is initially defined as an effect becomes the cause of yet a later event (Watzlawick, Beavin, & Jackson, 1967; Watzlawick, Weakland, & Fisch, 1998). With such cautions in mind, the therapist's empathy for a client is very important.

The context for the expression of empathy in an individual session focusing on marital issues needs to be structured and well thought-out. Empathy is essential for joining with the client and establishing a context for trust, openness, and hope. However, empathy needs to be balanced with systemic interventions, such as requesting that the client take personal responsibility for contributing to the couple's circular patterns and for making bilateral or systemic interpretations which examine the interrelationship and reciprocal nature of behavior. Again, along with empathy for the client must come a request to take responsibility for how she or he is contributing to the marital discord being described. For example, "Can you see how your behavior is intensifying the difficulty?" Furthermore, a therapist can share empathy for both partners of dyad. *When the circular nature of communication patterns is understood, the therapist can be sensitive to a couple's difficulty in a balanced way.*

In conclusion, while empathy is essential for the client–therapist relationship in the development of a therapeutic alliance, it can be problematic when the therapist is deemed to be more empathic than the spouse.

It can also align one spouse and the therapist against the other spouse or inhibit reflection when personal responsibility is not encouraged.

☐ Therapeutic Boundaries

An important area for consideration in working with one partner of a dyad concerns the issue of communication boundaries. Reporting the substance and process of a therapy session to the spouse can be very counterproductive to therapeuti . goals. The following two suggestions help to inhibit the inadvertent, inappropriate use of therapy material in the marital relationship.

The first suggestion is to establish the contract and the boundaries of the therapy during the intake session. The therapist might say to the client, "It is very important that you do not say to your spouse, 'The therapist said . . . ' or 'My therapist feels that you are . . . ' When a client triangulates a therapist in this way, the therapy can be used to gain a one-up position. A destructive coalition is formed between client and therapist which creates animosity and may result in an attempt by the absent spouse to denigrate the therapist. If the partner feels a comment by the therapist is important to share, then this idea should be integrated within the person's self and communicated as his or her own. Instead of saying "The therapist thinks," the spouse would say, "I believe" or "I have been feeling . . . " The spouse's response can then be focused on his or her partner and the therapist is not destructively triangulated into the marital discussion or relationship.

The second reason to boundary the communications of an individual session concerns lessening the energy of therapy and detracting from the potential power of a therapeutic intervention. For example, if a therapist confronts a husband by saying, "You are judging your wife for imperfections and weaknesses in yourself," what the husband should do is integrate this thought into his own thinking and have it make sense (or not) for himself. He should process the thought privately until he understands its truth or lack of truth when applied to self-understanding and personal experience. Instead, the husband went home and said without thinking, "The therapist thinks I'm judging you for weaknesses in me." The wife was not sophisticated psychologically and doubted the validity of the statement. She found it had no relevance for their relationship. "That is ridiculous," she said. The husband, who sought validation and approval from her, did not integrate the concept and dismissed it immediately. The power of the intervention was minimized because the husband did not keep it to himself long enough to have it affect his thinking or behavior. Apparently threatened with the growth of her husband and the change in the homeostasis of the couple, the wife later stated, "Going to that therapist is merely a waste of time."

☐ Systemic Interventions with Individuals

While individual therapy pays attention to the intrapsychic issues of a client, it also needs to have strong systemic foundations. Intrapsychic issues manifest themselves in circular ways in relationships. "Individuals are best understood within their interrelational contexts. A comprehensive systemic view of the family focuses on the evolving relationships of the family members within their environmental, historical, developmental, and ideological contexts" (Fleuridas, Nelson, & Rosenthal, 1986, p. 113). A circular perspective emphasizes cyclical sequences of interactions.

The following suggests several systemic and circular questions in response to individually expressed thoughts and concerns. Consider the systemic concepts and theoretical directions that could be taken by the therapist to deepen the understanding when an individual client states, "I feel very incompetent." Such a statement might be reflective of early introjected feelings.

Client: I feel very incompetent.

Therapist: That makes me sad. How long have you felt this way?

Client: For what seems to be all my life.

Therapist: How did you learn to think like this?

Client: I suppose from my father. I was never good enough. He always criticized me. I don't remember any encouragement.

The client's feelings might suggest a lack of differentiation from his family of origin . . .

Client: I feel very incompetent.

Therapist: When do you feel incompetent the most?

Client: When I am around my father.

Therapist: Have you ever talked to him about your feelings?

Client: No. I wouldn't dare.

The feeling of incompetence might be part of a specific reciprocal interaction between spouses . . .

Client: I feel very incompetent.

Therapist: How does your spouse relate to you when you feel this way?

Client: He puts me down even more.

The client's feeling could best be understood as an automatic thought, a concept used in cognitive theory.

Client: I feel very incompetent.

Therapist: Do you think this way in every context?

Client: No.

Therapist: Then when do you think well of yourself?

By nonverbally empathizing and asking circular questions from different systemic perspectives, the therapist works toward client insight (Penn, 1982). In terms of the marital dyad, the therapist who thinks in systemic ways can make an educated guess that the statement "I feel incompetent" reflects parental criticism and inferiority which was internalized by one spouse and then projected onto the other:

Therapist: You are very hard on yourself. How does your spouse respond and relate to your feeling of inferiority?

Client: She criticizes me all the time.

While such an intervention might initially place blame onto the spouse, the following intervention begins the steps toward true systemic understanding.

Therapist: Do you think you might "set up" your partner to criticize you?

Client: I never thought about that.

Therapist: The pattern does seem similar to your background, so I wonder what part you are playing in the repetition?

Systemic interventions, which seek personal responsibility, will also permit the client to examine his or her own behavior rather than undermining or criticizing an absent parent or partner.

A personal sense of power is often achieved through the ability to reflect upon and understand one's own functioning and responsibility in both the positive and negative aspects of a dyad. Taking personal responsibility for part of the difficulty in any relationship gives the individual an opportunity to stimulate change without waiting for the other's movement. Systems change most often when an individual understands his or her contribution to the relationship dynamics and works to alter his or her own behavior. In contrast, powerlessness is most often felt and enacted when a client is projecting all responsibility and blame onto another person.

A systemically oriented therapist practicing individual therapy will confront clients to help them become more personally insightful and self-responsible. Although the following interventions might seem harsh outside of the context of therapy, a spouse frequently feels empowered when she or he senses that she or he can do something to change the current quality of the marital relationship. Personal insight and self-responsibility are the keys when the therapist confronts from a systemic perspective. Examples of interventions that ask a client to accept responsibility are:

1. *Husband*: My wife is always critical.
   Therapist: Can you think about what you might do that leads her to criticize you? Try to answer without talking about her.

2. *Wife*: My husband is never emotional.
   Therapist: Would you be frightened if he were? Do you do anything that might contribute to it being safe or unsafe for him to express his emotions?

A common problem for couples is when one or both partners is critical or judgmental. Criticism and judgment can be turned into insight by exploring what part or role the client plays in creating or maintaining his or her partner's behavior and how the entire pattern may relate to issues in the client's family-of-origin. Further suggestions for interventions that seek to encourage personal responsibility are:

- What part do you play in what you describe?
- How do you contribute to that behavior in your partner?
- What is your investment in what your partner is doing?
- Do you look for verification of those negative thoughts?
- Is your partner responding to what you are asking for?
- How is what you are describing predictable from understanding your background?

An additional benefit is that interventions that seek to encourage self-responsibility help prevent the tendency of the therapist to become inducted into the individual client's way of thinking. For example, a woman comes to therapy complaining about what a tyrant her father has been all her life. The therapist, who has become inducted into the client's thinking over several sessions, develops a perspective that the father must be quite cruel. After several weeks, the daughter invites her father into the therapy session. Instead of meeting an aggressive, large man, as the therapist expected, the father is a diminutive, soft-spoken person who cried over the loss of his daughter. The image the daughter developed about her father when she was a child became fixed and never matured. If the therapist had asked some systemic questions such as "When your father is a 'tyrant' what do you do?" or "Have you tried to talk to him without being reactive yourself?," the perspectives of the client might have been challenged in a new way. By asking the client to examine her responsibility in the parent-child relationship she might have developed a more accepting position.

Individual Sessions in Conjoint Therapy

The intermingling of individual sessions with conjoint sessions can have both positive, and complicating, if not negative results. Positively, individual sessions can:

- create a closer tie of each partner to the therapist, often the result being an increased commitment to therapy.
- enrich the therapist's understanding of the clients' family-of-origin, and how it is related to current dynamics.
- assess the individual client's manner of relating outside the marital relationship.
- allow for a deeper psychological or psychiatric assessment without the client being self-conscious of the partner's involvement.
- establish a clearer understanding of a client's commitment to the relationship.
- allow for ventilation of intense feelings that might block the interaction in conjoint therapy.
- learn about secrets that might be blocking the progress of the marital work.

Negatively, individual sessions can:

- create difficulties with confidentiality.
- create an alignment between one partner and the therapist, possibly excluding the other partner.
- allow for one spouse to use the individual sessions as a weapon by putting the partner down.
- appear to or in fact label one partner as the "sick one."
- unwittingly split the couple as each partner begins to grow individually but apart (Berman, 1982).

When changing the structure of therapy from individual to conjoint work, the following issues should be considered. In many cases, one spouse has been asking the partner to enter therapy, but the partner has refused. With a sense of desperation, the individual goes into therapy alone to attempt to make progress in the relationship. If the therapist has been systemic in approach, the partner not in therapy often realizes that the therapist is not biased against him or her. The absent partner often observes his or her spouse working on the family-of-origin or taking personal responsibility for his or her part of the problem. The client might say to the spouse, "The therapist really confronted me about the way I _____ with you." If the therapy is approached systemically, the nonparticipating partner might grow to understand that the therapist can be fair and balanced. Although the absent partner might have interpreted being blamed, she or he now finds that the partner in therapy is growing and taking responsibility. This fact can change the status quo of the relationship.

Including a spouse or partner into an ongoing individual therapy can be problematic. Sometimes it simply should not be done. The alignment and loyalties of the individual spouse and therapist may be too strong. If the duration of the individual therapy is over two or three months, a very positive transference might have developed. In such a transference, the relationship between client and therapist can be very strong. As the individual client works out unresolved past relationships within the transferential relationship with the therapist, a level of inclusion is developed that seeks to boundary out other people, including a spouse. The longer the duration of the individual work, the greater the likelihood that a different therapist should do the couples work (See Chapter 3, Balanced Intervention).

With this taken into consideration, an advantage of using the individual therapist for conjoint therapy is that the therapist already understands some of the systemic issues. Furthermore, due to the systemic approach in which the client was being asked to take responsibility for a portion of the marital dynamics, the nonparticipating spouse might have already gained some trust in the process of therapy and the fairness of the therapist. The following are some suggestions for including a spouse or partner after individual therapy has already begun:

1. The client who has already established a relationship with the therapist needs to understand that when his or her partner is added to the therapy, and the therapist establishes a balanced approach in the session, she or he might experience some loss or anger at the absence of what heretofore had been a private loyalty and relationship. Forewarning often eases the intensity of these feelings. The therapist might say, "When your partner comes to therapy, I will listen and attempt to understand both your perspectives and you might experience this as loss. Please let me know if such is the case."

2. The joining spouse or partner might participate in two or three individual sessions to join with the therapist before the conjoint sessions begin. The therapist can share with this partner some concern about him or her possibly feeling sided against or not feeling fairly under-

stood. Again, if the new client is encouraged to share those feelings with the therapist in the session, and the therapist is balanced, they are rarely disruptive to the therapy.

3. At the commencement of the conjoint process, and at pertinent times thereafter, the therapist might verbalize all of the above with both partners present. This tends to create a commonly understood goal of balance and fairness among all parties.

☐ Conclusion

In conclusion, individual sessions can be conceptualized from a systemic orientation. If such is the case, personal responsibility and insight will be sought in order that the individual might enter his or her couple system in more effective and powerful ways. While it is sometimes difficult to create couples' cases out of individual ones, it can be done if a systemic approach has been practiced consistently.

8
CHAPTER

Working with Highly Reactive and Narcissistically Wounded Couples

The first chapters have been devoted to the basic principles and processes of working with couples. However, there is one particular type of couple interaction where some of these principles are not the intervention of choice. This chapter will describe this type of couple interaction and the therapeutic processes that are more likely to produce a positive outcome. Couples who are highly reactive, aggressive, and judgmental in their interaction often present the greatest challenge to a conjoint therapist (Nichols, 1998; Paolino & McCrady, 1978). Attempts to affect the process are difficult, emotionally draining, and often unsuccessful. Because the reactivity is so reciprocally driven between both partners, the homeostatic persistence of the dynamic is very strong. Each spouse expects the other to be totally devoted to the gratification of his or her own narcissistic needs (Feldman, 1982). Over the years, a couple may work with a number of different therapists trying to heal narcissistic vulnerability and pain. Narcissistic wounds are egocentric or psychic pain that inhibits or prevents an individual from being able to be sensitive to the needs or the perspectives of another. Narcissistic vulnerability "is manifested by a propensity to react to actual or imagined rejection or disapproval with conscious or unconscious self-fragmentation, identity and diffusion and/or diminished self-esteem" (Feldman, 1982, p. 417).

In most cases, highly reactive couples have common underlying process dynamics, albeit different stories. A process approach to working with them will be presented in this chapter. While the approach takes into consideration the process insights and techniques of the previous chapters, more sophistication is needed when hurt and pain are a couple's core interpersonal dynamic. The interpersonal dynamics of these couples include: (a) narcissistic wounds in both partners; (b) highly developed and organized introjects such as feeling abandoned or criticized; (c) a process of interpersonal repetition compulsion fed by negative projections that deepen the wounds; (d) an attributional process which feeds the reciprocal patterns of hurt and rejection; (e) an incongruence which prevents an individual or couple from sharing vulnerability; (f) a lack of safety which increases their sense of vulnerability; and (g) few skills to break the regressive slide from a couple's present day dynamic or content discussion into understanding the early regressive painful emotions and introjects that have created such a dysfunctional relationship.

The aforementioned process dynamics often work simultaneously in both partners to prevent differentiation and healing. Individuals most often find partners with similar narcissistic vulnerability and who are at similar levels of differentiation. The therapist who understands the power and persistence of these dynamics will approach such cases with different tools than might be seen in typical conjoint therapy. Some specific differences are (a) couples might be encouraged to suppress communication of what they feel; (b) the content of clients will be deemed as far less important than the process of communication; (c) couples will be asked to continually reframe the same experience to see it in a different light; (d) couple interaction may not be encouraged until understanding and new process communication skills are developed; and (e) each individual receives more attention as to their reactions of hurt and feelings of rejection.

☐ Highly Reactive and Enmeshed Couples

Narcissistic Wounds

The early underdeveloped self is highly susceptible to wounds from parents, siblings, or friends. While some wounds are incurred with isolated traumatic events such as a car accident or molestation, most narcissistic wounds are actually the result of ongoing dynamics of neglect, abuse, invasiveness, denigration, lack of safety, etc., from early childhood. Such woundedness occurs before and during identity formation and often prevents the psyche from developing a strong, balanced, integrated sense of self.

Such lack of safety for the psyche in early childhood often produces shame, destructive automatic thoughts, negative entitlement, and low self-worth. The defenses against psychic vulnerability can create distant and reactive interactional patterns in later interpersonal relationships. The list of individual defenses is long and ranges from denial and suppression to rationalization, grandiosity, or intellectualization. Interpersonally, the major defenses are anger and different styles of reactivity such as defensiveness, attack, and withdrawal. Through aggressive communication, an individual attempts to cover his or her wounds and distance an intimate partner for the purposes of trying to create individual safety. There is a need to not be seen as wounded or needy. Closeness increases the likelihood that the neediness is felt and perceived. The more intimate a relationship, the more a person is potentially vulnerable and exposed. Such aggression usually creates one or all of the following reciprocal patterns in a partner: (a) aggression creates more aggression; (b) aggression creates passivity and withdrawal in a partner, which in turn effects feeling rejected or unloved; or (c) aggression creates passive aggression. For example, a wife asks her husband to get milk, bread, and eggs at the store and he returns with milk, bread, and yogurt; she gets angry, he feels unappreciated, and they both become reactive. She says, "Just go to the store and get medium brown eggs," and he returns with extra large eggs. Reactive and aggressive feelings are the end interactional result, with the pain of feeling unheard, unloved, and criticized so deeply felt.

Narcissistic wounds communicated through reactivity and aggression need to be understood, grounded in early childhood stories, and healed through self-dialogue and new processes of healthier interaction. These processes are discussed later in this chapter.

Introjects and Couple Interaction

Introjects are the early emotions and thoughts developed and incorporated into a young child's self-concept through the interaction and quality of nurturing of his or her significant object relationships. These emotions and thoughts, organized as life experiences, tend to repeat and exaggerate themselves. In the development of identity, such emotions and thoughts became part of the self-concept with the corresponding negative automatic thoughts becoming ways of characterizing the self. For example, imagine that both parents of an individual are unable to nurture and express warmth. The child experiences this lack of emotional care with the feeling of being rejected. These feelings of rejection are organized over time and become labels of automatic thought such as "I am rejected" or "I am unloved." A second example is a parent who criticizes a child on a continuous basis. Responding to continual criticism, the child feels low self-worth and begins to think and say, "I am unimportant."

Such feelings can organize more and more of the individual's life experiences, with the interpretation of such experiences deeply affecting interaction in later intimate relationships. In many cases, the introjected emotions and thoughts can be sufficiently repressed or behaviorally controlled until the individual becomes involved in a committed intimate relationship. For this reason, the dynamics between couples sometimes can change quite precipitously when they become more committed to each other, live together, get married, or have a child. Once again, it is the matter of emotional closeness that triggers the underlying feelings of vulnerability. As long as emotional distance can be maintained, the pattern may not be revealed or manifested in a pronounced way.

The key issue is that, in later relationships, the psyche—having organized these emotions and self-thoughts in early childhood through young adulthood—begins to perceive and understand more and more interactions through the "lens"of these emotions; such that, the more rejection or criticism one feels, the more rejection or criticism one sees in interactions and interpersonal relationships.

Repetition Compulsion

Repetition compulsion is the tendency of an individual to take early negative feelings and thoughts and have them first define self-concept and then effect interpersonal and interactional dynamics. The early organized emotional experiences, consequent feelings, and thoughts tend to repeat and sustain themselves throughout life, specifically in more intimate relationships. A client perceives that he or she was rejected as a child. He or she organizes this emotion around many different experiences and projects it into many behaviors and interactions with a partner. Projection in this case refers to the dynamic of taking an internal negative emotion or thought and placing the cause or blame for the experience onto another. The first step of repetition compulsion is when a person feels rejected and then rehearses the cognitive statement of "I am rejected." The rejection is then projected onto a partner, and many behaviors—which could be interpreted from a variety of perspectives—are now seen as examples of rejection. For instance, husband or wife making a suggestion to the other is no longer an example of advice or caring, but an illustration of criticism and judgment. One partner refusing a request for sexual relations is no longer interpreted as a situational lack of desire, but a powerful statement of rejection to the individual who made the request.

Now that the person feels rejection, he or she rehearses the rejecting thoughts and sees the partner as a co-conspirator, if not the only cause of the rejection. He or she then defends him- or herself against the "partner's rejection." Possible defenses are to withdraw, get angry, attack, or became aggressive in some manner. As a partner perceives these dynamics and feels hurt, he or she in return gets angry that he or she is being treated in such a manner. Once the partner returns such anger and reactivity, reciprocal cycles of reactivity and defense take over in increasing patterns within a couple. Over time, these patterns became highly organized and very difficult to change. It is as if each partner was playing out a well-rehearsed script.

Negative and Externalizing Attributions

Added to the powerful persistence of narcissistic wounds and repetition compulsion are other interpersonal dynamics called upon to maintain the dysfunctional couple communication. For instance, the constant feelings of rejection are fed by automatic thoughts of, "I am rejected." An individual wounded by early life rejections will project negative behaviors or motives (attributes) onto an intimate partner and then use this perceived rejection as reason to get angry or to distance from that partner. Consider the following examples, illustrated by what figuratively could be called "above the line" interpretation, by understanding the input for what it is without personalization or agenda, or "below the line" interpretation, by understanding the input through the attributions of rejection, abandonment, criticism, etc.

1. Wife to Husband: "Would you pick up your shoes?"
   a. Without attribution of criticism: "I'd be glad to, sorry."
   b. With an attribution of criticism: "Nothing I ever do is right. Why are you always criticizing me?"
2. Husband to Wife: "I'll be working this Saturday."
   a. Without an attribution of rejection: "I'll miss you, sorry you have to work."
   b. With an attribution of rejection: "Why don't you ever want to be with me?"

When people interpret behavior "below the line," they are personalizing information and attributing negative intentions onto a partner. *The ability to change these attributions is crucial, even if a partner's behavior has not changed to date.* Attributions create circular patterns that increase narcissistic woundedness and interpersonal enmeshment. The power of altering attributions in interpersonal relationships is that each partner can learn the deeper meaning of these interactions and change them to a self-responsible stance. He or she does not have to wait for the insight or growth of one's partner before attempts at moving to a healthier interaction can take place.

Incongruence of Interpersonal Communication

The incongruence of content and process is almost a universal dynamic with couples who are deeply wounded and undifferentiated. Neither partner in the relationship is able to ask congruently for what he or she needs to heal or to create intimacy. Because of this mutual dynamic, dysfunctional dynamics repeat and what should be simple requests come out defensively and aggressively. The listener hears the negative process tone and responds negatively, often aggressively, with the couple remaining distant and hurt. Instead of being able to state, "I really want to talk with you," what is incongruently said is, "You never want to talk!" Negative judgment then reciprocally creates more negative judgment.

Lack of Emotional Safety

A core lack of trust and safety in highly reactive and enmeshed couples prevents most individuals from being able to give forthright caring, honest feedback, or to effectively listen. Safety is built on many dynamics including an attribution of a partner caring, an ability to be vulnerable and cared for, feeling heard and acknowledged, and a predictability of behavior. When feeling deeply hurt and vulnerable, safety is replaced with distance, doubt, fear, and most often aggression and defense for safety.

The marital therapist should not be discouraged if he or she is unable to establish a process orientation or a self-responsible stance in the couple interaction. The reciprocal negative dynamics in wounded couples is very difficult to break. There is often no feeling of safety or mutual understanding. Without safety, the couple will not tolerate the empathic interventions of the therapist. It is a reciprocal problem that requires the efforts of both parties to break the pattern of defensiveness. Defenses cannot be lowered because there is little safety. Safety cannot be established because of all the defensive and aggressive communications. The pattern of mutual misunderstanding and hurt continues.

In summary, a flow chart might look like the following:

Partner	Partner
Narcissistic wound	Narcissistic wound
from early childhood	from early childhood
Development of shame and	Development of shame and
distorted self-concept	distorted self-concept
A low level of differentiation	A low level of differentiation
develops	develops

Finds a person at same level of differentiation
↓
Marriage or intimate relationship based on
rescuing and repetitive negative dynamics
↓
Both partners perceive the other as not fulfilling their needs
↓
Development of negative attribution
↓
Eliciting behaviors of rejection and criticism from
one's partner, shaming and early dynamics are repeated
↓
Incongruence of speech where aggression and projection
replace vulnerability
↓
Lack of emotional safety resulting in distancing,
instability, and despair

☐ Interventions to Heal Reactive Interactional Patterns

The important transitional step is to help clients develop an understanding of their introjected feelings, how they repeat reciprocally in patterned communications in relationships, and new ways of thinking and behaving to break the patterns. The couple must move away from content of "who did what to whom" and move into individual process issues. In the following proposed treatment, insight, cognitive, and behavioral skills will be discussed for the purpose of breaking the power of repetition of early childhood pain in the later adult life and relationships. General skills that are needed include: 1) developing insight into family-of-origin issues; 2) labeling and naming the emotional "journey" into feelings of rejection, criticism, etc.; 3) identifying what interactions within the partner reinforce the "emotional journeys"; 4) teaching differentiation and responsive demeanor, communication with a balance of thought and emotion, and a desire to truly understand the perspectives and emotions of a partner; 5) encouraging counter-instinctual behavior—behavior which is not defensive or projective in both communicator and listener to break reciprocal patterns; and 6) encouragement and support of the couple by the therapist through the establishment of safety, hope, and patience. The therapist must become a mirror for each partner with the power to offer reflection, which could initially be perceived as adding to the narcissistic wound. Such mirroring is done through the use of an assertive tone of voice, a hopeful stance, and persistent encouragement to change existing patterns. It is difficult to alter the patterns of history when woundedness and vulnerability are so highly organized within an individual or couple. Highly organized means that, not only are these core emotions born of present day negative experience, there are historical self-concept and shame issues, cognitive distortions, and interpersonal process issues. Behavioral distance and destructive non-verbal language are also being recreated from the distant past, which is mostly unknown and unconscious. Similar interpersonal patterns continually repeated later in life feed the reality of the early introjected emotions. Couples tend to want to share emotions and the experiences or stories that justify how they feel. In most of these cases, the sharing is not helpful nor does it function as a catharsis in which both parties feel better after the sharing, but instead becomes the way of deepening the painful and negative feelings. These dynamics can be stopped and replaced with positive experiences and healing. Clients can take personal power over the intergenerational transmission of vulnerability, hurt, and pain.

Steps to Break Dysfunctional Patterns

The process of changing dysfunctional patterns is one that cannot be haphazard. The intentionality of the process, creating structures and homework for practice, and each partner's responsibility to alter specific communications is very important.

Step 1: The therapist must show empathy, a constancy of care, model differentiation, and be patient with the enmeshed couple. No couple interactional movement will be continuous and there will be many reversals and regressions. A couple therapist who normalizes the reversals for the client and paradoxically predicts the reversals will help a couple remain hopeful and persistent. Of course, the greatest likelihood of some regressive behavior is after a more intimate couple communication or at the conclusion of a more vulnerable and honest therapeutic session.

Step 2: Relate the many content arguments, disagreements, and fights a client has to certain organizing emotions or thoughts, which are often unconscious to the clients and stem from the earliest of years. Some examples of the unconscious mental schema are criticism, rejection, abandonment, incompetence, ignorance, etc., or thoughts such as, "I am unloved," "I am uncared for," and "He always rejects me."

Highly vulnerable clients usually group and organize experiences and interactions into one or two core vulnerable feelings and thoughts. These become highly organized and develop into highly generalized, all or nothing, repeated self- and other statements. For example the automatic self thought of, "I am rejected," creates insecurity and self-doubt, and the attribution of, "he or she rejects me," creates withdrawal and/or anger.

Step 3: Relate the organized emotions and thoughts to family history. In almost all cases, an individual who, for instance, feels constantly rejected or unintelligent will find the roots of these feelings in his or her family of origin. It is crucial that the client begins to understand that the feelings, usually solely attributed to the behavior of a partner, are actually grounded in historical experience. When there is a cognitive connection between historical experience and current behavioral patterns, a spouse can begin to understand the power and longevity of such introjects or organized emotions beyond the current relationship and will remove some blame and negative attributions toward the partner. The therapist might ask each client whether he or she has experienced the feeling they attribute to his or her partner earlier in life. Is the frequently experienced thought or feeling understood outside the context of a specific interaction and able to be applied to many interactions?

Step 4: Have the couple label the emotional journey into these organized emotions or thoughts. Naming and labeling begins the process of externalizing, controlling, bounding, and objectifying what prior to this was internal undifferentiated hurt and vulnerability. Through a process of externalizing, writing in a journal, objectifying, talking about, and describing, individuals can begin to step away from a more subjective undifferentiated emotional stance. Couples might say, "I was in my rejection feelings," "I was on my journey," or, perhaps, actually give the emotional or cognitive distortion a name. By labeling the emotions and the "journey" into the vulnerability, the clients begin to externalize the dynamic and take control. Key to this process is having the client understand that they are most often not victims, but creators of their emotional journeys into pain and hurt. As victims, they are not responsible and a partner is rejecting them. As creators, they recognize that the feelings of rejection are in large part created in their history and reenacted interpersonally through their interpretations and reactions.

Step 5: When the defenses against vulnerability and introjected emotions and thoughts are enacted interpersonally with the partner, it is important that the therapist use different process skills. For instance in most cases, reinforcing cathartic behavior, opening up the emotions of the clients, and having the client express their anger and hurt creates more woundedness. Strong and hurtful emotions and thoughts tend to prevent constructive communication. What is then said tends to deepen the pain not increase clarity or understanding. The therapist needs to realize that the content of many of the arguments is probably meaningless. A client can feel deeply rejected over almost any argument or discussion. If the therapist solves a content problem, there will be another to follow.

Instead, couple interaction is often discouraged and replaced with individual reflection, therapeutic mirroring and feedback, and a constant comparison of the currently felt emotion to early life experience. The hardest learning for a client is, that at one level, negative thoughts and emotions seem very appropriate for the interpersonal circumstance, but at another, they are not appropriate at all. They are actually the mechanism that maintains the negative repetitive cycles and continually create a client's woundedness in later life.

Step 6: The therapist, once insight, historical roots, and labeling have been identified, needs to encourage a client to reframe and reinterpret an experience in a healthier manner. What once led a partner to feel wounded, rejected, or criticized, now contains other possibilities for interpretation and response. Perhaps a spouse coming home late from work is not a sign of rejection, but is a simple miscommunication or an indication he or she is working hard to provide for one's family. The important concept in differentiation is that the client begins to choose different interpretations and develops new responses to a partner's behavior. The therapist knows that the client is beginning to disengage from the vulnerability when he or she can interpret a partner's behavior from a number of different perspectives rather than the singular negative perspective that was once so firmly entrenched.

Step 7: The behavior that eventually is most successful in breaking the repetition compulsion is one that is often the opposite or counter to what was before an instinctual or automatic response by the client. The therapist would explore with the client behaviors that would break the reciprocal cycles of the couple. Instead of feeling rejected and then withdrawing, the client learns to reach out. In the place of feeling invisible, a spouse expresses what he or she needs in a congruent fashion with requests shared vulnerably, not aggressively. An alternative to anger and aggression is a partner's vulnerability. The therapist by asking for more positive and creative options for a response assists the client to develop more constructive healing behaviors. The client learns to say, "I missed you," instead of, "Why don't you care for me?"

☐ Conclusion

The therapeutic process of altering negative patterns with highly narcissistically vulnerable clients is some of the hardest work the conjoint therapist may do. It can also be the most rewarding. There is great power and hope when clients begin to be able to change patterns and heal the wounds and the repetition of the wounds that could have been transmitted from generation to generation. Couples who so firmly believed that their spouse was intentionally hurting them learn that much of the dynamic is of their creation. Such self-responsibility and self-understanding helps to break the projective process and creates insight into how early wounds can unknowingly reenact in later intimate relationships.

II

BASIC APPROACHES
AND TECHNIQUES

CHAPTER

9

Enhancing Intimacy in Relationships

Marital and family therapists have focused primarily on eliminating pathology. Their interventions are usually designed to help resolve particular difficulties on problems such as marital conflict, poor communications, and conflicting sets of expectations. Such an emphasis is not surprising in light of the fact that theories of marital and family therapy stress pathology and symptom resolution in the same way that traditional theories of individual therapy stress pathology. Renewed interest dating back to the *Diagnostic and Statistical Manual of Mental Disorders,* 3rd Edition-Revised (DSM-III-R; American Psychiatric Association, 1987) has refocused attention on pathology rather than on normalcy and health.

Most of the techniques presented in this volume will address the question of how to reduce or eliminate marital pathology. This chapter will do just the opposite. The purpose of this chapter is to present concepts and techniques that can be used to *promote healthy functioning* in the couple. A clinician working from a problem-solving model is only concerned with the presented problem(s). This clinician may not have a sense of how to proceed beyond symptom resolution because he or she is lacking a conceptual framework of intimacy and the skills to create higher functioning. He or she may also lack a growth-oriented framework in which to use various techniques designed to enhance the relationship.

Marital therapy is unique among the psychotherapies because it involves the treatment of a relationship defined in a very specific way in our culture. The word that captures the essence of this relationship—love—has been considered taboo in the professional literature. Marital therapy involves the treatment of a *love*(ing) relationship, yet theories of marital and family therapy rarely mention the word love. Love has been dismissed to "softer" disciplines such as drama, poetry, and fiction. Therapists who adhere to the scientist–practitioner model find the concept of love difficult because it cannot be operationalized or measured. Researchers have found the concept elusive; clinicians find it troublesome because they usually think of asking only whether the partners love each other. This question is often responded to negatively at the beginning of therapy.

An exception to the clinical non-use of the concept of love is in the area of marital enrichment. The marriage enrichment movement predated and subsequently merged with the human potential movement of the 1960s. Although this movement never established a large foothold in the clinical field, many psychotherapy programs were developed to promote healthier, happier, more loving relationships.

When two people are married, the fact is that we are treating a type of relationship uniquely defined. Marriage is a voluntary yet (ideally) permanent relationship, as opposed to family, which is permanent yet involuntary. The basis for marriage is emotional, and the emotional attachment is defined in terms of love. Finally, marriage is the only relationship in which there exists sexual permission and expectation. This fact adds another dimension to the relationship, which in turn may become another area for relational problems.

In this chapter, we will focus not only on love, but also on sex and intimacy. These concepts are inseparable, in spite of the fact that marital therapists have indirectly claimed love and intimacy as their territory and sex therapists have claimed sex as theirs. Committed couples do not split these concepts unless they are experiencing difficulties. However, couples in treatment frequently split off certain aspects of their relationship. For example, a couple might split sex off so that they claim to be close without having sex, or partners might engage in an extramarital affair claiming the sexual relationship is meaningless. These couples need an explicit idea of love just as much as the clinician. Until recently, the psychological literature did not have any models of love that were clinically useful. A model now exists that is extremely useful when taken as one part of the comprehensive program that follows. This model of love consists of three components—commitment, intimacy, and passion.

☐ The Triangle of Love

In working with couples, the first step is to ask them to describe what they think comprises a loving relationship. At this point, the clinician wants a general answer in order to move to a description of the triangular

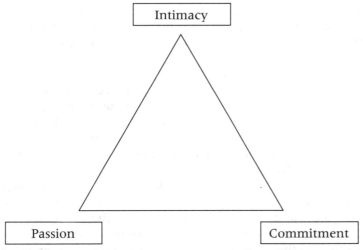

FIGURE 1. Copyright © 1986 by the American Psychological Association. Reprinted with permission.

theory of love. After the couple has responded, the clinician begins a description by drawing a triangle with three equal sides and labels them as shown in the figure above.

Sternberg (1986a, 1986b, 1997) developed a triangular theory of love based on research in social psychology and personality. Love is defined here as the combination of three components that need to be defined for the couple.

Definitions of the Three Components

Commitment

The first component is commitment. This component is cognitive or "cold." At some point in the couple's relationship, a decision was made to commit to each other. They made certain societally sanctioned promises to each other regarding exclusivity. Commitment may also be manifested through sexual fidelity, engagement, marriage, and so on (Sternberg, 1997).

The first issue to discuss with the couple is their definition of commitment. Do they share the same definition? Are they committed, uncommitted, ambivalent, or unequally committed? We believe one of the most important factors in the outcome of marital therapy is commitment. When a couple comes for therapy and they both say they are equally committed to the marriage, we usually see the couple resolve their problems. The couple can also be congratulated for maintaining their commitment to each other as people, in spite of the fact that each may be doing things the other does not like.

When the couple is ambivalent, has unequal commitments, or is lacking in commitment, an open discussion needs to take place so that each partner's thoughts and feelings are understood. The purpose of this technique is to obtain a commitment to treatment long enough to explore the relationship. This will allow the couple to see whether marital functioning can be restored or whether there should be a separation. When couples end therapy prematurely, they frequently continue to go "back and forth" and never have an opportunity to thoroughly understand the part each played in the marriage not working out. In short, when couples cannot commit to each other, they need to make a commitment to the therapeutic process.

In cases where the commitment is weak or one partner is ambivalent about continuing the relationship, a number of different approaches may be taken to help increase commitment. These approaches are based on social-psychological research. Harold Kelley (1983) reviewed major findings related to the process of commitment, that is, those intra- and interpersonal processes that help to establish and to sustain stability. One way to sustain commitment is to improve the reward-cost balance in the relationship. In clinical terms, two tactics may be taken with the client. The first is to ask the partner to think back to what has been rewarding about the relationship. As the partner begins to remember these positive interactions, it helps to remind the person of past rewards. The partner is next asked, if those rewards could be reinstated would she or he be willing to continue in the relationship. The second tactic is future-oriented. The partner is asked to think about what she or he would need to feel happy or satisfied in the relationship. The person's partner is asked whether he or she would be able to meet these needs. The less committed partner may be willing to sustain the relationship in the hope of receiving future rewards. The therapy would then involve working towards the fulfillment of the needs stated at this point.

Another factor related to commitment is that of irretrievable investments. In any relationship of significant duration, the partners have made intangible investments that will be lost if the relationship ends. It is useful to talk about these investments. The therapist might ask, "What kinds of investments have you already made in this relationship?" The most useful investments are those that tap into what the partner has contributed emotionally.

A third factor in commitment deals with the understanding that occurs between partners. Over time partners develop a sense of mutual understanding. A sense of "we-ness." They have an identity as a couple. They know their roles, develop a history together, and create their own private language. All these attributes would be lost if the relationship ends, and the process would have to occur again in any new relationship. Having the partner think about the value of this understanding and its replacement can further promote commitment.

A final factor that has clinical relevance is that of considering the attractiveness of alternative relationships. Any time a partner considers leaving one relationship, there is always the thought of whether there will be another to replace it. One way to increase commitment to the process of therapy, as well as the relationship, is to discuss the need for understanding what happened in the current relationship in terms of that person's contribution to the problems. The therapist may point out that ending a relationship without this understanding may result in a repetition of the same problem in the next relationship. By suggesting that the problem can be carried over into the next relationship, it is obvious that the attractiveness of the next relationship is being reduced. In addition, leaving a relationship with ambivalent feelings also may result in indecision and a pattern of moving in and out of the current problematic relationship. If the clinician can engage the ambivalent partner in treatment for an extended period of time, the prognosis for the couple is very favorable. Commitment should not be underestimated as a variable in the treatment process. A high degree of commitment to the process is highly correlated with a successful outcome.

Intimacy

The second component of the triangle is intimacy. More has been written about intimacy than about the other two components (Sloan & L'Abate, 1985). Prager (1995) lists thirteen different concepts of intimacy and 45 measures of intimacy and related constructs. Sternberg (1986, 1997) refers to intimacy as the sense of feeling close, connected, or bonded, having a sense of welfare for the other, wanting happiness for the other, regarding the other highly, being able to count on the other in times of need, experiencing mutual understanding, sharing oneself and other possessions, talking intimately, giving emotional support, valuing the other, expressing empathy for the other, communicating honestly, and finding the other person predictable (trustworthy). These feelings give rise to "the experience of warmth in a loving relationship" (Sternberg, 1997, p. 315).

Schaefer and Olson (1981) differentiate between two types of intimacy. An "intimate experience" is a feeling of closeness or sharing with another person in one or more of seven areas of what they define as intimate behavior. They define an "intimate relationship" as one in which an individual shares in several areas with the expectation that the experiences and relationship will persist. They believe intimacy is a process that can never be fully completed, one that requires constant attention and work. Seven types of intimacy are identified: 1) *emotional intimacy*, which involves experiencing a feeling of closeness; 2) *social intimacy*, which involves, among other things, having common friends; 3) *intellectual intimacy*, which involves sharing ideas; 4) *sexual intimacy*, which involves sharing affection and sex; 5) *recreational intimacy*, which involves doing pleasurable things together; 6) *spiritual intimacy*, which involves having a similar sense regarding the meaning of life and/or religion; and 7) *aesthetic intimacy*, which involves sharing in the experience of a sense of beauty.

Crowe and Ridley (1990) divided intimacy into four categories that are basic and rely on common sense rather than any theoretical framework of discourse. These categories are:1) *physical and non-verbal intimacy*, the giving and receiving of affection by means of hugging, general body contact or simple mutual grooming; 2) *sexual intimacy*, the ability of the partners to be comfortable with the level of sexual closeness acceptable to each other including the partners' possible different needs for sexual intimacy in relation to frequency or intensity of sexual contact; 3) *operational closeness*, the daily relationship of the partners including possessions in common, the wish and right of knowing the whereabouts of each partner when apart, the sharing of tasks, the working together on upbringing of children, and the planning and organizing of time together; and 4) *emotional intimacy*, the wish to exchange feelings and confidences and the ability to relate empathetically to each other.

The Waring Intimacy Questionnaire is a true–false self-report questionnaire containing 90 items, that is used to measure the quantity and quality of intimacy in a marriage. Based on pilot studies, Waring defined eight components of intimacy: 1) *affection*, expression of emotional closeness; 2) *autonomy*, independence from family of origin; 3) *compatibility*, ability to play and work together; (4) *conflict resolution*, ease in how differences are resolved; 5) *cohesion*, commitment to the marriage; 6) *identity*, self-esteem and self-confidence of the couple; 7) *sexuality*, sexual needs are communicated and fulfilled; and 8) *expressiveness*, sharing beliefs, feelings, attitudes, and thoughts (Hickman, Protinsky, & Singh, 1997).

After mentioning a few words to describe intimacy, the clinician should point out that every couple and individual has his or her own definitions of intimacy, and ask each partner to briefly define intimacy with the idea that this question will be discussed later in much more depth.

Passion

The third component of the love triangle is passion. Passion has been described as romance, sex, physical attraction, affiliation, nurturance, and the longing to be with the other person. Other needs such as those for succorance, self-esteem, dominance, self-actualization, and submission may also contribute to the experience of passion. Passion may be manifested through the actions of touching, making love, gazing, and so on (Sternberg, 1997).

Hatfield (1988, p. 193) defines passion as "a state of intense longing for union with another. Reciprocated love (union with the other) is associated with fulfillment and ecstasy. Unrequited love (separation) with emptiness, anxiety, or despair. A state of profound physiological arousal." This passionate desire is a combination of cognitions, behaviors, and emotions. The Passionate Love Scale (PLS) was developed by Hatfield (1988) to measure passion and includes indicants for cognitions, behaviors, and emotions.

Once again the technique is to describe this term briefly and then ask about the partners' definitions.

Clinical Application of the Triangle

The triangle serves as the structure for much of the subsequent work. It is used initially to explore commitment and for purposes of assessing where the love relationship is lacking. In the process of describing the triangle, the clinician wants to ask five diagnostic questions. These questions may be posed directly or indirectly depending on the openness and sophistication of the couple and the style of the therapist.

1. The first question is *whether both partners desire all three components*. This is basically a yes/no question. Each partner either wants the three components or not. There are obvious cases in which one partner may deny any commitment (e.g., "I want a divorce") or deny having any sexual interest (passion) in the other (e.g., inhibited sexual desire). In less obvious cases, one partner may say he or she wants a particular component but fails to have any grasp of what that component involves. A common case is the husband who wants intimacy but equates intimacy to such things as sex, a backrub, or helping in his business.
2. The second question is *whether each partner wants the same level of intensity for each component*. The three components exist in approximately equal intensities. If the strength or intensity of any one component is altered, then another kind of relationship is defined. Sternberg (1988) described eight kinds of love based on the presence of the three components: 1) *non-love*, the absence of all three components; 2) *infatuated love*, the presence of only passion; 3) *empty love*, the presence of only commitment; 4) *liking*, the presence of only intimacy; 5) *companionate love*, the presence of commitment and intimacy but not passion; 6)

fatuous love, the presence of commitment and passion but not intimacy; 7) *romantic love*, the presence of intimacy and passion but not commitment; and 8) *consummate* or *complete love*, the presence of all three components. The partners should be asked whether they believe they desire the same level of intensity in these three areas or whether they experience discrepancies. The clinician should note whether one or more areas is given too little or too much emphasis. For example, a couple might emphasize how great sex (passion) is to the exclusion of the other areas. When there are discrepancies, the therapist needs to guide the couple toward developing an agreed upon level.

3. The third question is *what prevents the identification and expression of these three components?* Each partner should be able to: (a) identify and define the components, and (b) express each component openly and freely. For many couples, there may be an intellectual identification and definition of a component without the concomitant ability to express the component emotionally or behaviorally. The therapist should ask the partners to think directly about what prevents him or her from being able to express certain feelings. The clinician should carefully examine the question from the perspective of the Intersystem Model described in the Introduction, and fears of intimacy to be discussed later in this chapter.

4. The fourth question is *whether each partner has a realistic perception of what love involves.* Some partners think of loving relationships in ways that are highly distorted and unrealistic. As mentioned earlier, the clinician should ascertain whether the three components are given too much or too little emphasis. At this point, it is useful to listen for some of the common myths of marriage such as, "If she (or he) really loved me, she (or he) would automatically know what I want." In some relationships, partners do not desire intimacy or passion. They want a highly committed relationship that looks like a marriage, but in fact is a permanent friendship or companionate relationship.

5. The fifth question is *whether each partner has a realistic perception of what she or he can offer or has been able to offer.* As the couple talks about the three areas, it will become apparent whether an individual is able to actually deliver on what is being stated. The partners' feedback and the way in which the partners interact provide information about their limitations.

Teaching the triangular model of love and asking these five diagnostic/ therapeutic questions sets the stage for the task of promoting intimacy in the couple. The next step involves asking the couple to identify the specific components of intimacy and then to think about what behaviors constitute an intimate relationship. In addition to the list generated by the couple, we add additional ideas from L'Abate's (1977) work on intimacy and marital enrichment.

In addition to Sternberg's model of love, Zick Rubin (1973) conducted an empirical study in which love was found to have four major components. These components are 1) *needing*, the desire to be with and cared for by the other; 2) *caring*, wanting to help the other; 3) *trusting*, exchanging confidences; and 4) *tolerance*, overlooking the other person's faults. Rubin also found that partners did not desire these four components in the same degree. In fact, in some relationships low correlations existed between some components. These components can all be incorporated in Sternberg's (1986) model under the heading of intimacy.

The component of tolerance is one that should be more carefully considered here because it is not mentioned elsewhere in this chapter. Successful couples learn where each other's faults and perceived weaknesses lie. Of necessity, they need to find ways to work around these areas rather than continue to press or nag each other for perfection. The perspective of a loving couple needs to be on the positives and not the negatives. Part of the process of marital therapy is learning to accept those aspects of the partner that this person does not desire nor need to change in order to improve the overall level of marital satisfaction. *The therapist can encourage the growth of tolerance by focusing the couple on expressing more caring, positive verbal and behavioral exchanges, and clarifying and fulfilling each other's expectations. When good feelings are being generated it becomes easier to overlook negative events and feelings.*

☐ Components of Intimate Interactions

Our technique then involves reviewing the seven components of intimacy listed below, followed by ways the couple will move from a conceptual level to a behavioral level. The clinician reviews these items and then starts at the top of the list to allow the couple to discuss each one in order. The couple decides whether they like the ideas that have been generated and how to implement the ideas. The couple then starts with a new set of ideas or attitudes about what constitutes intimacy. Once they agree to these ideas mutually, the next step is behavioral. They are asked to describe exactly what they are willing to do to carry out the idea. In the following sessions, the therapist asks about the behavioral progress. In addition, an affective component is added by asking that the partners comment on how they feel when they receive some of the intimacy behaviors. In the session, they are also asked to discuss their feelings toward their partner in light of the behavioral changes.

The seven components of intimacy L'Abate (1977) has identified are:

1. *Seeing the good.* Each partner should be able to see the good, both in him- or herself as well as in the other. Each should be able to say what is good in him- or herself and express what he or she likes about the other. The behavioral implementation could involve statements of *affirmation, appreciation,* and *affection.* We refer to this triad as "the three A's" and suggest couples practice it daily. The most difficult concept is affirmation. Statements of *affirmation* are "I like you" in nature. These statements affirm the value of the other person. For example, saying "I'm glad I'm married to you" or "I like being with you" refer to the love for the other person. Statements of *appreciation* deal with what the other person does. When the other person does something that is liked, it should be verbally noted. For example, a partner might say, "I appreciate the fact that you brought me a cup of coffee this morning" or "I appreciate your thoughtfulness." The third A is *affection.* Affection refers to showing signs of liking and loving with words or actions. Touching, holding, kissing, and making verbal statements of affection are also important.

2. *Caring.* Caring means being concerned about another's welfare, happiness, needs, and feelings in a consistent and dependable way. It is an attitude of respect for others, which derives from our own ability to care about ourselves. Caring begins with an awareness of what we need in order to feel safe, secure, esteemed and growing. These needs must then be competently communicated to others and acted upon in order to achieve some level of satisfaction. Caring for another requires tuning in to what the other says she or he needs and being willing to meet some of those needs.

3. *Protectiveness.* A couple is a social system embedded within other social systems. Many forces impinge on the couple such as work, in-laws, and children. Mutual protection means taking the other person's side when necessary and seeing issues from the other's perspective. The couple must protect the integrity of their relationship by drawing boundaries around it. To protect the relationship requires reaching some agreement on the priorities (i.e., self, marriage, children, and work) and then carrying them out in ways that serve the relationship as a whole. They must also give each other the time required to be a couple.

4. *Enjoyment.* Enjoyment refers to being together and doing things together that are pleasurable. Achieving pleasure may be accomplished by doing something for oneself or by sharing pleasure with another. In our society, many people have been taught that pleasure is not a goal in itself nor even desirable. These individuals have been trained to believe that performance is all important. The emphasis is placed on doing, achieving, and competition. This need to perform in order to

win approval and love needs to be examined and a healthy attitude fostered to replace it. This new attitude should involve learning to give pleasure and enjoyment to oneself in order to share it with one's partner. Couples can be encouraged to negotiate activities they both enjoy just for the sake of pleasure. Part of this process also requires that each partner accept some responsibility for initiating enjoyable activities.

5. *Responsibility.* When problems emerge in a relationship, there is a tendency to deny personal responsibility by externalizing blame onto one's partner. In an intimate relationship, each partner must take responsibility for his or her part in the relationship not working. Healthy interdependence rests on personal responsibility, not on one partner taking all the blame or on one partner giving all the blame. Partners must assume responsibility for making the relationship work. They must realize relationships require maintenance and that one partner cannot do all the work.

   We also think of responsibility in terms of being able to express emotions in a manner other than a reactive one. An emotionally reactive response is raw or lacking in thoughtful modulation. Emotional reactivity simply means that emotion rules. Being emotionally responsible means the partner is emotionally self-aware and is able to ask for what is needed in order to resolve the feelings.

6. *Sharing hurt.* L'Abate (1977, 1999) believes that sharing one's hurt is a most intimate act. He points out that we can share our good feelings and success with most anyone. With whom do we share our hurt feelings? Pain is difficult for a lot of people to feel; many defend against the feeling by denying it or by transforming the feeling into something else—often, anger. It is no wonder we only share our pain when we trust someone deeply and can safely expect that person to be empathic.

   An intense level of anger often characterizes unhealthy relationships. In such cases, the only feeling expressed or in evidence seems to be anger. In these relationships, all the underlying feelings have been buried by the anger. These buried feelings may include hurt, depression, resentment, frustration, guilt, remorse, and so on. Hurt is especially prone to be buried because it is seen as a weakness. When anger is used to cover over other feelings, the expression and resolution of the underlying problem(s) are impossible, rendering each partner powerless. Learning to share hurt rather than burying it is critical in promoting understanding and empathy. The therapist may ask the partners to consider all the feelings felt, but not expressed, and then facilitate the expression of the underlying feelings in the session, focusing on hurt.

7. *Forgiveness.* This concept is one that most couples overlook in their list of components of intimacy. Yet, it is implicitly working in every healthy

couple relationship. It is also impossible to live in a close relationship and not from time to time hurt the person we love. When this happens, it is essential to be able to deal with the hurt directly and not focus on some feeling used to cover it up. If these acts are not or cannot be forgiven, a state of resentment is established which erodes the relationship. Several questions are useful to facilitate forgiveness. Forgiveness is not achieved by making a simple apology. It is achieved through an understanding of oneself and others. First, the person who committed the hurtful act should question him- or herself about motivations. This self-inquiry is most salient when hurting the other is part of a pattern. Second, the partners must understand each other. The person who was hurt needs to be validated for feeling hurt and the partner who did the hurting needs to be understood in terms of his or her motivations and intents. The intent should ultimately be that of not wanting to hurt the other.

Once again, the review of these components is best accomplished over a number of sessions. The ideas are developed and then techniques to implement them discussed. Each week, the therapist should check in to see how progress is going on those items discussed.

One final note on intimacy has to do with how couples conceptualize closeness. Many couples simply equate intimacy with physical closeness. A technique to help make this expectation explicit is to ask them to draw two circles to show their level of closeness, each circle representing one of the partners. The partners are told to draw two circles representing how they see themselves now and two circles representing how they should ideally like to be. The circles can then be used to facilitate a discussion in which the clinician would point out that intimacy is a balance between closeness and distance and that couples need to negotiate these two ideas in some practical way. The idea of negotiating distance is new to many couples. Usually they ask for distance indirectly or by creating a fight. In one young couple, the assumption was that all free time would be spent together. Each partner believed the other expected him or her to give up any interest that might take him or her away from the relationship. Once they realized how counterproductive this idea was, they were able to schedule time for personal interests and be in the house together without feeling compelled to be together.

☐ Fears of Intimacy

Fear of intimacy is directly related to the issue of conflict in the couple. Fear has a biologically programmed response. In humans, the response is to fight or to flee. Patterns of chronic fighting, intermittent fighting and making up, fighting and fleeing, or simple withdrawal from each other are common responses to a fear of intimacy. These patterns regulate the distance, but do so in a way that is unacceptable to most couples.

Many couples experience difficulty in becoming more intimate, although they have some awareness of what it means and what they want. When this problem is apparent from the outset, the following technique should be used *first*. In addition, if the problem appears in the process of working through developing greater intimacy, work should be halted and the Intimacy—Fear Awareness technique used.

The technique involves making the implicit, and sometimes unconscious, fears of intimacy explicit. It is often helpful to normalize these fears by noting how some of them are found in most everyone. The couple would then be asked to consider what fears each brought to the relationship. It is essential to keep the discussion framed in terms of fear. A slow and careful therapeutic examination will usually uncover one or more fears that can then be worked through. Other authors have offered a psychodynamic approach to the fear of intimacy (Firestone & Catlett, 1999). Unfortunately, their text is so theoretical that it provides little guidance for the clinician.

The clinician may need to supply some ideas based on observations made of the couple and their individual dynamics, including family-of-origin information. A number of the common fears are historically based in the family of origin. The following list is helpful for the clinician to keep in mind. This list is not exhaustive. It represents some of the most common fears.

Fear of Dependency

This fear is found in partners who believe it is absolutely essential to be emotionally self-sufficient, insulated, and independent. In extreme cases, the partner exhibits counterdependency or the need to constantly remain aloof from the other as if to say she or he does not need the other at all, but finds the partner a financial or social convenience. This pattern can be found in marriages which Sager and Hunt (1979) have called *parallel*. These couples do not rely on each other to fulfill their emotional needs. The marriage is characterized by emotional distance, with both leading separate lives. In some relationships, the counterdependent partner will select a very dependent partner who carries their dependency needs for them. They can then take care of the dependent partner without having to look at themselves, because the dependent partner needs or demands so much.

The fear of dependency often stems from early parental influence. Parents, usually fathers, share the importance of being able to stand alone in the world without having to rely on anyone. During childhood, children who grow up to fear dependency are pushed to be on their own with little, if any, guidance or support from the parent. When these children do need help, they are told they are weak or that they should be able to do it alone. This fear appears in men much more often than in women and is passed from father to son.

To illustrate this pattern, one 40-year-old man stated he could never ask his wife for anything. He believed to ask her for something meant he was weak and "a nothing." As a child, this man had been physically punished and ridiculed whenever he showed any emotional weakness such as crying, and he was ridiculed as being a baby when he expressed needs of his own. He had internalized his father's expressed emotions so strongly that he actually felt he would die should he express his needs. Although he realized this feeling was irrational, he could not stop feeling it on his own. His fear was based on the belief that only the strong have the will to survive.

Fear of Feelings

Expressing intimacy involves sharing a feeling with another person. Self-disclosure is important and might include revealing thoughts, beliefs, attitudes, opinions, and especially, feelings. Some partners have learned to fear their feelings. The feelings such individuals fear are not specific ones such as the fear of hurt, rejection, or abandonment, but a general fear of *all* feelings. Originally, this general fear might have been related to fear of specific feelings. Unfortunately, the specific fear has generalized to include a fear of expressing any feeling.

Partners who have obsessive-compulsive personality structure use their defenses to avoid feelings, and indeed these individuals seem devoid of feeling. They hide behind rationality, denial, projection, rationalization, intellectualization, and a rigid sense of what they believe to be right. Satir (1967) referred to these types of partners as "computers" because of their mechanical non-feeling approach to others. "Computers" think rather than feel, think rather than act, and stay detached from others in order to avoid having their own feelings touched. Being so devoid of an emotional life of their own, they sometimes enter into a relationship with a histrionic partner. On the surface, they act as if the other partner was sick or crazy, but unconsciously they derive some gratification. The feelings obsessive-compulsive partners find uncomfortable may be projected onto their partner so that they can then deal with the feeling in the other and not in self.

Individuals reared in families where feelings were out of control may also learn to avoid their own feelings. In situations where child abuse or alcoholism was prevalent or if a parent suffered from depression, a manic depressive reaction, or was emotionally unpredictable, the child might fear being overwhelmed by feelings and losing control or going crazy. In these partners' minds, the idea of feeling is synonymous with craziness. The same dynamic may also occur in individuals who have suffered from long-term depression. In several of our client cases, men with long un-treated depressions felt that allowing any feeling is the same as inviting an occurrence of depression.

A final pattern of fear occurs in those individuals who were emotion-ally discounted and/or told how to feel by their parents. Being emotion-ally discounted means the parents would ignore, criticize, or punish the child for having a feeling. Because emotional discounting is a verbal pro-cess and less severe than other types of abuse, it is often overlooked. However, repeated emotional discounting can have several long-term ef-fects. Adults we have treated believe their partners will discount them should they attempt to express a feeling. They learn to ignore, minimize, and rationalize their feelings. The pattern is further complicated because these clients do not disclose their feelings to the therapist, giving the im-pression that everything is satisfactory. The therapist must learn to listen for what is not expressed as much as to what is expressed.

Fear of Anger

The fear of anger may manifest in two ways. First, partners may fear the anger they have toward others. They may fear that getting too close to another person may elicit or release this hostility, aggression, anger, or rage. Individuals with this fear keep their distance from others. They realize anger is inevitable in a close relationship so they rationalize that the only way to avoid it is to not have a close relationship. Several types of familial environments may create this type of fear in an individual. In one type of family, the child may be parentified. Parentified children are asked to assume responsibility far beyond their capacity. They must act like pseudo-adults, often having been cast in the role of taking care of a parent. The loss of the child's sense of security, the excessive demands, and the pent-up feeling of anger that was not allowed to be expressed, builds up over time. Many partners who were parentified as children carry deeply bur-ied resentment and anger that is displaced onto their current partner.

Another family situation that generates fear of anger is one in which anger pervaded the client's family system. Child abuse, spouse abuse, or both of these may have taken place. As a child, this individual witnessed how anger got out of control and how members of the family got hurt. In an effort to never repeat this pattern, as an adult partner he or she tries to suppress anger. As a result of the model set by his or her parents, this partner believes anger can only have destructive consequences. The opposite type of family environment can have the same effect. In these families, the parents are reported to have never been angry or in conflict. The parents implicitly transmit the message that anger is bad, unacceptable, destructive, and so on. In many of these families, children are told directly it is not nice to be angry or that something is wrong with them if they feel anger.

In other cases, partners simply may not have the skills to deal with anger. As a result, angry feelings never get resolved, and build up over a period of time. The feeling may escalate to the point of violence, scaring themselves and their partner so much they vow never to be angry again. Of course, this effort is doomed to fail, but the fear still remains.

The other major manifestation of this fear is that of being the recipient of angry feelings. These individuals are very fearful that their partners will become angry with them. They will go to great lengths to placate the partner in order to avoid anger. Just as in the above case where partners fear their own anger, these individuals may have been reared in families where anger was expressed too much or too little. Most commonly, they were reared in families where the anger was explosively and unpredictably expressed. Children of alcoholics come to realize that the alcoholic's anger is unpredictable, unwarranted, and intended as destructive. These children then live in a state of constant fear waiting for something bad to happen to them or to another family member.

Fear of Losing Control or Being Controlled

Control is an important part of every relationship. Healthy relationships are based on mutual control. Partners share the power and control in the relationship. When a partner fears losing control or being controlled by the other, she or he may actively resist or passively give in to the other. This fear has two levels of meaning. On the surface, it refers to the feeling that getting too intimate will result in a loss of control in one's life. This partner believes the other person will begin to take over and run his or her life. Essentially, it is a regressive feeling of being a child again with the other partner assuming a parental role. Individuals with this fear do not know how to assert themselves appropriately. They unconsciously sabotage themselves in order to have the other partner take control. This feeling parallels what happened in the person's family of origin. The parents were overcontrolling, did not promote competency and maturity, and may have actually set the child up to fail by pushing him or her into tasks beyond his or her capabilities and then withholding guidance and support. Intimacy suffers in these relationships because of the parent-child nature of the relationship. Those who fear losing control will not let their guard down to let others know them. They assume this knowledge would be used against them to keep them in their place.

At a deeper, intrapsychic level, losing control means feeling engulfed by the partner. Engulfment refers to losing oneself in a relationship; the person's tenuous sense of self-identity gets lost. These individuals are poorly differentiated, and they have a poorly defined sense of self. Paradoxically, they search out others to help them complete their sense of self, but then they need to recoil from the relationship to preserve the sense of self they already possess. They simply do not know who they are or what they want. They tend to move back and forth searching for a balance. These individuals must search out their own identity and actively seek others who will support them and respect individual boundaries.

Fear of Exposure

Early on in a relationship, people only expose what they choose to expose. The partners only see the facade. As the relationship develops, the couple becomes closer and more self-disclosing.

The level of self-disclosure zigzags to deeper levels, with partners taking turns risking more disclosure as trust builds. The question for every partner early on is, "How much to disclose and when?" However, self-disclosure may stop at a surface level out of the fear that exposing oneself will be too painful. A partner with a low sense of self-worth or self-esteem will not want his or her partner to know. She or he will pretend to feel good about him- or herself.

The incongruence between how they feel inside and how they act leads them to see themselves as impostors: "If they only knew who I really am or what I really did, they would never. . . . " For these partners, the family did not provide sufficient development of self-worth. In many of these families, the love for the child was contingent on performance and not the person. The parents were demanding, critical, and never satisfied with the child's performance. Contingent love teaches the child to value only doing well and not self. The child learns she or he is loved only when things are going well and that the parent's love is not for the child, but for what she or he can do, which is never enough. If a problem or unpleasant feeling is expressed, the child immediately loses sight of the fact that love can be a constant in the relationship. In order to protect themselves from feeling unloved, they would not consider telling their partner how they feel if the feelings were negative, and would expect their partner to do likewise. The basic assumption of these individuals is that if you really knew me, you would not like or love me (because I do not really like or love myself).

Fear of Abandonment/Rejection

The more a partner emotionally invests in a relationship, the greater the hurt is experienced should the relationship end. Partners who were hurt in the past by rejection/abandonment become sensitive to getting too close too soon or to getting close at all. In more serious cases, the partner has been traumatically rejected or abandoned. This situation might have occurred through death, divorce, or desertion of a parent. Children who have lost a parent and have not been aided in working through the loss sometimes carry a fear of abandonment to all subsequent relationships. Children who learn they were adopted may also carry a deep sense of rejection and abandonment. In other cases, the family of origin did not contribute to the fear. The fear may have evolved through adult relationships that were extraordinarily hurtful.

In some cases, we have seen partners suddenly abandoned just prior to a wedding without any explanation or further contact with the person. In one case, a person's partner had been killed in an airline accident and, simultaneously, it was discovered that the surviving partner was having an affair. These events left the surviving partner with a deep sense of loss, rejection, and hurt. In a case like this, never getting close to another person is seen as a way to protect oneself from ever having to relive such a painful trauma.

☐ Conclusion

A number of concepts and techniques have been reviewed in this chapter. The clinician should use them flexibly, creatively, and according to the type of couple. There is no formula for developing intimacy. The ideas in this chapter constitute a blueprint, with the couple providing the bricks, mortar, and sweat.

10
CHAPTER

Reframing

Reframing is the most generically used strategy in the systems therapies, particularly strategic therapy, as well as psychotherapy in general. It is fundamental for psychotherapy because it helps the client change perspective or make different attributions toward the same behavior(s), thereby facilitating a change in attitude and behavior. Systems therapists have referred to this concept by a variety of terms: *relabeling* (Haley, 1973; Minuchin, 1974); *reframing* (Watzlawick, Weakland, & Fisch, 1974); *content reframing* (Bandler & Grinder, 1982); *redefinition* (Andolfi, 1979); *seeing the good* (L'Abate, 1975); *positive connotation* (Palazzoli, Boscolo, Cecchin, & Prata, 1978); *ascribing noble intention* (Stanton, Todd, & Associates, 1982); *nonblaming* (Alexander & Parsons, 1982); and *context markers* (Bateson, 1979; L'Abate, Ganahl, & Hansen, 1986; Viaro, 1980). For some reason, reframing has been virtually ignored in the secondary literature on couples and family therapy. Nichols and Schwartz's (1998) textbook on the concepts and methods of family therapy virtually ignores reframing. In fact, their discussion of reframing suggests they believe it is a technique that makes the therapist appear phony. They make such statements as "reframing was often transparently manipulative" (p. 59) and that positive connotation was "often as sincere as a car salesman's smile" (p. 59). In their 555-page text, they devote less than a page to reframing. Becvar and Becvar (1993) published another very popular textbook on family therapy. Out of 378 pages, they devote a little over a page to reframing with only one citation to a 1974 reference. In a book that is so well researched, one can only wonder why they chose to ignore a topic of such importance. Likewise, Young and Long (1998) only offer a page on framing and reframing with little attention paid to the existing literature. We can only speculate that these authors have failed to recognize the importance of reframing in our field or they have a strong bias against anything associated with strategic/paradoxical therapy. On the other side of the coin, Bagwell-Reese and Brack (1997) discuss the importance of reframing in mental health in terms of changing worldviews.

Watzlawick and colleagues (1974) were among the first to discuss the central role of reframing in therapy. They defined reframing as changing the conceptual and/or emotional meaning attributed to a situation and said that a behavior reframed is the behavior that has been defined or framed by the client as being symptomatic.

A reframing statement is quite different from an interpretation. For example, interpretation carries some truth-value and the therapist actually believes the statement represents some aspect of reality. On the other hand, reframing statements are not intended to have the same validity. The theory of truth that is used by the therapist in reframing is pragmatic. In the pragmatic theory of truth, that which works is considered true (James, 1907). The therapist is attempting to construct a view of reality that is more conducive for change to occur, rather than replace the client's faulty worldview with one that is correct (G. Kelly, 1955). Tennen, Eron, and Rohrbaugh (1985) have stated:

> Adaptive functioning does not require being in touch with reality and having an accurate view of the world. Rather, any world view that interdicts problem sequences is considered in planning interventions. This position is nested not only in "functional theory," but in growing empirical literature pointing to the healing effects of illusion (Lazarus, 1983; Taylor, 1983). Adaptive functioning has been associated with denial (Lazarus, 1983), the illusion of control (Alloy & Abramson, 1979; Tiger, 1979) and the misperception of one's success and its causes (Greenwald, 1980; Miller & Ross, 1975). High self-esteem (Tennen & Herzberger, submitted for publication; Tennen et al., submitted for publication), lack of depression (Lewinsohn et al., 1980; Abramson & Alloy, 1981) and better adjustment to illness and injury (Bulman & Wortman, 1977; Taylor, 1983; Tennen et al., in press) have been associated with non-verdical and illogical perceptions and beliefs. The shift from psyche to system and from reality testing to useful illusions may represent the most significant contributions of the strategic therapist in his/her use of paradox (pp. 199–200)

In order to effectively reframe the symptom, the therapist must first join with the client system and understand the meaning of the symptom. Unfortunately, many therapists have viewed strategic/paradoxical therapy as a bag of tricks that the therapist unilaterally imposes on the client(s). In order for these techniques to be effective, the therapist must understand the problem from the inside out. This means comprehending the meaning and function of the symptom. Acquiring this information is an essential part of the assessment phase.

Every system of therapy attempts to change the meaning of the problem or symptom in some fashion (Weeks, 1977, 1990). The use of reframing in the literature usually has two meanings (Weeks & L'Abate, 1982). One is to change the way in which a symptom is defined in terms of some polarization such as good versus bad, crazy versus sane. This use of reframing stems from the various models of psychotherapy. Clients and others frequently attribute bad intent to behavior. In couples, this attributional process leads one partner to the moral perspective that they are okay and the other is bad. Reframing can be used to change the meaning attributed to the problem or to the dynamic that exists in the relationship. For example, couples usually believe their fights are exclusively negative behaviors. They have framed their fights as destructive, negative, and so on and seen them as representing negative intent. In reframing the fighting behavior, the therapist wants to change the meaning attributed from bad to good. The therapist can say, for example,

> The two of you must care a great deal about each other and yourselves, because you invest so much of your energy in fighting. Couples who don't care or are indifferent don't fight. Your fighting shows there is something worth fighting for in spite of the fact that you may end up appearing to fight against each other.

The second use of reframing is to move the focus from the individual to the system. When couples or families present with problems, there is usually a symptom bearer (identified patient) who is carrying the problem for the rest of the family. The other member(s) do not see the connection between what they do and the behavior of the "sick" one. In couples, the "healthy" spouse externalizes and/or denies any responsibility for the problem. The attributional strategy in the couple is linear, not circular. One of the therapist's tasks is to get them to see how the problem stems from their interaction or relationship or both. Reframing is the method whereby the therapist can move the couple from a linear attributional strategy to an interactional or circular attributional strategy.

In other words, when couples present in therapy, there is often an overt or covert belief that the other partner is wrong, sick, crazy, and so on. Thus, it is the other partner's place to change. The symptom presented is usually seen as "belonging" to just one partner and not a result of the partners' interaction. The therapist must find a way to get the couple to see the problem systemically. Unless and until they see the problem as shared or bilateral, couples therapy is impossible. This is the reason reframing is essential if any systems approach to therapy is to work.

The two types of reframing described above are usually combined in a statement given to the couple. Palazzoli and coauthors (1978) called this technique positive connotation. The symptom is given a positive meaning and all the members of the system are linked together. Reframing changes the definition of the relationship, changes the meaning of the behavior by altering or disrupting the interpretative framework, and disrupts one's ability to predict another's behavior. It also puts the participants on the same level. One goal of the reframe is to prescribe a shared meaning in the relationship (e.g., "fighting means you care"). It also increases interdependence by suggesting they both want the same goal for the relationship.

Finally, one of the most significant effects is to change the attributions from linear to circular and from negative to positive. If the reframe is successful and the couple believe they both deserve the same thing, then they must ask themselves if there aren't better ways to achieve it than to engage in the same endless game. The result should be new efforts to change the other's impressions of self by changing one's behavior.

☐ Developing the Reframe

The art of reframing has been poorly described in the literature. Most literature describes the reasons for developing a new frame and some of the typical content of reframes, but not the process involved in creating new frames. Weeks and L'Abate (1982) reviewed the literature on reframing and gave numerous examples of reframes throughout their text. Many of these examples were couple focused. In addition, Protinsky and Quinn (1981, p. 139) developed a few standard reframes to deal with common couple and family dynamics. In one of their cases, a husband became suicidal after the last child graduated from high school and went to college. His wife had been overinvolved with rearing the children and felt a profound sense of loss. The couple were given the following reframe:

> The team is very impressed with the great lengths that Joe has gone to in order to protect his wife from her feeling of loneliness. It was Joe's intuitive belief that Mary could not survive the emptiness she felt when John graduated and left home. Thus, Joe acted in helpless ways so that Mary might fill her emptiness. This is a highly caring act on Joe's part. However, it is the team's belief that Mary does not need Joe to rescue her from loneliness in the way that he has chosen. The team perceives many hidden strengths to Joe; it is the team's belief that he will continue to act in his present protective way.

L'Abate and Samples (1983, p. 38) developed an invariable reframe for couples with intimacy problems. They used the following statement:

> Dear _____ and _____:
> After working with you for so long, I am fairly convinced that you need to defeat each other to avoid getting too close. Intimacy can be a very scary and dangerous condition, and I can understand how it affects you in that way. For some people, intimacy means loss of control, loss of mind, loss of self, loss of strength, and in some cases, loss of life.

Weeks and L'Abate (1982) and Jessee and L'Abate (1985) also developed a paradoxical approach to treating depression that included reframing depression in the context of the relationship. Jessee and L'Abate (1985, p. 1139) used the following reframe in one case:

> I think you are to be congratulated for being depressed to help your husband. It is obvious that you have become depressed in an attempt to take his mind off being unemployed. I cannot think of anything else you could have done that would have demonstrated your caring and loyalty to him so convincingly.

It should be noted that in many of the abovementioned cases, the reframe was given to the couple in written form with instructions that they should read it on some ritualized basis. Reading and re-reading the reframe is a powerful maneuver that helps the reframe "sink in." Commonly, one partner is pathologizing the other and needs to repeatedly get the message that he or she is part of the problem.

While examples are very helpful, the therapist also needs to know the process involved in developing a reframe. Only one article in the literature focuses on this issue exclusively (Jones, 1986). Jones briefly touched on the importance of joining, using the client's language, and asking focused questions. All of these elements are essential in reframing. Reframing is not something the therapist does to the couple. In other words, the therapist cannot just offer up a reframe and expect it to be accepted.

The first step in reframing is for the therapist to develop an idea or ideas about what kind of reframe would be helpful in facilitating change. As stated earlier, for systemic change to occur there must be a systemic definition of the problem by the couple. The therapist may anticipate that several possible reframes may be useful and consider what is most likely to help facilitate change. The therapist must think ahead and then gently guide the couple toward a new definition of the problem. The therapist cannot guide the couple unless he or she has joined with them. To join means to be seen as an ally of each and both simultaneously.

Understanding each partner's perspective and the couple's common goals helps to achieve joining. The therapist can note the couple's language and use similar language. The therapist's definition of the problem and the couple's definition of the problem start out incongruent. The goal is to bring the couple in greater congruence with the therapist. The key way in which this task is completed is by slowly weaving together a series of questions that gets the couple to change their perceptions. Imagine the couple's relationship as a giant jigsaw puzzle. As the pieces are put together, several possible images begin to emerge and then one image dominates and sets the pattern for filling in the rest of the pieces. The therapist uses questions to elicit different pieces of the puzzle. The questions may be designed to elicit new information, to punctuate the information in a different way, or to change the meaning given to certain facts. The couple may spontaneously articulate a new frame as a result of considering these questions. If a spontaneous reframe is not forthcoming, when they are sufficiently "primed," the therapist may offer the reframe. If the process has been carefully completed, the reframe will take root; if not, it will be rejected sooner or later. Some couples are ready to accept a reframe with little cultivation. Others require the careful process described above. A case helps illustrate the points made above.

> A couple in their mid-30s presented with a variety of problems. The major problem was that they had been dating for several years but had not been able to decide whether to marry. One of the problems that was revealed later in therapy was Ann's insomnia. Insomnia has always been conceptualized as an individual problem in the clinical literature (Ascher, Bowers, & Schotte, 1985). Ann had tried a number of remedies to eliminate her insomnia but none had worked. In fact, she failed to mention this problem early on in treatment because she had given up on believing there was any help. It was her partner, Jeff, who mentioned it. Ann saw her insomnia as an individual problem and Jeff agreed. Neither one saw any connection between her problem and their relationship problems.
>
> The goal of the reframe for her insomnia was to give it a positive meaning for her relationship and to help them see how the insomnia was an interactional phenomenon. After careful questioning about how the couple managed conflict, the therapist suggested that Ann's insomnia served several very useful functions for their relationship. The most important function it served was to keep Ann from showing anger. A person who does not sleep does not have the energy to get angry, and her inability to become angry seemed to protect the relationship because Jeff, who always equated anger with rejection, could not deal with an angry partner. Rejection was a central theme in Jeff's history, as he felt both his parents had rejected him as a child.
>
> The reframing statement was put in written form as follows: The insomnia protects your relationship by keeping you, Ann, from getting angry with Jeff. Jeff would see your anger as rejection and leave.
>
> This reframe can be analyzed as follows:

INTRAPSYCHIC COMPONENTS

1. *Definition.* The insomnia is redefined as protective for both partners. In a more general sense, the partners are defined as being in a relationship characterized by protection. They must now ask, "Are there better ways to be protective?"

INTERACTIONAL COMPONENTS

1. *Congruence.* Ann attempted to control her anger through insomnia in order to protect Jeff in the relationship. Jeff had sent her messages that he could not tolerate anger. Hence, they were in an incongruent relationship regarding the expression of anger. The reframe made this incongruence explicit, showed how they both participate in her symptom, and allowed them to share a common goal of protection.
2. *Interpretation.* The change in definition changes how the symptom and relationship are interrelated. They will now attribute positive meaning to the symptom.
3. *Interdependence.* By showing how they both satisfy unconscious needs in the other, the level of interdependence is increased.
4. *Prediction.* Ann can no longer predict that she will experience greater loss of sleep when angry. This connection had been unconscious. Jeff can no longer predict how Ann will deal with her anger or how he will deal with his sense of rejection. In fact, he requested that she let him know when she was angry, even if it felt bad to him.
5. *Attribution and Impression Management.* The linear attribution strategy was disrupted. They both attributed a positive meaning to the symptom and to the other's intent. This in turn lead them to invite the other to try something different. Ann was asked to express her anger and Jeff was asked to express his sense of rejection more directly.

The use of reframing in psychotherapy and marital therapy deserves considerable attention. The reader who wishes to gain a greater understanding can consult several classic reviews: Jones (1986); L'Abate et al. (1986); Weeks (1977); and Weeks and L'Abate (1982).

In summary, reframing the symptoms has multiple effects. The most important effects in systems therapy are its ability to change the linear attributional strategy of the couple to a circular attributional strategy, and to change the attribution of meaning given the symptom to one that is positive. "Positive" in this case actually refers to some aspect of the relationship that helps the couple bond. The positive dynamic (e.g., protection) helps to create greater congruence by defining something that both desire. Once both partners see how they participate in the symptom, they are ready to work cooperatively rather than competitively. Additionally, by attributing positive intention(s), each partner is more open to try different strategies in dealing with the other—which means each partner must change.

☐ Research on Reframing

Several studies have investigated the effect reframing—used alone or in conjunction with other techniques—has had on changing behavior. Feldman, Strong, and Danser (1982) divided moderately depressed college students into several groups. Some students received messages that their depression was a negative condition and should be avoided while others were told it was something useful and should be experienced. These researchers found that paradoxical reframing produced more symptom remission than that found in any other group. In a similar study using depressed college students, Beck and Strong (1982) told students depression was something that should either be avoided because it was negative or it should be embraced because it was positive. Both groups evidenced change, but the positive group had the lower relapse rate. Another group of researchers found that the nature of the directives (paradoxical vs. non-paradoxical) did not affect outcome. However, depressed subjects given the positive reframe had lower Beck Depression Inventory scores than those in the no-reframe condition (Kraft, Claiborn, & Dowd, 1995). Another group of depressed and lonely college women were divided into three conditions—reframing, self-control directives, and a waiting list group. Those in the reframing group experienced the greatest reduction in depression (Conoley & Garber, 1985). All four studies showed similar findings and were characterized by a high level of experimental control and objective outcome measures.

Two more recent studies also confirmed these earlier findings. Swoboda, Dowd, and Wise (1990) used a sample of 116 depressed clients from a mental health center. Three treatment conditions were used: paradoxical reframing, paradoxical restraining, and a pseudotherapy control group. Multiple outcome measures of depression were utilized. Subjects in the paradoxical reframing group showed the greatest change.

Another study examined the effects of three therapy sessions with couples in conflict (Davidson & Horvath, 1997). Forty couples were treated in a mental health center. The therapists used two interventions. The first was a positive reframe of their conflict and the second was a message to go slow (a restraining message). Of the forty couples, some received treatment immediately and others were treated after being on a waiting list. Couples in the treatment group showed a 39% improvement compared to the 10% on the waiting list. Interestingly, when the couples approved of the reframe, they were more likely to benefit from treatment. All the couples were given the same reframe in this study.

Akillas and Efran (1995) researched socially anxious males who were assigned to three groups: symptom prescription without reframing, symptom prescription with reframing, and a waiting list control group. The only group to show significant improvement was those who received reframing with prescription.

In an attempt to broaden the theoretical scope of reframing, Morris, Alexander, and Turner (1991) experimentally manipulated blame using attributional theory. They found that messages that were positive significantly reduced the intensity of blaming attributions. These researchers suggested that "blaming schemata" may be developed predisposing family members to construe each other's behavior more negatively than would be if the schemata did not exist.

☐ Conclusion

Reframing is an essential part of psychotherapy and has been demonstrated to bring about change. Weeks and L'Abate (1982) were among the first to propose that reframing alone could effect change. Reframing can also be used to set the stage for other interventions such as a restraining message or other paradoxical messages.

Unless the therapist pays careful attention to the first therapeutic stage of reframing, it may be difficult or impossible to proceed. A problem that is defined by the couple in a fixed, immutable way will be resistant to change. The clinician begins the therapeutic process by redefining the problem, even if only slightly altering meaning at first. The slightest alteration in meaning can grow over time into a much larger alteration. In traditional individual therapies, problems are often redefined as having underlying origins outside the client's awareness and control. This type of redefinition moves the client away from the originally defined problem to that of having an underlying or unconscious issue. Another common type of redefinition is to move from content to process. This type of reframe tends to be systemic and shifts the couple's focus from the content of their behavior toward the fact that they have established a dysfunctional dynamic between them.

In this chapter, we have stressed the concepts of moving from negative to positive frames and from individual to systemic frames. Many other frames are possible to co-construct with clients. These two are probably the most common and useful for the couples therapist. The remainder of this volume describes basic techniques that may be used with couples.

Communication Techniques

Communication does not belong to one approach in therapy. It is part of all therapeutic approaches and constitutes an approach in and of itself. The purpose of this chapter is to present a number of communication techniques that can be used as part of strict or exclusive communications work with a couple or as part of an integrated approach, for example, communication training blended with contracting. Techniques to improve a couple's communication cut across all other techniques in this book. The sine qua non of couples therapy is communication training whether it's conducted explicitly or implicitly. Because communication is the foundation for all therapeutic work, it is a transtheoretical concept. Much of the work on couples' communication that has been reviewed shows that it is psychoeducational (L'Abate & McHenry, 1983; Young & Long, 1998). In other words, couples require an individualized educational training or coaching process to help eliminate deficits and to create more effective means by which to communicate.

Because the purpose of this chapter is to describe techniques of communication enhancement and not theories of communication, only a basic schema of couples' communication will be presented to help guide the clinician. This schema will help the clinician facilitate communication of the type that is helpful to couples rather than to individuals. It was developed by Bernal and Barker (1979) in an effort to draw together different theories of communication. Part of what this theory addresses is linear versus circular and content versus process communication.

Gottman (1994) reported that studies among couples that have remained married have shown the significance of communication in predicting the longitudinal course of marriages, thereby predicting divorce and marital satisfaction. Predictions from three separate studies were consistently over 90% accurate. A recent longitudinal study with violent couples made similar predictions with the accuracy of predicting divorce remaining high (Gottman & Gottman, 1999).

The "core triad of balance" (Gottman & Gottman, 1999, p. 3), emotional behavior, cognition and perception, and physiology, can predict divorce. Each couple establishes a balance of positivity and negativity in these three areas with the balance(s) determining the ultimate fate of the marriage. Gottman (1994) found that couples headed for divorce showed more negativity than positivity in their emotional behavior and marital interaction. Four negative interactions (complaint/criticism, contempt, defensiveness, and stonewalling) were most predictive of divorce. Gottman labeled these interactions as the "Four Horseman of the Apocalypse" (1994, p. 110), defined as:

> *Complaint/criticism*: Complaint as an expression of disagreement or anger about a specific issue which may escalate into criticism becoming more judgmental, global, and blaming after repeated and frustrating attempts to resolve the issue.
>
> *Contempt:* A mockery, insult, derision, or sarcasm of another individual indicating incompetence or absurdity (e.g., disapproval, disdain, judgment, putdowns, etc.).
>
> *Defensiveness:* An attempt to ward off or protect self from perceived attack. A response may be denial of responsibility for a problem, a counterattack, or a whine.
>
> *Stonewalling:* Listener does not provide any cues to the speaker that a "stonewall" is being placed between the listener and the speaker. Emotionally, the speaker perceives the listener as being detached, smug, hostile, disapproving, cold, or disinterested.

When couples are having communication problems they recast the entire relationship in terms of "the distance and isolation cascade" (Gottman & Gottman, 1999, p. 306). This is a pattern of (a) viewing the marital problems as severe; (b) believing there is no point in working out the issues with the other partner; (c) feeling flooded by the other partner's complaints; (d) arranging lives in parallel fashion so less and less time is spent together; and (e) loneliness.

Communication that is linear in nature reflects cause–effect thinking and is other- (outside of self) focused. When a partner is engaging in this type of communication, she or he does not talk about or disclose self, or he or she talks about self as simply reacting to others. Circular communication reflects a more mature, differentiated, and abstract form of thinking. At this level, partners can talk about their reciprocal, interlocking patterns of relating. For example, a husband might say he is angry over the tone in his wife's voice. She could clarify the meaning of her tone once she has this information and add that her tone was in response to his withdrawal. This couple can see how they each affect and are affected by the other. Patterns of communication begin to become clear to them through this type of discussion.

Content-oriented communication deals with just the specific content issue at hand for a couple. In content communication, the couple can only think about *what* they are thinking and not about *how* they are thinking. Process communication is more mature, differentiated, and abstract. Partners can step outside themselves in order to become their own observers. They can talk about how they are talking (metacommunicate) and how they need to change dysfunctional patterns in their communication.

A couples therapist needs to facilitate moving from linear to circular and from content to process communication in order to promote healthy communication. Unfortunately, there are not any specific techniques to accomplish this goal. This process unfolds during the therapeutic interactions as the therapist points out these different communications, asks different questions, directs communication in different ways, and models these concepts. Bernal and Barker's (1979) schema may also be used psychoeducationally. It can be taught to couples so they can begin to analyze their own level of communication. There are five levels of communication in this system. These are organized from the least mature and helpful to the most mature and helpful. They could be described in the following ways:

1. *Object level:* The couple focus on issues outside of self exclusively (e.g., money, sex, in-laws). Issues related to self and the relationship are objectified and concretized; for example, an attorney is upset that he lost a case. He tells his wife he "feels bad" and then describes the events of the case in detail. He fails to talk about himself and ends up telling her a boring story.

2. *Individual level:* Each partner focuses on the other as the cause for his or her behavior. Responsibility for one's actions is disowned and projected onto the other; for example, making statements such as, "You make me angry" or "You made me do that."

3. *Transactional level:* At this level, patterns of behavior can be observed and commented upon. The reciprocal nature of the relationship is recognized; for example, making statements such as, "You got angry with me, and I withdrew, and then you got angrier and I withdrew even more."

4. *Relational level:* Couples who have achieved this level are aware of the underlying assumptions and rules that govern their relationship; for example, they may know that anger is triggered by not feeling loved.

5. *Contextual level:* The most important contextual factor would be aware-ness of how one's history, especially experiences in one's family of origin, affect the current relationship; for example, a wife who is an-gry with her husband might be displacing old anger toward her father.

A couple can be taught these levels with the idea that the first two levels are content-oriented and linear. They may be asked to work on developing themselves in the other levels by first developing greater aware-ness of themselves and then discussing these ideas.

☐ Assumptions Facilitating Communication Work

A major deficit in communication training models is in the area of the assumptions couples hold. Attempts to teach a couple new ways of com-municating will be met with resistance and eventually fail *unless* their underlying assumptions are addressed first. By the time many couples enter therapy, a long history of miscommunication, misinterpretation, and misattribution has developed and is rigidly held in order to protect each self. Two techniques are useful in order to create a different attitudi-nal set and prevent the problem of miscommunication, misinterpretation, and misattribution from reoccurring: The first technique is to help the couple differentiate between intent and effect; the second is changing assumptions.

Unfortunately, many partners develop the idea that intent and effect are exactly the same, and thus a communication that was experienced as hurtful is automatically assumed to have been intended as hurtful. It is impossible to be in a close relationship without experiencing some com-munication as hurtful. When this experience occurs, it is essential to check out the intent of the sender. In order to do so, the couple must first un-derstand the difference between intent and effect. The therapist can dis-cuss these concepts until the couple understand the difference.

Examples of how these may differ are very useful. In one case, when-ever a wife asked her husband how he felt, he became angry and with-drew. He would counter her question with the response that she was trying to put him down because she was more articulate with expressing her feelings. The fact was that he was the one ascribing hurtful intent to her because he was hurt by her question. The husband had been repeat-edly punished whenever he expressed a feeling in his family of origin. The hurt he experienced over simply being asked how he felt was deeply rooted in his history and not in his wife's efforts to understand his feel-ings. Once they were able to check out her intent, her husband's negative attributions toward her stopped.

The ability to differentiate intent versus effect is essential in teaching the technique of effective listening, which is described later. Differentiating intent and effect results in cognitive restructuring. Rather than thinking, "Because that message hurt, she or he must have wanted to hurt me," the partner now thinks, "I am feeling hurt by that message; what did my partner intend to say and why am I feeling the way I am?"

The second technique, changing assumptions, is preparatory for all the others. Many couples enter treatment both assuming that their partner does not care about them, wants to hurt them and, in spite of their best efforts, will never really be able to understand or be understood.

The therapist may suggest that both partners adopt three new assumptions to help their relationship:

1. The assumption of commitment;
2. The assumption of goodwill and intent; and
3. The assumption of understanding.

The first assumption highlights the fact that the couple are committed to each other and to the therapeutic process. This assumption should of course be checked out and validated before proceeding.

The second assumption addresses some of the issues in differentiating intent and effect: The partners need to believe goodwill exists in the relationship. This assumption draws out their sense of caring for one another. They learn that even though a statement may be hurtful, its intent was not necessarily to hurt the other.

The third assumption is that of understanding. When couples begin therapy, they often feel their partner does not care about them or understand them. Then, when a miscommunication occurs, the partners are ready to give up on the relationship and the communication stops. The point of this assumption is that no matter how muddled the communication becomes, if the partners keep trying, they will at the very least be able to understand each other. The assumption *normalizes miscommunication* and implies that communication is a difficult, time-consuming process. This assumption does not imply agreement. The therapist should explain how understanding the other person does not mean agreement with the other person's perception or giving in to what she or he wants. Most couples will readily agree to these assumptions. The couple should remind themselves of these assumptions every day and then every time they feel their communication is deteriorating.

☐ Creating a Context for Communication

Effective communication requires a context with three basic structural elements. This context is taught and modeled in the therapist's office and then extended outside the office. Thus, the first technique involves teaching the couple how to create the context.

1. The first element is to talk to each other. Do not talk through other people or things. In the therapist's office, the task is to keep the partners focused on each other. The therapist should be like a coach on the sidelines providing feedback and directives. At home, the couple need to speak directly to each other without using the children or others to talk for them. They should not use the TV or other activities to dilute the intensity of their interactions.

Communication should be as free of distraction as possible. The couple should be taught how to create "islands of experience" with each other by establishing boundaries around the dyad and setting limits when others attempt to intrude on those boundaries.

2. A second element of the context is proximity and contact. Partners should not attempt to talk from room to room or on the run. They need to move close together and give each other strong eye contact. In the office, contact needs to be monitored and strengthened when necessary. It is useful to have the couple agree on a talking place and time. The place should be comfortable, free of distraction, and associated with pleasant activities. Touching, if only hand-to-hand or fingertip-to-fingertip, can create even more intensity in the experience.

3. Third, communication is a process and takes time. A couple should not expect to resolve every problem in 5 to 15 minutes or to build a relationship in such short bursts. The couple will need to make a commitment to talk on a regular basis every day. At first, the time spent talking at home should be short and gradually lengthened, as they become more successful communicators. If a regular time is not established due to fluctuating schedules, then after each talk a time could be agreed upon for their next communication. Consistency and repetition are important to the successful learning of new communication skills.

☐ Communication Techniques

For this section, we will describe the combination of techniques that usually promotes improved communication. Conversely, these techniques tend to diminish or to eliminate many of the common problems found in communication. These problems will be treated in the next section on obstacles to effective communication.

"I" Statements

Each partner should be encouraged to make "I" statements. "I" statements refer to: *I* think, feel, believe, wish, wonder, and so on. An "I" statement reflects the fact that the speaker is taking responsibility for self. On the other hand, "you" statements (e.g., *you* said, *you* did) are blaming or provoke defensive reactions. "It" statements (e.g., *it* seemed to me) are either too logical, impersonal, or vacuous to be helpful. Each partner should practice using "I" language, avoiding "you" and "it" language. Whenever the couple catch themselves using the latter two forms, they should stop and convert the idea to "I" language. Each partner should monitor self and be open to reminders that he or she has lapsed into other styles, without getting caught in blaming the other partner when a lapse is made.

Listening

Many couples will state that their problem is one of not talking or communicating enough. There are times when it is useful to reframe this statement by saying that the problem is not one of talking, but one of *knowing how to listen*. Listening is more than sitting quietly, nodding, or saying "um-uh" now and then. Listening means letting the sender know what was heard and how the statement was interpreted. The listener's responsibility is to reflect back the content and affect that was registered. The content (literal) is the meaning that was extracted, while affect refers to the emotion stated or inferred in the statement. Examples of what a listener might say include:

> "I heard you say you felt hurt because of my comment regarding what you said to your mother."

> "I heard you say you felt okay about my comment, but the way you said it gave me the feeling you were sorry."

> "I interpreted what you said to mean that you really do want to do it, but your body language said to me that you weren't sure."

The purpose of reflective listening is for the couple to share the same meaning. Words by themselves are not always sufficient to communicate meaning, especially in cases where affect is essential as part of the understanding. The sender needs to provide a clear message that includes a statement of feeling. The sender should not assume the receiver will automatically know his or her feelings. It is the responsibility of the sender to communicate both affect as well as content. The couple need to be trained to follow a format that goes something like this: "I'm feeling _____ because of _____." In other words, make an "I" statement. Once the sender has been coached to make this kind of statement, the receiver is next coached to reflect back the affect and content.

If the reflected statement is accurate, then the discussion may proceed. However, the reflected statement may be highly discrepant with the intended communication. If this happens, the couple again start the cycle over of stating the thought and having it reflected back. When the communication has failed, many couples feel frustrated and want to give up or start blaming each other. An assumption couples make is that communication should be easy and problem-free. This assumption should be checked out with the couple and if it is present, it should be discussed.

Additionally, when couples begin to blame, the whole process comes to a halt. Blaming should not be permitted. Miscommunications need to be normalized. The couple need to see themselves as being on the same team with each partner willing to help the other when a miscommunication occurs. The therapist may predict miscommunications for the couple as a way to prepare them for dealing with these occurrences.

Another common problem occurs when the sender gives contradictory verbal and nonverbal messages but denies that such messages were sent, because of a lack of awareness. The couple need to know that such communications are going to take place, and be given a strategy to handle mixed messages. Assuming the receiver has accurately detected a discrepancy and reflected it back, the sender may continue to deny certain feelings. For example, a husband might deny that he is angry, although his nonverbal behavior reveals this feeling to the partner and the therapist. The receiver should be taught to reflect back the *specific behavior* that conveyed the feeling. In this example, the wife might say, "I thought you were feeling angry because your voice became loud, you clenched your jaw and fist, and your face turned red." The therapist may then validate these perceptions of the receiver. If the sender continues to deny the feelings, the therapist should deal with the issue by trying to explore the reason for the denial.

The therapist should also note that a denied feeling will keep resurfacing, which means further interaction will help reveal the true feeling. If the sender of a contradictory message continues to deny certain feelings at home, the couple need to have an agreement. The sender should agree to accept the feedback and think about it seriously. In most cases, the feedback is discounted and then forgotten. The receiver must be willing to stop after providing the feedback. If he or she insists the other agree, a no-win is set up. The receiver must also consider whether he or she is reading a feeling not present. The couple may return to the matter later to try to sort it out. If they are unable to do so by the next session, then it should be worked through with the therapist.

Reflective listening is essential when a couple get trapped in what has been termed the *self-summarization syndrome*. Couples need to be taught about this concept. The concept refers to each partner saying essentially the same statement over and over again, usually with increasing emotional intensity.

Self-summarization is a misguided attempt to get the other person to understand. Repeating the same message does not create understanding.

Interrupting this destructive process by using reflective listening will change the interaction. One partner might suggest starting over by going back to the original point and asking for a reflective statement. Self-summarization usually occurs when the partner fails to respond in an appropriate way, but it may also occur when an individual has a fixed agenda and will not consider negotiation and compromise. In these situations, the only voice the person hears is the one in his or her own head. For example, the husband may have the agenda of proving his wife wrong; all of his statements will be designed to prove his point. His wife might try to respond, but he is so fixed in his agenda he cannot hear her statements.

The therapist can help couples learn about these obstacles and learn how to work through them in the session. They may then begin to practice at home. When communication techniques fail to correct self-summarization, it is time to explore for hidden agendas. Using this concept alerts the couple to the existence of hidden agendas and may help them to do this type of exploration if they become hopelessly stuck.

Validation

Validation is related to "I" statements and reflective listening. To be validated means to be understood as a person. The opposite of validation is discounting. Discounting means being ignored, misunderstood, or told that one felt or said something she or he did not. In other words, this type of misinterpretation occurs when certain feelings or words are wrongly ascribed to a person. This concept is known as "mind raping" (e.g., I know you really felt hostile even though you deny it). Couples often confuse validation with agreement, thinking that if they see the other person's point of view, they must agree with him or her. It is possible to validate another person without agreeing.

The first step in communication is to validate the other person. Then and only then can a discussion be held over differing perceptions, beliefs, opinions, and so on. *When the couple try to skip the validation phase, they inevitably end up arguing over the content in an effort to get validated.* They assume agreement is the same as validation once again. Confusing these concepts can be lethal to communication. The therapist must teach the couple how to validate and still be able to disagree or see things in different ways. The therapist should constantly monitor communication in the session in order to point out when validation is needed.

Editing

Written communication is usually clearer and more concise than the spoken word because the former has been thoroughly edited. Editing has several useful functions in couples' verbal communication. First, when dealing with a difficult topic, it is best for partners to think through what they want to say before they say it. The couple can be instructed in the use of *mental rehearsal* as a way to prepare for a discussion. This involves carrying out a mental dialogue designed to sharpen the ideas the person wants to communicate. Second, one can never say all that one thinks, nor should one have to. Extraneous, distracting, nonthematic comments only confuse the process of communication. The couple need to stay focused on the theme or problem. Each partner also knows what kinds of comments "push the other's button." These comments distract the couple by reengaging them in a discussion with no end. Both must agree to edit out comments designed to create conflict and sabotage the process. Each individual must also try not to take the bait if such a comment is made.

Time

Communication is a process that takes time. Couples need to learn that good communication requires not just their energy, commitment, and understanding, but also their time. They must learn how to create time to communicate. Communication should not be compressed to fit their time, but time should be expanded to fit the need to communicate. Getting couples to make dates or appointments is helpful. Sometimes the block of time will be insufficient, requiring one or more session on the same topic. The idea of doing a little at a time helps to dispel the myth that every conversation should bring about closure. When communication is extended, the need for continuity is absolute. Both partners must know when the dialogue will continue.

☐ Obstacles to Effective Communication

The couple must be taught how to communicate effectively and be coached in the session. Effective communication does not just happen. It is a skill that can be taught in a systematic way. The role of practice can be emphasized repeatedly as each session begins. A review might be done of skills that are in the process of being acquired. These skills will not work unless the couple also know what obstacles prevent them from communicating more effectively. They should be aware of some of the common obstacles. This information will allow each partner to do a personal self-analysis and to agree to self-monitor in order to stop destructive habits. A few of the major obstacles are reviewed below.

Mind Reading

Mind reading refers to the idea that one really knows what the partner is thinking, feeling, and so on, without checking out those assumptions. In other words, a partner's assumption is elevated to the level of reality. The therapist may ask partners to think about how they know when they are mind reading and agree to check out their assumptions. The therapist can ask partners to think about what signals, both internal and external, tell them they are mind reading. An internal signal might be a common assumption a partner makes when certain events are happening. An external signal could be as simple as giving legitimacy to the idea that the other person said, "I never said that."

Personalization

This concept pertains to attacking the person as well as the problem. The problem should be defined in terms of what a person does, not who he or she is. Thus, when discussing a problem in the relationship, the couple should stay focused on the behavior and not attack each other personally. Attacking the other person's character or blaming the other is counterproductive. The two most common types of personalizations are labeling (e.g., "you're stupid") and generalizing (e.g., "you never listen to me").

Distracting

There are two ways of distracting. One involves leaving the theme of the discussion by bringing up other past, present, and predicted future problems. The couple should adopt the rule of staying on one topic at a time. A related distraction involves one person bringing up an issue and the other person bringing up another issue, and so on. This strategy is one of attack and counterattack.

Polarized Language

Certain concepts in our language only serve to polarize couples. These include right versus wrong, always and never, truth versus a lie. Language that is black and white can be eliminated. We teach couples that these concepts are polarizing, judgmental, and troublemaking. A simple rule is to ask them not to use these terms when they speak. They may think in these terms, if they must, just avoid expressing them.

The couple will then be forced to find other language. They might be encouraged to use terms such as opinions, beliefs, perceptions, feelings, values, likes, and so on. For example, a wife might say she thinks oral sex is wrong, which implies there is something wrong with her husband for suggesting it. He might reply that it isn't wrong and that something is wrong with her for not wanting it. They are now polarized around the issue of rightness and wrongness. Had she said she didn't like it because it made her feel embarrassed, then a discussion of her feelings could take place.

☐ Research-Based Communication Interventions

During therapy, two key goals in reducing risk factors are to aid the couple in evaluating and clarifying expectations and to improve conflict management and communication strategies. The two key goals in reducing risk factors are to enhance positive bonding through friendship, fun, and sensuality and to boost the understanding of and the choices reflecting commitment. Utilizing cognitive-behavioral strategies, cognitions and behaviors associated with marital success may be established (Stanley, Blumberg, & Markman, 1999).

Gottman and Gottman (1999) listed eleven goals in their intervention strategy, which when met, would signal the termination of therapy. The markers of divorce, particularly the Four Horsemen mentioned earlier, must be significantly and meaningful reduced as the couple work out their conflicts. The ratio of negativity to positivity must also be reduced. A buffer must be established that will allow a partner's anger to be seen as valuable information rather than a personal attack. A love map should be created and maintained on a daily basis providing a means for the partners to continue learning about each other's worlds by periodically updating their knowledge. The admiration and fondness systems also have to be activated and reactivated. Most of the time during daily nonconfrontational interactions, partners are now turning toward each other in a positive way rather than away. The couple creates a positive sentiment override (POS) defined as "a discrepancy between insider and outsider perspectives such that messages an observer might describe as objectively negative, say irritable, are taken as neutral or even positive by the receiver of the message" (Gottman & Gottman, 1999, p. 313). Maintenance of the POS is done by resetting the point of turning towards versus turning away, thereby suggesting the couple is more emotionally connected and engaged with each other. Much of this connection is nonemotional, occurring in the daily mundane happenings of the marriage in fairly neutral contexts. Each person needs to accept influence from his or her partner, especially the husband from his wife. For resolvable conflicts, the couple:

- Uses a softened rather than a harsh start-up when dealing with conflict
- Effectively repairs negative interaction chains
- Uses positive affect for de-escalation
- Learns how to physiologically soothe partner and self
- Learns the tools to make each conversation better than the last without the help of the therapist.

One study supported Gottman's findings of belligerence, defensiveness, and contempt as being destructive patterns during conflict resolution (Gottman, Coan, Carrere, & Swanson, 1998). Analyses suggested that the active listening model, the most common component of current marital therapy models, was not predictive of differential marital outcomes and occurred infrequently in the resolution of marital conflicts. Instead, a particular pattern of model that did predict divorce was found through the quantitative analysis of process. The predictive pattern of divorce involves a negative startup by the wife; the husband's refusal to accept his wife's influence; the wife's in-kind reciprocity of low intensity negativity; and the husband's absence of low intensity negativity. Among stable couples, the only variable predicting both marital stability and happiness was the amount of positive affect in the conflict. This study reported that positive affect could be utilized to de-escalate negativity and was found only in couples who eventually obtained stable and happy marriages.

☐ Conclusion

The practice of communication skills training with couples appears deceptively simple. This chapter has demonstrated the myriad factors involved in carrying out this task effectively. Once the therapist has a grasp of these techniques, it is then a matter of monitoring the communication process, assessing it moment-to-moment, and intervening actively and directively when communication fails. This last requirement of active, immediate, and directive intervention may not be comfortable for the therapist. A reexamination of the therapist's own beliefs and methods of working may be needed if these simple techniques are to be used effectively.

CHAPTER

Conflict Resolution

Conflict is inevitable in every close relationship. Some couples exhibit their conflict openly and directly while others attempt to deny and suppress or exhibit their conflict covertly. The question is not whether conflict exists in a couple, but how they manage conflict when it arises. Virtually every couple coming for treatment is in a state of conflict. They may be in conflict over a variety of issues, from expectations, needs, and wants; to money, sex, children, in-laws, and so on. The conflict may be expressed overtly or covertly and with varying degrees of emotional intensity. When the level of intensity is high and the couple lack the skills to successfully resolve the conflict, the first task of the therapist is to de-escalate the feelings, to teach the couple conflict resolution skills, and to help them resolve their particular issues.

The exception to this approach would be when the level of intensity is so high and the need to blame each other is so entrenched that the couple are not yet ready to work together. It is best in these situations to see the partners separately until the level of anger can be reduced and the blaming can be stopped. Of course, in cases involving spouse abuse, the type of conflict must be carefully assessed. In cases where the conflict and anger is instrumental or purposeful, couples therapy should not be undertaken (Mack, 1989).

The first step in helping the couple deal with conflict is to inform and to help them recognize that conflict exists in all close relationships, thereby normalizing the existence of conflict. Some couples have the idea that their marriage should be conflict-free. In their minds, any hint of conflict means they have made a serious mistake or have failed. The therapist can point out that it is not a question of whether conflict exists, but rather whether the couple have managed it destructively or constructively. The couple can be asked directly, "How do the two of you manage conflict?" The therapist is probably going to hear that conflict results in getting stuck, unresolved hurt, and angry feelings. At this point, the therapist can begin the change process by suggesting the idea that conflict can be a constructive force in their relationship. Toward this end the therapist may point out how constructive management of conflict can help each of them get what she or he wants, allows each of them to be heard, understood, and respected, and leads to a sense of competence and closeness.

This initial discussion of conflict is designed to change a couple's attitude that conflict is bad and can only have destructive consequences. In addition to the work done in the sessions and the homework, it is useful at the outset to use some bibliotherapy. Although a number of popular books are available on this topic, we generally ask our couples to read *The Dance of Anger* by Harriet Goldhor Lerner and *Your Perfect Right: A Guide to Assertive Living* by Robert Alberti and Michael Emmons. The second book is not exclusively about assertiveness in couples but covers many of the basics, including communication techniques, conflict resolution, and anger.

Before proceeding to talk more about what the therapist does, it is essential to consider how the therapist uses his or her self in dealing with conflict. Beginning therapists are often afraid of losing control of a session or of not knowing how to manage intense conflict. The therapist may have the mistaken idea that his or her job is to prevent or minimize conflict and consequently, to rescue the couple from their conflict. Some therapists will experience a strong countertransference reaction in which they fear anger emerging in the session because of their own difficulties in experiencing anger. All of these possible reactions mean that the therapist must believe what she or he is proposing and be free of fear of conflict and anger. The therapist may need to seek supervision or therapy to deal with personal issues. Conflict resolution is actually not that difficult a process, yet we have seen many beginning marital therapists find it impossible to implement this type of approach due to their own personal limitations. The therapist can keep a watchful eye on himself or herself to determine whether he or she is avoiding, minimizing, or denying the conflict and anger present in the couple.

☐ Anger

Conflict and anger are intimately related. Where there is conflict, there is usually anger. It is usually the anger that frightens the couple and the therapist. According to Kassinove (1995) "we define *anger as a negative, phenomenological (or internal) feeling state associated with specific cognitive and perceptual distortions and deficiencies (e.g., misappraisals, errors, and attributions of blame, injustice, preventability, and/or intentionality), subjective labeling, physiological changes, and action tendencies to engage in socially constructed and reinforced organized behavioral scripts"* (p. 7). Anger is associated with losing control and being destructive. Much of what has been emphasized in conflict-resolution work focuses on the mechanics of resolving conflict in a behavioral way. It is assumed these skills will reduce anger, but this approach does not address the problem of dealing with conflict that begins with anger. In working on this problem, a significant amount of time needs to be spent exploring attitudes, beliefs, and feelings before the behavioral work is started.

Our first task then is to help the couple understand the meaning and function of anger in their relationship. A number of questions help reveal the meaning of anger. These questions may be asked as the exploratory process unfolds. They should not be asked as a simple list of questions.

Meaning and Function of Anger

1. What is anger?
2. What does it mean when you are angry?
3. What does it mean when you are angry with your partner?
4. What does it mean when your partner is angry?
5. What does it mean when your partner is angry with you?
6. How do you respond to your partner's anger?
7. How do you respond to your own anger?
8. How do you let your partner know you are angry?
9. How long does your anger usually last?
10. What other feelings are associated with anger?

The meanings attributed to anger are derived from several sources. The two most important are the experiences with one's mate and the experiences in the family of origin. Getting some history from the couple will reveal their beliefs and attitudes about anger. If a person's partner uses anger destructively, that fact will certainly influence the partner's perception of what anger means. The family of origin is also a strong factor in developing this belief system. Children learn a great deal about anger and conflict from what they see, or fail to see, in their parents' behavior. The strength of this influence cannot be overstated. It is therefore useful to know what those experiences were for each partner. Preparing an anger genogram will further illustrate these influences (DeMaria, Weeks, & Hof, 1999). The following questions are answered for the anger genogram:

1. How did your parents deal with anger/conflict?
2. Did you see your parents work through anger/conflict?
3. When members of your family (name each one) got angry, how did others respond?
4. What did you learn about anger from each of your parents?
5. When a parent was angry with you, what did you feel/do?
6. When you got angry, who listened or failed to listen to you?
7. How did members of your family respond when you got angry?
8. Who was allowed and not allowed to be angry in your family?
9. What is your best/worst memory about anger in the family?
10. Was anyone ever seriously hurt when someone got angry?

These questions often reveal two patterns in the family-of-origin. In one pattern, a member of the family, usually the father, is the only person allowed to be overtly angry. In many of these cases, this pattern is associated with drinking. Father used anger to manipulate, control, and express his aggression. Mother and other members responded in fear, not knowing whether father would lose control. The adult children might use this same pattern or might be so frightened of their own anger or that of others that they go to great lengths to avoid anger and its expression.

The other typical pattern is the family that attempts to deny anger and conflict. Children from these families do not understand their experience of anger or that of their partners. Thus anger is an unknown and fearful feeling and often is out of awareness.

The type of training one experiences in one's family of origin may actually play a significant role in the selection of one's mate. A partner who grew up in a home pervaded by anger might choose a mate who appears to be devoid of anger, perhaps of all feelings. Another partner might choose a mate perceived as weak and dependent so she or he can safely displace old, unresolved feelings of anger. Helping partners understand these early experiences can be validating and enlightening. They might have been told as children that they should never be angry, which invalidated their experience and led them to question and doubt their perception of the world. They may be unconsciously repeating old patterns or carrying out a mission for a parent. The therapist may see the same dynamic in the couple that was present in the parents. These unconscious scripts and repetitions cannot be effectively treated with a set of behavior-based skills. This work involves family-of-origin exploration, awareness, and an understanding of psychodynamics.

Another facet of understanding the meaning of anger is how it can be used as a shield to protect the person from experiencing feelings that are more difficult or painful. In short, the overtly expressed and felt anger may act as a defense and, at the same time, the anger may serve to give the person a sense of power, energy, and control. Anger may be used to cover up many feelings, and the therapist can explore what these other feelings might be. In many cases, the client will not know, which makes some interpretations necessary. Some of the common feelings underlying anger are frustration, guilt, sadness, depression, powerlessness, dependency, and mistrust. The therapist should keep these possibilities in mind, exploring those that appear plausible.

Many partners are not in touch with these feelings or find it unacceptable to feel or to express the underlying feeling. For example, one man from a cold and rejecting family entered his marriage with strong unresolved dependency needs. Yet, he could not admit that he needed anyone or wanted anything. He could not ask for what he wanted out of fear of not getting it and being rejected, so he expected his wife to automatically know and give him what he desperately wanted. He became chronically angry toward her for failing to meet his unexpressed needs.

There are two feelings that deserve special note. One is hurt. When there is anger there is almost always hurt. Hurt, unlike anger, usually elicits an emphatic response, yet it is difficult for many partners to say they feel hurt. The other feeling, which has been grossly ignored in professional writing, is fear. Organisms have an innate response to fear, which leads to fleeing or fighting. This fight or flight response accounts for much of our behavior during conflict, that is, a fear response once elicited leads to withdrawing or to attacking. This explanation may be offered to the couple in order to explore the basis for fears that are elicited. What is so fascinating about this concept is that some of the fears are related to intimacy and were described in Chapter 8. For example, a partner may have been reared in a destructive family where he felt neglected and abandoned. This fear follows him to his current relationship. As this person gets closer to his partner, a paradoxical situation occurs. He wants closeness; yet wanting closeness in the past was associated with rejection. During conflict, the partner's fear of rejection is unconsciously triggered and results in an angry fight. This type of trigger reaction is the reason we say skills alone will not resolve the problem. The fears of intimacy we have identified are useful to explore as part of the underlying force driving the anger.

Functions of Anger

Berkowitz (1993) stated that anger may not have a particular goal. According to the author, "angry feelings stem from an unpleasant occurrence that yields internal physiological reactions, involuntary motor reactions (clenched fist, postural changes, etc.), facial changes (muscle-induced changes that yield dilated nostrils, frowning brow, etc.), and thoughts or memories that arise at the time of the unpleasant occurrence. He thought of anger as the experienced combination of these inputs, and believed it is not aimed at achieving any particular goal and does not serve any useful purpose of the person" (p. 206). In contrast, there is much research that stresses the goals, functions, and purposes of anger in relationships.

In the previous section, it was pointed out that anger may result from a fear of intimacy. Anger then may function to regulate distance in a relationship. When a partner is getting too close and eliciting unconscious fear, there is a need to create distance. Because the need is unknown and fear is experienced as anger, the partner has no conscious methods to negotiate for the distance. A fight can serve to alleviate the underlying feeling of fear by creating distance. Conversely, when partners become too distant, anger can be used in order to serve as a means of gaining the attention of and interaction with the other partner, thus bringing the pair closer.

Anger may also be used in a similar manner to test the degree of commitment in a relationship. If a partner believes her partner may reject or abandon, then it is possible to test this belief by trying to push the person away through anger. If he keeps coming back, then the partner knows she will not be rejected. In more extreme cases, the partner may discover that he or she can engage in highly disruptive behavior because of the other person's high dependency needs. Such situations occur among people with low self-esteem, especially for those in a relationship with an addict. For example, the alcoholic husband may be chronically abusive to his codependent wife. She is in need of therapy just as much as he is because of her dependence on the relationship.

Anger may be used to assert power and control in a relationship. The partner who needs to bolster his or her sense of power by controlling another will usually find that anger is an effective method. This partner will also choose someone who can be intimidated by anger. The therapist should consider the individual dynamics and pathology of such a partner. These partners may fall into diagnostic categories such as narcissistic, paranoid, aggressive, or sociopathic.

Anger may also function in at least two healthy ways in a relationship. When a boundary is violated, anger is likely to emerge. The boundary may be related to any subsystem of the couple's relationship. The two most common boundaries are associated with self and marriage. In the first case, an individual may feel she or he is having personal rights violated. For example, a couple might agree that the husband can have an evening to work at home before a major presentation the next day. As the evening unfolds, his wife begins to interrupt him over things that could have waited. He might assert himself with anger to let her know that she has violated the agreement they made.

Anger may also stem from a violation of a marital boundary. In one case, a young married couple came to therapy because the husband would tell his parents things that his wife considered private. They had never discussed this problem calmly in order to clarify expectations, but they had fought over it many times after getting certain information back from his parents. It is useful to help such a couple think about both the meaning and function of their anger. Once they have developed some awareness, it is much easier and usually much more successful to learn and to utilize fair fighting skills.

The therapist and the couple must also recognize anger when it is disguised as something else. Anger is not always expressed openly as anger. Anger may be thinly disguised or so well disguised that even the therapist has trouble seeing it. The thinnest disguise for anger from most therapists' perspective is passive-aggressive behavior. As the term implies, the aggression is expressed indirectly or passively. Some of the common methods of being passive-aggressive are forgetting, procrastinating, misunderstanding, and overreading the other person's behavior.

An example of passive-aggressive behavior involved a husband who forgot to pick his wife up at a designated time; he claimed he forgot the time. Procrastinating in doing something for one's partner is another expression of anger; for example, a wife had promised to organize some household files and six months later it still was not done. Misunderstanding and overreading the partner's behavior are similar; if one partner has been clear, but the other continues to misunderstand, then a payoff is to be found in not understanding. Likewise, a partner may read certain things into the other partner's behavior and despite that partner's protest that it is not true, insist that it is in order to justify the behavior.

A second way to disguise anger is to take a position of righteousness. By asserting that one is right, moral, true, good, and so on, the other person is cast in the role of being wrong, immoral, deceitful or lying, and bad. This hostile and indirect way of putting one's partner down allows the partner to try to get away with his or her anger.

A third method to hide anger is through self-victimization. The victimized partner (e.g., "You absolutely must take care of me and not upset me") may either pretend to be sick or develop psychosomatic problems. In one of our cases, a woman had married a distant, cold, and self-righteous husband who was totally inaccessible. His wife developed numerous aches and pains that could never be medically diagnosed. Because of her history, she had not learned to express anger in direct form and her various ailments served to get her husband's attention and also served as a way for her to express her discontents, albeit indirectly.

The final method is the most difficult to see as anger, because in this strategy the partner uses the ploy of reason and rationality to vent anger. These partners tend to be obsessive-compulsive personalities who use intellectualization as both a defense and as an offense. One of our cases demonstrates this point in a dramatic way. The wife had been decorating the house and decided to purchase new curtains. When the husband discovered how much money she had spent, he was unquestionably upset. However, when he discussed the curtains with his wife, he gave her one logical reason after another why the curtains had to be returned. He even claimed they lacked the proper thermal properties. In addition, he said she could not be trusted to make good decisions without him, so he decided to take away all of her credit cards. When initially confronted in therapy about the denial of his anger, he vehemently denied any feelings of anger toward her. This case points out how difficult it can be to help partners recognize and acknowledge their anger.

Giving clients permission and providing a safe, secure environment in which to explore facilitates the expression of feelings. Although the focus may be on one partner, the reactions of the other partner should be monitored. Partners may actually collude to keep the pattern intact. They may be too frightened of anger to deal with it openly.

☐ General Principles of Fair Fighting

In order to have a fair fight, a number of rules must be remembered. A fair fight starts with the individual who has the problem doing a self-assessment. Prior to saying anything to the partner, it is important to sort out one's own feelings. Earlier in this chapter, it was suggested that anger may only be the tip of an iceberg which contains a variety of other feelings. During the first part of a fair fight, the feelings need to be expressed. If anger is the only expressed feeling and many others are withheld, then the other person cannot respond appropriately. In many cases, the angry person wants the partner to see how hurt she or he is, but when the partner fails to acknowledge the hurt, she or he does not get what is needed, feels frustrated, and becomes even angrier. Taking time to explore one's feelings in some depth helps to facilitate the expression of those feelings.

The second major task of the angry person is to identify the source of the anger before beginning an argument. In some cases the source of anger is clearly unrealistic. For example, a man might be angry because his wife spent a few minutes talking to another man at a party. He expected her to stay with him and talk only to couples or other women. This expectation is unrealistic and engenders anger. It is each partner's responsibility to determine whether his or her anger has a rational basis. If it does not, then the partner needs to use the cognitive therapy approach (see Chapter 12) discussed in this volume. The partner may be informed about the feeling and the fact that the other partner is attempting to take responsibility for it by changing his or her thinking.

On a practical level, several ideas need to be discussed before the actual steps to fair fighting are reviewed. First, the couple need to be reminded that in a fair fight the attitude must be one of win–win. This attitude consists of being willing to give up something in order to bring about a compromise. The therapist can point out that unless each person feels she or he has given up something, they probably do not have a compromise solution.

Second, fair fighting is a skill and it takes time to acquire a skill. During the process, mistakes will be made. When mistakes are made, the partners should not blame each other or give up. In fact, they may agree to help each other by pointing out times when the partner deviates from the rules. The couple should begin to use these rules with issues that are not emotionally laden. We suggest the couple divide these issues into three categories: cool, warm, and hot. They begin to use fair fighting with the cool issues in the session, practice more at home, and then move on to the warm issues. The couple can be reminded that fair fighting requires practice, practice, and more practice.

The third rule deals with time. Fair fighting requires time. Ideally, the couple would be able to discuss a disagreement as soon as it occurs. This idea assumes they have plenty of time. The reality is that many fights occur when there is not time to talk or the conditions are not right (e.g., when guests are over). In these situations, the partner may express the feeling discretely and agree to talk later. A fixed time needs to be set in order to contain the problem. If a time is not set, the partner is likely to keep bringing up the anger. When the discussion does take place, resolving the fight may take more time than was allotted. A fight can be broken up into segments. Some disagreements take many hours to resolve. Fights should not be hurried in order to meet some time limit or the need for quick resolution.

Having a fair fight assumes the anger is under conscious control. Sometimes a fight will deteriorate into a destructive situation because of escalating anger and decreasing self-control. A rule we suggest is that either partner may call a time out during an argument unilaterally and without question. The partner who is getting angry may call a time-out to cool off. The partner on the receiving end of the anger may call a time-out because he or she is afraid of the anger or sees a deterioration in the argument. The cooling-off period should be as short as possible but as long as is needed to bring the emotion down to a manageable level. The person who calls the time-out is also responsible for setting the time to resume the argument.

The couple should understand and be in agreement with these ideas before proceeding to the mechanics of fair fighting. Fair fighting consists of a number of do's and don'ts. The first task of the therapist is to make each partner responsible for how he or she fights. We give each partner a copy of the Essential Do's and Don'ts (see box). They are asked to read this list and rank order the items where they have trouble. In the next

---

ESSENTIAL DO'S AND DON'TS

1. Be specific when you introduce a gripe.
2. Don't just complain, no matter how specifically; ask for a reasonable change that will relieve one gripe at a time.
3. Confine yourself to one issue at a time. Otherwise, without professional guidance, you may skip back and forth, evading the hard ones.
4. Always consider compromise. Remember, your partner's view of reality is just as real as yours, even though you may differ. There are not any totally objective realities.
5. Do not allow counterdemands to enter the picture until the original demands are clearly understood, and there has been a clear-cut response to them.
6. Never assume that you know what your partner is thinking until you have checked out the assumption in plain language. Never assume or predict how your partner will react, or what your partner will accept or reject.
7. Never put labels on your partner. Do not make sweeping, labeling judgments about your partner's feelings, especially about whether or not they are real or important.
8. Sarcasm is dirty fighting.
9. Forget the past and stay with the here-and-now. What either of you did last year or month or that morning is not as important as what you are doing and feeling now. The changes you ask cannot possibly be retroactive. Hurts, grievances, and irritations should be brought up at the very earliest moment; otherwise your partner may suspect that they may have been saved carefully as weapons.

session, each partner is asked to talk about their bad habits and how she or he might change the habits. The therapist may praise their constructive comments as well as offer additional suggestions to help overcome habits that are not helpful.

The next task is to go over the steps of constructive conflict resolution (see box on Steps to Fair Fighting). These steps are broken down so they are easy to understand. The therapist may wish to point out that Steps 1 through 4 deal with feelings about the problems and mutual understanding. Before a problem is "solved," it is essential to acknowledge the other person's feelings about it first. Couples make two common mistakes in this area. The first, as we have implied, is to fail to discuss the feelings about the problem rather than the problem itself. Acknowledging the feelings of the other does not imply accepting the other's position. This fact often keeps partners from acknowledging the other because they equate acknowledgment of the other person's position with acceptance.

The fact is that in many cases the person who expressed the problem just wants to talk about his or her feelings and not about the problem. This situation frequently occurs when the problem is outside the relationship. In a typical scenario, a wife may be having a problem at work. When she tells her husband how she is feeling he begins to give advice or problem-solve. The wife in turn feels discounted emotionally. She believes he is problem-solving in order to make her problem go away. The couple need to be aware of when to and when not to proceed to the problem-solving steps (Steps 5 through 11) in this model.

As we said earlier, these steps should be put into practice in the session in which the couple are working on easy issues or just role-playing some dispute. The first session may require a half an hour to a full hour just for one argument. After they have practiced the steps once, the pace usually increases and the steps will become less mechanical and more natural. In order to help the reader pull together the techniques described in this chapter in a systematic way, we have developed a flow chart that shows when various techniques should be used (Figure 2, p. 161).

In addition to the behavioral techniques of fair fighting discussed in this chapter, negotiation is also an important technique to teach partners experiencing anger and conflict. Dayringer (1976) developed a series of steps very similar to those of the Fair Fighting technique. He views the goal of fighting as learning how to negotiate. He sees anger as a response to being blocked from attaining one's goals. Some of his steps include learning how to engage to fight, selecting a "beef," giving feedback, asking for change, discussing change and different alternatives, and closing with goodwill. In order to develop a truly comprehensive approach, his steps in effective negotiation need to be compared, contrasted, and merged with the steps developed by Fisher and Ury (1981) and Ury (1991).

STEPS TO FAIR FIGHTING

1. The person who has the problem is responsible for bringing it up as soon as possible. Before you bring the problem up, think it through in your own mind.

2. State the problem to your partner as clearly and concretely as possible. Use the following format: "I am feeling (e.g., angry) because of (e.g., the way you put me down at your parents' house)."

3. It is important that you both understand the problem being brought up. The partner who is on the receiving end should reflect back what was said using the following format: "I hear you saying you feel _____ because of _____." After reflecting back what was said, ask clarifying questions so you know exactly what your partner meant. For example, "Describe." "Tell me." "What is it that upsets you?"

4. When both partners agree on what is being said, the first partner may proceed.

5. The partner who brings up the problem should take responsibility for offering a possible solution in terms of changes both can make (e.g., "I can make sure you know what I want. I would like to suggest you _____").

6. This solution can be discussed and then your partner may offer a counterproposal. Again, the solution should involve changes both of you can make.

7. Discuss several options until you agree that one proposal is most workable (not right or wrong, but workable).

8. Once you have agreed on an idea, proceed to talk about how you will put it into action. This means being able to clearly answer the questions: Who will do what, when, and how.

9. Once everything has been worked out, think about what could happen to undermine it. Each of you can think of how you might sabotage the agreement.

10. Working through a conflict stirs up a lot of feelings because it means you had to give up something. Congratulate each other for the hard work and willingness to compromise. Reaffirm your relationship in as many ways as possible. You have good reason to celebrate.

11. Agree to come back to this problem after some specific period of time to reassess how the agreement is working. You may need to change it or fine-tune part of it.

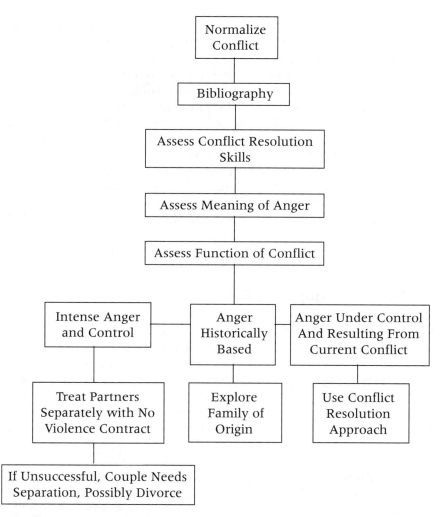

FIGURE 2. Flow Chart for Conflict Resolution

They stress the following points for effective negotiating: (a) differentiating the problem from the persons involved, with each person treating the other in an empathic and respectful manner; (b) actively listening to oneself as well as the other while attempting to resolve the issues on merit in an objective, unbiased fashion; (c) avoiding polarized and combative stances, focusing instead on specific concerns; (d) creating a variety of potentially mutually satisfying outcomes; and (e) using standards of judgment that are fair, reasonable, and impartial.

Ury (1991) developed the negotiation model further by focusing on modifications that need to be made when the other person is strongly confrontational. He emphasizes the following: (a) the need to maintain the ability to mentally separate oneself from the interaction and "observe" what is happening rather than responding in an oppositional or aggressive manner; (b) the need to respond in an empathic manner to the ideas, issues, and feelings raised by the other person; (c) the need to positively reframe the issue at hand; (d) the need to search for ways to enable both persons' expressed and unexpressed interests to be met in a win/win manner, avoiding I win/you lose or I lose/you win outcomes; and (e) openly and clearly identifying the consequences for both parties if a mutually satisfying, negotiated agreement cannot be reached.

The need for conscious utilization of negotiation skills in a relationship is nowhere more evident then when marital roles are being addressed. Sherwood and Scherer's (1975) concept of "planned renegotiation," as expressed by Hof and Miller (1981), highlights the need for such skills.

☐ Deeply Rooted Conflict

The fair fighting approach presented here is highly effective for most arguments. When the conflict resolution model described above fails to work, it is usually because a hidden agenda exists in the couple's relationship. What does the hidden agenda actually mean? In conflict-resolution models, a basic assumption is that the couple lack the interpersonal or social skills needed to fight constructively. Of course, this assumption does not take into account the intergenerational factors described in this chapter. New models are needed to suggest how clinicians can motivate clients to change and avoid resistances to treatment. Prochaska and DiClemente (1988) investigated the process of change both inside and outside of psychotherapy. They identified five stages of attitudes people have about change. In the first stage, the Precontemplative stage, people are not even thinking about changing. In the second stage, the Contemplative stage, people are evaluating the pros and cons of changing, but have not yet made the decision to change. During the third stage, the Readiness stage, people have decided to change and are preparing to take some action. During the fourth stage, the Action stage, people actually implement some change strategies. Finally, the fifth or Maintenance stage encompasses peoples' attempts to continue and strengthen changes that have already been made (Prochaska, DiClemente, & Norcross, 1992).

Conflict needs to be understood within the Intersystem Approach as having multiple dimensions. Traditional conflict-resolution programs focus on the conflict from the interactional perspective. In some cases, work at the interactional and intergenerational levels is not sufficient. Couples who do not respond to a behavioral approach need to be examined from this perspective. They may carry intrapsychic issues that make them appear "impossible" or difficult to manage as a couple. In these cases, the conflict needs to be conceptualized at the individual level in terms of intrapsychic components. The conflict could be an expression of a personality disorder such as the passive-aggressive personality or as an expression of depression.

Feldman (1982) developed one of the most clinically useful intrapsychic models to account for marital conflict. In this model the underlying cause is what he calls narcissistic vulnerability. The phenomenon refers to low self-esteem, self-fragmentation, and a lack of sense of identity. This weakness in the partners leads to hypersensitivity and narcissistic expectations. The partners are very sensitive to rejection, disapproval, and criticism and have difficulty controlling their emotions and behavior. To compensate for their vulnerability, they develop unconscious expectations that the other partner will be totally admiring, attentive, loving, and so on. Because these expectations are so pervasive and unconscious, each partner is wrapped up in self and appears unempathetic to the other.

Obviously, no partner could fulfill these expectations, and so this leads to narcissistic rage and anxiety. If the process stops at this stage, the other partner becomes the scapegoat for the vulnerability. However, for some individuals the process involves a phenomenon known as projective identification. This defense mechanism involves splitting off some disowned or unacceptable part of self and projecting it onto the partner. The other person may become all good, or most commonly, all bad. The "all bad" partner holds those parts that cannot be allowed in self. Once this unacceptable material has been projected onto the other person, the projection process continues. The projector then attempts to destroy this behavior in the partner. The image of the partner is now grossly distorted and results in an unconscious escalation of conflict.

Figure 3 shows the various stages schematically, as well as the various approaches to treating different parts of the cycle. A model such as this requires in-depth, insight-oriented work over an extended period of time. When factors such as narcissistic vulnerability come into play, social skills training may be only one part of what is needed.

In addition to this model, it is useful to remember couples operate in collusion. They may both need the conflict and anger in order to protect themselves from dealing with other feelings. They may both fear intimacy and need a relationship in which intimacy is set up to be an impossibility. In examining the conflict from an intrapsychic perspective, the therapist must explore the unconscious needs being met by maintaining the pattern of conflictual interaction.

Another way to deal with conflict in couples is to employ paradoxical

<table>
<tr><th>DYNAMIC</th><th>APPROACH OR TECHNIQUE</th></tr>
<tr><td>Narcissistic Vulnerability</td><td>Emotional Awareness Training
Dream Work</td></tr>
<tr><td>Blocked Empathy</td><td>Communication & Empathy Training</td></tr>
<tr><td>Narcissistic Expectation</td><td>Cognitive Awareness Training</td></tr>
<tr><td>Narcissistic Rage</td><td>Self-Instruction/Control Training</td></tr>
<tr><td>Cognitive Distortions</td><td>Cognitive Awareness Training
Focusing on Positives in Relationship</td></tr>
<tr><td>Overt Marital Conflict</td><td>Behavioral Contracting and Problem-Solving</td></tr>
</table>

FIGURE 3. Dynamic processes and treatment techniques in Feldman's (1982) approach. Reprinted from the *Journal of Marital and Family Therapy.* Copyright © 1982. American Association for Marriage and Family Therapy. Reprinted with permission.

intervention. Weeks and L'Abate (1982) describe cases that involve the use of one or several paradoxical strategies. The two most common techniques are to positively reframe the conflict and then prescribe it. The positive reframe helps the couple see that there is something they derive from the conflict, that it serves some function in the relationship. The prescription paradox brings the heretofore out-of-control conflict under control.

For example, the therapist might say the following: "It is clear the two of you care a great deal for each other. You keep a fight going almost constantly in order to protect each other from having to confront your depression. For now, you should continue to help each other by carefully noticing when the other person looks 'down' and picking a fight immediately. If you miss how your partner is feeling, then you should cooperate fully by fighting back when your partner picks a fight with you." If the couple follows this directive, they learn to see how fights are connected to depression and begin to take some control over the process. If they do not follow the directive, then they do not fight, which was one of the goals of therapy.

A well-constructed paradoxical intervention is a win–win proposition. This particular approach requires a good deal of skill to implement. It should be attempted only after some study and, ideally, with the help of a supervisor experienced in this approach.

☐ Theoretical Approaches to Conflict Utilization

In the literature on conflict, two terms are commonly used to refer to work in this area. These terms are "conflict resolution" and "conflict utilization." Turner (1982) suggests that the term conflict resolution denotes that the ideal goal for a couple to achieve is to resolve conflict. On the other hand, conflict utilization refers to an active, dynamic process that connotes the idea that the couple can make use of the conflict for more than simply resolving a problem. He believes conflict can be positive, productive, and growth enhancing, and he lists eight positive functions of conflict including 1) using energy rather than repressing it; 2) using conflict creatively to raise new questions and ideas; 3) surfacing heretofore hidden thoughts and feelings; 4) creating new methods in the couple for handling conflict; 5) reassessing power in the relationship; 6) creating a climate of cooperation; 7) learning to see problems rationally; and 8) renegotiating old contracts and changing expectations in the relationship.

One of the first tasks in dealing with conflict is to help the couple develop some positive ideas about subjects they have been avoiding or dealing with poorly. The therapist should ask the couple about their beliefs regarding conflict. Once these beliefs have been made explicit and challenged, the therapist may suggest looking at conflict as a positive and constructive force in the relationship, one that could be intimacy enhancing if handled well, but relationship debilitating if handled poorly. The couple can be asked to list positive aspects of conflict. As we suggested earlier, if the couple does not have a positive attitude toward conflict and anger, no amount of education, coaching, or therapy will help. The couple will resist efforts to begin the work because their belief system tells them it is something to be avoided.

At the beginning of therapy, some bibliotherapy may help to instill this positive attitude. A book such as *The Intimate Enemy* (Bach & Wyden, 1968) makes this point both implicitly and explicitly. A positive attitude can also be demonstrated through self-disclosure or sharing specific case examples demonstrating the many benefits of conflict.

Cognitive Approaches to Conflict

Attribution and Efficacy

In spite of the fact that cognitive therapy is a major force in psychotherapy and attribution theory is a major force in social/clinical psychology, very little has been written on cognition and conflict. Doherty (1981a, 1981b) published two articles describing cognitive processes in conflict and although there are many practical applications both articles were primarily theoretical in nature. His work helps us to better understand the nature of conflict from the inside out. He clarifies the underlying mental processes that occur when conflict exists and identifies the factors that inhibit and facilitate conflict being utilized.

Doherty's two key concepts are attribution and efficacy. Attribution theories deal with causal explanations of how we attribute meaning to an event and the information on which it is based (Kelly, 1973). For the partner in a relationship, the basic question is, "Who or what is causing this problem?" In a sense we are all attributional theorists. This question is ubiquitous in couples therapy. The causal attributions have several dimensions. In other words, there are several possible sources of the problem. This is the "who" or "what" of the problem. Partners may assign blame and responsibility of self, partner, relationship, context, and possibly to theological sources or to just plain luck, fate, or chance.

In Schachter and Singer's (1962) two-factor theory, and in various scientific clinical and appraisal theories (e.g., Ellis, 1973; Lazarus, 1991), anger has been hypothesized to come from people's interpretations of an event (Kassinove, 1995). The therapist must also discover how the partners conceptualize the conflict, that is, the "who" and "what." In most couples, blame is assigned to the other partner. As long as this kind of attributional strategy is present in the couple, change will not occur. Perhaps the most common reason that anger is not owned is because individuals do not see it as belonging to them. It is believed that someone or something outside the person causes anger, and therefore they have no responsibility for it. That is, clients' belief structures define situations in irrational (Dryden, 1990; Ellis, 1977) or absolute (Beck, 1976) ways, and then they attribute blame and deflect responsibility for their anger to other people or events (Kassinove, 1995).

In a previous book, Weeks and Hof (1995) discuss the importance of helping the couple shift from a linear to a circular attributional strategy. A linear strategy involves the partners blaming each other or externalizing responsibility. A circular strategy involves partners defining the problem in terms of their relationship or system. In order to help couples make this shift, the therapist uses reframing (Weeks & Treat, 1992). Reframing has been defined as changing the meaning of an event, and is used in two ways. The first is to redefine an event (behavior) that had been viewed negatively as one that is viewed positively. The second meaning is most applicable here. For couples, to reframe is to redefine behaviors so that they are no longer seen in terms of cause and effect but rather as circular, interlocking, or reciprocal. Reframing is described in Chapter 9.

Doherty (1981a) also identifies several other attributional dimensions and strategies that contribute to marital conflict and that need to be examined, namely, intent, stability, voluntariness, and specificity.

Intent refers to the meaning attributed to the person who performed the behavior. The partner is trying to determine the real meaning of the behavior. In most cases, intent actually refers to the judgment the partner makes regarding whether a behavior was perceived as having a positive or negative impact. For example, if a wife tells her husband to change his clothing because the outfit does not match, he might ascribe negative or positive intent to her statement. He could say to himself that she cares about him and how he looks. On the other hand, he might feel personally criticized and ascribe negative intent to her statement. Intent and effect often become confused in couples. Just because something "feels" negative, or is perceived to be negative, does not mean it was intended to be negative.

In couples therapy, it is important to help the partners eliminate distortions and projections around intent. Having each other discuss what is intended is a beginning. If partners persist in seeing the behavior differently, then the two issues need exploration. Perhaps, the response to a behavior is over determined. For example, if he or she had learned to respond only one way to a particular behavior in a family, the original conceptualization and its corresponding responses may persist, regardless of partner or context. The other possibility is that the initiating partner does not know the real intent of his or her behavior. He or she may be in denial of the actual intent or may distort the meaning of the behavior. The therapist will have to use some judgment in sorting out what the real intent might be.

The second attributional dimension is stability. Stability refers to the extent to which the behaviors represent stable personality characteristics in the other person. A behavior may be viewed as an isolated event related to some environmental situation, such as getting angry when the car has a flat tire. It may also be viewed as representing some stable characteristic in the other person as "he is always angry; therefore, he is an angry person."

This attributional phenomenon helps explain why therapists find it useful to frame problems in terms of behaviors rather than personality traits or characteristics. By definition, a personality trait is believed to be rather stable and probably not changed easily. When the partner believes that a trait is being dealt with, as opposed to a behavior, he or she may be less likely to attempt to change the situation. In fact, the person may be likely to give up immediately because a favorable outcome is not foreseen. The couple may feel they cannot change when problem behaviors are defined as immutable traits. By redefining the problem in terms of behaviors, which are transitory and determined by context, a greater sense of hope and change potential is inspired.

Voluntariness or deliberateness of a person's behavior is the third dimension of attribution. Partners make assumptions about how voluntary behaviors may be, and are likely to believe the behavior was voluntary or involuntary, controllable or uncontrollable, spontaneous or contrived. When the behavior is defined as voluntary, or in any of the parallel ways listed, the behavior carries much more import. Obviously, if one partner has done something perceived as hurtful, and the behavior was deliberate, the other partner will feel personally attacked. It may be easier to forgive a hurtful behavior if it is defined as involuntary.

The final attributional dimension is specificity. The attributions made may generalize to the person or the relationship; they may range from global to specific. More problems occur when the attributions generalize, assuming these are negative attributions. For example, a newly married couple may have a few fights. They may begin to believe that all they ever do is fight. They become defined as a "fighting couple," and they believe they should divorce because that is all they will ever do. The generalization could have been to the individual in this example. One partner could be defined as always wanting to fight. Global negative attributions are demoralizing for the couple and represent a distortion.

The therapist can work toward specificity by challenging these distortions directly. A cognitive therapy approach may be used in which the couple are taught about distortions, how to identify them, and how to stop them (Burns, 1977). The therapist's use of language and the questions asked also lead the couple in the direction of seeing the problem specifically rather then globally. Specific questions about the "who, what, where, when, and how" of the argument encourages less global thinking in the partners.

Doherty (1981b) uses the concept of efficacy to refer to beliefs about future events, a central aspect of readiness. He proposes "efficacy refers to the individual's expectation for the couple or family as a group to engage in effective problem-solving activity" (p. 4). Bandura (1977) proposed that it was the individual's expectation for being able to bring about a particular outcome. Efficacy is similar to having hope, feeling masterful and competent, and being able to make a positive prediction happen. For the couple, the question is "Can the problem be solved by us?" Doherty (1981b) suggests that if the efficacy expectations were low, the members of the family would not be persistent in trying to solve their problems and they would show a learned helplessness response. One of the goals of therapy, therefore, is to help create a generalized high efficacy belief and response, a sense of hope.

The level of efficacy determines the amount of effort partners expend in trying to solve a problem. Individuals with high efficacy expectations will predict positive outcomes and be very persistent in their problem-solving efforts. Low efficacy expectations results from repeated failures in problem solving. Doherty (1981b) states that individuals with low efficacy expectations develop a cognitive deficit of ceasing to learn new information; a motivational deficit of giving up; a behavioral deficit of avoiding the issues or the partner or ritualizing the conflict; and an affective deficit of "feeling" that the conflict is uncontrollable.

Rational Emotive Behavior Therapy

Albert Ellis (1976) described how the theory and techniques of his Rational-Emotive Therapy (RET; updated in 1995 to REBT, emphasizing the behavioral component) can be applied in working with anger. His theory is based on the assumption that anger stems from irrational beliefs held about one's partner or relationship. It is an individually oriented approach, because the change must take place within the individual and not the relationship. The dissipation of the anger is accomplished through the A-B-C-D theory of rational therapy. A is the activating event, B is the belief system, C is the emotional and behavioral consequences, and D refers to the act of disputing the irrational belief. This particular theory and cognitive therapy in general are described in Chapter 12, Cognitive Techniques.

Ellis (1976) proposed that much marital anger grows out of the "shoulds," "oughts," and "musts" in relationships. For example, if one partner thinks, "I absolutely must feel loved by my partner all the time and he or she must verbalize it," then disappointment, anger, and conflict will result when those needs are not met. By eliminating the irrational ideas, the basis of the anger and conflict is removed.

He suggests two strategies for dealing with anger, the first of which simply involves a cooling off period in order to set the stage for thinking the anger through. The second strategy incorporates the following eight steps: 1) acknowledging the anger of oneself; 2) assuming full responsibility for the anger; 3) accepting oneself with the anger; 4) putting an end to making oneself anxious and depressed, and being self-deprecating; 5) looking for the belief leading to the anger; 6) differentiating among wishes, demands, and commands; 7) removing the absolute "musts"; and 8) changing the behaviors and emotions that support the feelings of anger.

This model can work well when applicable. In some cases, the anger and conflict are certainly being driven by irrational thoughts and an individually oriented approach is appropriate. Each partner may need to change some thinking in order to remove the anger.

The disadvantage of the REBT approach, in our opinion, is that it is asystemic, and thus nonrelational. In the intersystem model described by Weeks (1994), the partners co-determine the relationship and the relationship influences the partners. Ellis's approach does not examine how the relationship influences the thinking or actions of the partners.

Affective Approaches to Conflict

L'Abate (1977) states that in most cases anger is the result of feeling hurt and the fear of being hurt. The hurt feelings may by based in unresolved grief, past frustrations, and feelings of personal inadequacy. The failure to recognize these feelings means the clinician only treats the symptom and not the underlying emotional difficulties.

L'Abate (1977) and L'Abate and L'Abate (1977) suggest five steps for dealing with the feeling. The first step is to recognize that when anger is experienced, there is also an underlying feeling of hurt. The second step is for the partner feeling the hurt to express it directly and appropriately to his or her partner (e.g., "I felt hurt when . . . "). Third, the individual with the feeling must assume responsibility for the hurt and not project it onto the partner. Normally, it is the anger that is projected in terms of blaming the partner as the source of the anger. Fourth, the person must be able to forgive him- or herself for denying the hurt and not being invulnerable to this feeling. Finally, one must recognize that feeling hurt is a human reaction. It is important to redefine oneself as having weaknesses and vulnerabilities. Only by accepting this can the person stay in touch with the hurt. This aspect of conflict utilization, dealing with the feelings of hurt and anger, too often has been underemphasized or ignored in the literature.

☐ Conflict Utilization: A Synthesis of the Whole

The practicing therapist needs to integrate ideas from all the approaches discussed (cognitive, affective, and behavioral) to develop a comprehensive Conflict Utilization Model. We hope to provide a basic framework in which this integration may occur. The following ideas are presented to help synthesize much of what has already appeared in the literature on conflict, communication, problem solving, and contracting. It is not that all of the ideas are original, but that the particular combination of ideas is new and comprehensive.

A word of caution: This approach works when the anger and conflict have not reached the level of abuse. If violence exists, this approach may be contraindicated. Safety is always the primary concern in these cases. In situations where violence exists, it is necessary to first assess the nature of the violence and if the violence is instrumental, then the partners should be seen separately or referred for individual therapy. Instrumental violence is designed to control or coerce the partner. It may be frequent and unrelated to the emotional life of the couple. A description of how to work with spouse abuse can be found in *Treating Couples: The Intersystem Model of the Marriage Council of Philadelphia* (Weeks, 1989a).

Another factor that must be considered is the therapist's own ability to work with anger and conflict. Beginning therapists are sometimes afraid of losing control of the session so they keep feelings of anger to a minimum and do not encourage enough emotional intensity to emerge. The therapist must balance how much affect occurs at any given time and pace the couple in how quickly they move into conflicted areas. It would be inappropriate to move into highly conflicted areas in the evaluation phase of therapy. During this phase the therapist is collecting information about the different conflicts, but not actually encouraging the couple to talk to each other until certain conditions have been met (i.e. setting up some ground rules for fighting).

The therapist may also have a number of countertransferential reactions to dealing with anger and conflict. We believe it is also useful for the therapist to do their own anger genogram (DeMaria, et al., 1999) and to answer the questions regarding the meaning and function of anger and conflict. Perhaps there is an inclination on the part of the therapist to minimize, ignore, or deny some of the anger and conflict in couples. He or she may have grown up in a family that minimized anger or where conflict was out of control resulting in the therapist fearing these feelings just as much as the clients.

Any number of countertransferential reactions is possible. Therapists in training need to be monitored carefully and asked about these types of reactions directly. Some therapists may need supervision or therapy to help them work through unresolved feelings of anger, fear of conflict, or other feelings that hinder doing this kind of work effectively.

Levels of Conflict

Before beginning direct work with the couple in the area of conflict utilization, it is important to assess the level of conflict that is present within the couple. Stages of marital conflict are discussed in *The Evaluation and Treatment of Marital Conflict: A Four-Stage Approach* (Guerin, Fay, Burden, & Kautto, 1987).

Low-Level Conflict

Low-level conflict is often issue-focused with minimal projection. The individuals are able to maintain a responsible, balanced, and differentiated view of the situation, themselves, and their partner. There is usually a strong sense of "coupleness" present and a willingness (though skills are often lacking) to engage each other effectively, cognitively, and behaviorally. There are legitimate differences or preferences and the negotiation process generally works quite well. This level of conflict responds well to education and skill-building efforts alone.

Medium-Level Conflict

Medium-level conflict often involves deeply ingrained family-of-origin patterns of relating, and significant, individual life "script" issues (James & Jongeward, 1971). There is a modicum of projection and some loss of "self focus" (Guerin et al., 1987) with an increase in emotional reactivity and blaming. One or both partners appear less differentiated, responsible, objective, and balanced (affectively, behaviorally, and/or cognitively) than individuals in the low-level conflict category. Historically-based, unresolved issues may have prevented the individuals and/or the couple from learning or employing the appropriate conflict utilization skills. This level of conflict often responds well to insight. At this level of conflict, techniques that may be used include Hendrix's (1988) approach to the resolution of projection-related issues; the resolution of life "script" and family-of-origin issues through "reparenting" (James & Jongeward, 1971); and significant focusing on differentiation and individuation with an appropriate emphasis on addressing deficits in social learning through remodeling, skill practice, and reinforcement.

High-Level Conflict

High-level conflict has a chronic quality to it. There is a high degree of emotional reactivity, blaming, and vilification. The couple is consistently and negatively polarized, and there is little sense of positive "we-ness." In one or both partners, differentiation is low, as is responsibility, objectivity, and balance within and among the affective, cognitive, and behavioral dimensions of the individuals. There are severe object relations issues with significant narcissistic vulnerability and the use of rampant projective identification as an ego defense. The more severe and primitive or early the trauma, the greater the likelihood these issues will occur.

High-level conflict generally requires long-term therapy including a conjoint emphasis to build the "coupleness"; provision of a buffer against the intrusion of the early trauma; experiences of healing intimacy; and frequent individual sessions to provide individual support and nurturance to diminish the severity of the emotional wound and to promote healing. The relationship therapist may not be able to do the individual therapy for several reasons including narcissistic vulnerability, fear of abandonment, or jealousy of one or both partners.

Even if there is a positive transference and scrupulous balance and fairness on the part of the therapist, the narcissistically vulnerable individual may feel abandoned or rejected by the therapist. Great care must be exercised if the therapist endeavors to do both aspects of the therapeutic work. An appropriate referral for concurrent individual therapy is often the best course of action.

At all levels, skill deficits, unhelpful patterns learned in the family of origin, and intrapsychic issues may be at work, contributing to the perpetuation of the conflict. In order to decide at which level(s) to intervene, the therapist needs to assess the individuals and the couple from a intersystem perspective. The nature of the individual/intrapsychic issues and the psychosocial/whole-world context issues (e.g., issues of race, ethnicity, and spirituality; current economic conditions) involved in the couple and the conflict must be evaluated.

Once an assessment has been made of the meaning and function of the anger and conflict, the extent of the couple's conflict utilization skills, and the level of conflict, the therapist can utilize appropriate steps and creatively incorporate the conflict into the therapy.

☐ Conclusion

The reduction of conflict and anger is one important barrier to couples' intimacy. Couples who move through conflict resolution successfully begin to feel a greater sense of competence and relationship bonding. They begin to realize conflict is a challenge that they can overcome as a couple. This process affirms their relationship.

The model presented in this chapter is more comprehensive than most other models (L'Abate & McHenry, 1983). From the model presented in the flow chart, the clinician can see that we view the problem from multiple perspectives consistent with the Intersystem Approach. For example, at the *individual* level we might think about the meaning of anger for the individual partner; at the *interactional* level we might consider the function of the conflict for the couple; and at the *intergenerational* level we might see how familial patterns of dealing with anger are being repeated. Keeping all these levels in mind gives conflict a complexity not often appreciated in working with this issue.

13
CHAPTER

Cognitive Techniques

The marital therapist has the choice of using interventions that are affectively, behaviorally, or cognitively oriented. The first two categories of interventions have been widely discussed in the marital therapy literature (L'Abate & McHenry, 1983). The use of cognitive interventions has received little interest in spite of the fact that cognitive approaches have been highly influential in individual psychotherapy. For the most part, cognitive approaches have only been applied to individuals. Most of Albert Ellis's (1962) early work in Rational-Emotive Therapy (RET) and Aaron Beck's (1976) early work in Cognitive Therapy (CT) were individually oriented. In 1988, Beck discussed how cognitive therapy might be applied to couples. In 1995, Ellis renamed his approach Rational-Emotive Behavior Therapy (REBT) acknowledging the further role behavioral responses have with individual's interpersonal problems and in family and couple relationships.

The exception is Ellis and Harper's (1961b) book on how Rational-Emotive Therapy might be applied in understanding and treating marriages, and the more recent text by Ellis, Sichel, Yeager, DiMattia, and Digiuseppe (1989). These ideas clearly did not take hold in the field of marital therapy. We believe the reason for this is because they promoted RET as a singular approach, just as Beck did later with Cognitive Therapy. Cognitive approaches have their utility, but they also have limitations. In fact, for most couples the use of any single approach is too narrow and ineffective. In our opinion, promoting change and growth in a couple requires the clinician to use a variety of approaches and to fit the approaches to the couple, not the couple to the approach.

Although this chapter will describe cognitive techniques, we do not advocate that they be used exclusively. These techniques need to be blended with the techniques found in other chapters of this book. Baucom, Epstein, and Rankin (1995) state, "cognitions, behaviors, and emotions are inextricably interwoven" (p. 65) and should be considered during marital therapy. Epstein and Baucom (1998) state that research has documented how the quality of couples' intimate relationships is impacted by their cognitions, behavioral interaction patterns, and emotional responses (Epstein & Baucom, 1993; Fincham, Bradbury, & Scott, 1990; Gottman, 1993; Weiss & Heyman, 1990). The marital therapist must be skillful in integrating the couple's internal cognitions with their overt interactions, which include the behavioral interchanges as well as the affective expressions of each partner (Epstein, 1982).

☐ The Theory

In order to use cognitive techniques, the clinician must be familiar with the basic theory and principles of both Rational Emotive Behavior Therapy and Cognitive Therapy. Both of these theories obviously focus on cognition, that is, what and how people think. These theories postulate that behavior and affect follow from thinking. In other words, if the clinician wants to alter what a person does or how a person feels, the first step is to change the person's thinking. What has not been pointed out in the literature is the basic difference between the Rational-Emotive and Cognitive theories.

The cognitive therapist focuses more on *how* the person is thinking, while the Rational Emotive Behavior therapist focuses more on *what* the person is thinking. Thus, Rational-Emotive Behavior therapists are *content-oriented* and cognitive therapists are *process-oriented*. The combination of these two approaches is essential in as much as thinking is both content and process.

For example, a wife concluded that her husband did not love her because he was acting sad and withdrawn following the funeral of a friend. A cognitive therapist would examine the process of her thinking and might conclude she had made what is called an arbitrary inference—drawing a conclusion without substantiating evidence. A Rational Emotive Behavior therapist would examine the statement itself along with the irrational belief(s) on which it is based, and help her change the self-statement—"I absolutely must have everyone's love and approval."

☐ Rational-Emotive Behavior Therapy

Albert Ellis's (1962) basic theory consists of the *A-B-C-D* model. *A* stands for actions. An action is an event that can be observed. *B* refers to the person's belief or belief system. *B* is commonly referred to as the person's self-statement. The self-statement is what the person says (thinks) to self about *A*. The self-statement gives *A* its meaning. At the same time, it also determines *C* in the formula. *C* is the consequence of *B*. By consequence is meant: 1) what the person does; and 2) how the person feels. *D* is short for dispute. Once the person understands *B* is an irrational or nonproductive thought, she or he may dispute the original belief and substitute a rational or productive statement. In sum, the basic theory can be outlined as follows:

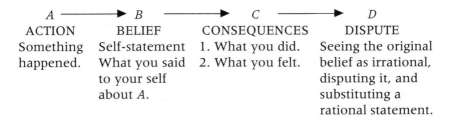

A	*B*	*C*	*D*
ACTION	BELIEF	CONSEQUENCES	DISPUTE
Something happened.	Self-statement What you said to your self about *A*.	1. What you did. 2. What you felt.	Seeing the original belief as irrational, disputing it, and substituting a rational statement.

This theory and model can be easily explained to the client. Ideally, it is also useful to give an example—an example drawn from the client's own experience as well as a general example. One such example involves a husband who comes home angry and begins to displace his anger onto his wife. He might be critical of her and get annoyed and angry about minor occurrences such as the house not being clean enough, supper not being ready, or his mail not being in the right place. His wife might respond to his behavior by going to another room and crying. Given her behavior, what must she be thinking about his actions? She might be making self-statements like, "It's all my fault" or "I'm a bad wife." Neither of these statements is productive. She needs to change her belief about what happened so she does not feel bad, withdraw from him, and make further assumptions about his actions. She might think, "He had a tough day and is irritable, so it's not me he is angry with, but his situation."

Common Irrational Thoughts

In addition to the basic theory of REBT, it is also useful to know some of the common irrational thoughts that creep into people's thinking. Ellis and Harper (1961a) have catalogued some of these thoughts in their book, *A Guide to Rational Living*. The following is a general list of these irrational thoughts, followed by some of the ways in which these thoughts get played out in couple relationships.

Irrational Idea #1

The idea involves thinking that it is a dire necessity for an adult to be loved or approved of by virtually every significant other person for everything she or he does. This thought is common in couple relationships. The partners usually expect acceptance, approval, agreement, and love for virtually everything they do. When this idea is taken to the extreme, every action is equated to love and approval. An action that does not meet the expectation is then seen as rejection and disapproval, which creates an emotionally intense situation. In couples, this irrationality can be succinctly stated as, "My partner must absolutely love and approve of everything I do." Of course, this belief is a prescription for not feeling adequately loved, since it cannot be totally and completely met.

Irrational Idea #2

This idea involves thinking that one should be thoroughly competent, adequate, intelligent, and achieving in all possible respects. Failure, says Ellis, is construed as the worst possible crime in our society, and the fear of making a mistake brings unhappiness plus a refusal to take risks. The rational individual strives to *do*, not to *do perfectly* and accepts himself or herself as a fallible creature that is imperfect because of human limitations.

In couples, this idea translates into the "perfect partner syndrome." The perfect partner should be able to do everything that is expected. These partners overachieve, push themselves to the limit, rarely ask for help, and pretend to be forever cheerful. One of the most destructive ways in which this particular idea manifests itself is when the partner is not only trying to do all that is expected, but also guesses (mind reads) what is expected and not expressed. In short, the partner tries to anticipate the needs of the other and imagines a need where none exists. In spite of striving for perfection, this partner always feels that he or she is failing.

Irrational Idea #3

This idea involves thinking that certain acts are wrong or wicked or villainous and that people who perform such acts should be severely punished. In couples, this idea gives the partners a right to punish each other because it legitimizes the idea that when there is a victim, there is a villain. Thus, if one partner does something the other defines as wrong, the wronged partner has the right, if not the obligation, to punish the other. This situation does not allow for forgiveness—only punishment and revenge. Affairs are a classic example. The person who committed the affair is often seen as wicked, while the other partner is just an innocent bystander. By polarizing the thinking into right versus wrong, there is no way for the betrayed partner to see his or her role in the marital pathology that lead to the affair. The partner who had the affair (hereafter, the "affair partner") may also believe that they deserve to be severely punished and to feel guilty.

Irrational Idea #4

This idea involves thinking it is terrible, horrible, and catastrophic when things are not going the way one would like them to go. According to Ellis, frustration is normal and events in life can be unpleasant or unfortunate but rarely are they catastrophic unless we think they are. The rational person accepts the fact that it is too bad when things are not the way one would like them to be and one should certainly try to change or control conditions so that they become more satisfactory. However, one does realize that if changing or controlling an uncomfortable situation is impossible, one had better become resigned to its existence and stop telling oneself how awful it is.

All partners have expectations of each other. Under normal conditions, the expectation is that not all expectations will be fulfilled. However, some partners enter relationships with little tolerance for frustration, disappointment, or impulse control. They are so narcissistically vulnerable that if something does not turn out their way, they feel personally injured or attacked. This type of partner makes situations into catastrophes.

In one case, a husband expected his wife to keep her personal items on the chest in the bedroom in exactly the way he had shown her. When she failed to follow his instructions, his immediate reaction was to believe the marriage was a mistake and that she did not love him.

Irrational Idea #5

This idea involves thinking human unhappiness is externally caused and is forced on one by outside people and events. The rational person realizes that virtually all human unhappiness is caused or sustained by our interpretation of things rather than by the things themselves.

Partners frequently use this idea to blame their unhappiness on the other person. By externalizing responsibility for happiness onto another, they do not have to examine their own behavior. In couple sessions, the partners may only want to talk about the other person or the relationship and never themselves. The other person becomes an object who acts upon them in a purported cause-effect manner. The unhappy partner is unable to see how his or her interpretation of the event or person creates the feeling.

Irrational Idea #6

This idea involves thinking that if something is or may be dangerous or fearsome, one should be terribly occupied with and upset about it. In couples, the idea that one should be upset and preoccupied with fear is enacted in two ways that initially may appear to be opposite. The first way involves the fear of intimacy or getting too close. For many partners this fear is initially unconscious. For others, they may keenly know it. For example, a partner who had been rejected by two previous husbands may fear rejection again. This partner may set up a situation in which she rejects first or keeps so distant that rejection is perceived as making little difference to her.

At the other end of the spectrum is the partner who fears too much distance or divorce. Partners with this concern are in a chronic state of fear over loss and being alone. Codependent partners fit this description. They marry addicted people and stay with them, because of their own fears of being alone and unlovable and because of their extremely low self-esteem.

Irrational Idea #7

This idea involves thinking that it is easier to avoid facing many of life's difficulties and self-responsibilities than to deal with them directly. Ellis links this irrational belief to our biological tendency to seek pleasure now, rather than to delay the pleasure in order to work for long-range goals, which may be more difficult to achieve. The rational individual realizes that the challenging, responsible, problem-solving life is the enjoyable life and that self-discipline is required to face difficult problems.

One of the common myths of marriage is that all will be bliss after the honeymoon. Partners who ascribe to this myth assume marriage is or should be easy. Love, they believe, will be the great panacea. When confronted with the reality that relationships are difficult, require constant attention, effort, and hard work, they sometimes choose to flee through divorce, distraction in work, or substance abuse. The understanding that one builds a relationship over time is missing. Couples operating with these myths believe problems must be solved immediately; if they aren't, it means they will never be resolved. In many cases young couples believe conflict is all bad and that all problems must be solved immediately and without angry feelings. To fail in this task represents a failed marriage.

Irrational Idea #8

This idea involves thinking that the past is all-important and that because something once strongly affected one's life, it should do so indefinitely. This idea can lead a person to overgeneralize from past events to present situations so that she or he does not look for new options, but rather transfers feelings about others from the past onto people in the present surroundings. The rational person learns from past experiences, but is not overly attached to or prejudiced by them.

Couples can use this irrational idea in a variety of ways. One way would be for a partner to focus on one specific event in the history of the relationship and use that event as the basis for the relationship. For example, a wife believed her husband had to control her sexually on their honeymoon. From that point onward she construed every comment in terms of how controlling her husband was. This line of thinking tends to be based on relationship trauma, such as a major fight, affair, or difference in values, which is never resolved and is played out again and again around different content.

Another way in which couples use this idea is to justify their behavior on the basis of childhood experiences. For example, a woman who was abused by her brother claimed she could never trust any man in spite of the fact only one man had mistreated her.

Irrational Idea #9

This idea involves thinking that human happiness can be achieved by inertia and inaction or by passively and uncommittedly "enjoying oneself." Ellis often sees inertia as a defense against an irrational fear such as failure. Rational individuals realize that they are happiest when they are actively and vitally absorbed in creative pursuits, or when they are devoting themselves to people or projects outside of themselves.

In couples, this idea is similar to Irrational Idea #7. In this case, the partners assume no responsibility for their own happiness, expecting the other to now take on this responsibility. The key to treatment in such a case is to get each partner to identify and work toward taking care of their own needs. In one case a husband assumed his marriage would somehow magically cure a long-standing depression. He had not sought treatment nor taken any responsibility for his mood. He thought the occasional good feelings he felt in being with his wife would "take over his personality."

Irrational Idea #10

This idea involves thinking that one should be quite upset over other people's problems and disturbances. Ellis says that being involved with others' problems that do not directly affect us is a way to avoid facing our own behavior and problems. Partners cross over the line of normal concern when they become engrossed in the other partner's problems in order to avoid dealing with their own.

This pattern is classic in dysfunctional couples. One partner will be defined as the sick one while the other one is the well one. What is not obvious is the pathology in the "well" partner. Frequently, these partners have selected a sick mate who actually carries their underlying problem. For example, a partner who cannot confront depression himself may marry a depressed individual.

Irrational Idea #11

This idea involves thinking that there is a right or perfect solution to every problem and it must be found or the results will be catastrophic. There is no perfect solution and a desire for perfectionism only results in not seeing the alternative solutions. The rational person attempts to find various solutions to a problem and accepts the best answer, recognizing there is no perfect answer.

Some can get hooked on the idea of absolute right and wrong. If there is a right and wrong, then every problem has a right and a wrong answer. Such a couple is not capable of generating alternative solutions or of being creative. They think the right answer must be somewhere. It may be in logic, authority, divine wisdom, an expert, or part of family tradition. The only way to avoid this problem is to discard right and wrong thinking, replacing it with likes, preferences, needs, opinions, and so on.

Irrational Idea #12

The idea involves thinking that one has virtually no control over one's emotions and that one cannot help feeling certain things. The rational person sees that he has enormous control over his emotions if he chooses to work at controlling them and chooses to practice saying the right kinds of sentences to himself.

Partners can claim they do not have control over how they feel. When partners make this claim, it is often with the idea that their partner should overlook their feelings because they couldn't help it or take responsibility for creating the feelings. When partners make assertions like these, they must be challenged with information on how to take control and confronted on the process of not accepting personal responsibility. Some partners believe marriage gives them permission to give up emotional control.

This list of irrational thoughts can be supplemented with an additional list that focuses exclusively on love and approval (Ellis, 1987).*

Irrational Beliefs About Love and Approval

OBVIOUS OR BLATANT IRRATIONALITIES:

1. Because I strongly desire to be approved by people I find significant, I absolutely must have their approval (and am an unlovable and worthless person if I do not)!
2. Because I strongly desire to be approved by people I find significant, I absolutely must ALWAYS have their approval!
3. Because I strongly desire to be approved by people I find significant, I absolutely must have OUTSTANDING approval!
4. Because I strongly desire to be approved by people I find significant, I absolutely must have TOTAL AND PERFECT approval!

SUBTLE OR TRICKY IRRATIONALITIES:

1. Because I strongly desire to be approved by people I find significant and BECAUSE I VERY STRONGLY WANT TO BE, I absolutely must have their approval!
2. Because I strongly desire to be approved by people I find significant, and BECAUSE I ONLY WANT A LITTLE APPROVAL FROM THEM, I absolutely must have it!
3. Because I strongly desire to be approved by people I find significant, and BECAUSE I HAVEN'T HAD MUCH LOVE AND APPROVAL FOR A LONG PERIOD OF TIME, I absolutely must have their approval!
4. Because I strongly desire to be loved and approved by people I find significant, and BECAUSE I HAVE BEEN WARMLY APPROVED IN THE PAST, I absolutely must have their approval now!
5. Because I strongly desire to be approved by people I find significant, and BECAUSE I AM A SPECIAL KIND OF PERSON, I absolutely must have their approval.
6. Because I strongly desire to be approved by people I find significant and, BECAUSE I HAVE BEEN SO DEPRIVED IN OTHER AREAS OF MY LIFE (AS I MUST NOT BE!), I absolutely must have their approval!

---

*Copyright © 1987 by the American Psychological Association. Adapted by permission.

7. Because I strongly desire to be approved by people I find significant, and BECAUSE I FEEL SO ANXIOUS AND DEPRESSED WHEN I AM NOT APPROVED, MY POWERFUL FEELINGS OF NEEDINESS PROVE THAT I absolutely must have their approval!

8. Because I strongly desire to be approved by people I find significant and BECAUSE THE LACK OF THEIR APPROVAL MAKES ME BEHAVE SO BADLY, MY DYSFUNCTIONAL BEHAVIOR PROVES THAT I absolutely must have their approval!

Notice how in this list, statements are framed in terms of absolute *musts*. Ellis has pointed out how statements that include *must, ought*, and *should* create trouble. Whenever these words are detected, they need to be immediately challenged. The client can be asked to eliminate these words and insert statements such as "I would prefer" or "I would like." A simple change in wording can create a major change in thinking and lessen the severity of consequences. For example, changing "I must have his approval" to "I would like his approval" brings about a lessening of the behavioral and emotional consequences if approval is not forthcoming.

Ellis and Harper (1961a) laid the foundation for the application of REBT to couples. They proposed that marital problems occur when spouses have unrealistic (irrational) expectations of each other and then make extreme negative self-statements on the basis of these expectations. To illustrate, a husband might think his wife should spend *all* her time with him. When she fails to do so, he thinks because she does not want to spend her time with him, she cannot love him. The clinician's work is to expose the irrational thinking and the negative judgments made on the basis of it and replace the irrational thoughts with more productive thinking.

☐ Cognitive Therapy

This approach to treatment was developed by Aaron Beck (1976) and popularized by David Burns (1980) in his book entitled *Feeling Good*. Beck and Burns focus on the process of thinking. They both assert certain ways of thinking may be *automatic*. "Automatic thoughts" are moment-to-moment ideas, beliefs, or images an individual manifests which are often elicited by specific events. These thoughts are often biased or stereotypes and may be either positive or negative, but mostly negative in confrontation situations. An individual will commonly accept these thoughts as plausible rather than questioning their validity (Dattilio, Epstein, & Baucam, 1998). A person automatically uses a habitual pattern of thinking in assessing a situation. These patterns in turn create what are called *cognitive distortions*.

Cognitive Distortions

The most important part of cognitive theory is an understanding of the types of cognitive distortions. Burns (1980) has described these in terms that are easily comprehensible for the layperson. The chapter in his book (Chapter 4) that reviews these concepts is essential bibliotherapy for the couple when this approach is being used. The following list summarizes the cognitive distortions that Burns considers most common:

1. *All-or-nothing, either/or thinking.* The person's thinking is dichotomous and polarized. For example, a wife might ask her husband to sit down and talk with her. When he agrees to talk, but at a later time, she might conclude, "He never wants to talk with me.

2. *Overgeneralization.* A single event may be viewed as establishing a pattern over one's marriage. For example, a husband brought his wife flowers only to be told there was not a vase in which to put them. The husband generalized from this event that he could never bring his wife anything because she would find some problem with it.

3. *Mental Filter.* This distortion involves allowing one negative event to color all subsequent events. This distortion means all new experiences are filtered through the original negative experience. For example, after many years of a husband never being turned down sexually, his wife finally became sexually assertive and said "no" on one occasion. Thereafter, the husband believed his wife would never again be interested in him sexually.

4. *Discounting positives.* A positive change is not accepted as real and the negatives continue to receive attention. For example, a husband started to give his wife compliments after starting therapy. His wife discounted his remarks as an act designed to get her off his back and to placate the therapist.

5. *Jumping to conclusions.* This distortion involves drawing inferences without checking out the other person's intent. For example, a separated couple was working on getting back together. Because the primary cause of the separation had been defined as sexual, the wife believed the first time they had sex would be a pass–fail test for her. She had assumed he would be grading her performance and determining the outcome of the marriage based on one sexual encounter.

6. *Magnification.* An event is given more emotional weight than it should. For example, a wife had lunch with a male colleague whom she knew her husband envied. He reacted to the lunch with great jealousy, claiming the other man had it all and he had nothing, including his wife's attention.

7. *Emotional reasoning.* This idea deals with emotionally based logic. The

person believes that because he or she feels a certain way, life must really be that way. For example, a divorced man said, "My wife rejected me, my mother rejected me, I feel rejected by women. Women do not really like men, they just use them and reject them." The emotional reality becomes reality. If something feels a certain way, it must be that way.

8. "*Shoulding.*" This distortion involves raising a wish, want, or preference to the level of a *should*. In one case, a husband wanted his second wife to have the same close relationship to his children that his first wife had. He insisted that she *should* make this happen.

9. *Labeling.* This distortion involves putting a label on another person rather than being descriptive and behavioral. For example, a husband made an insensitive remark to his wife. Rather than saying, "Your remark hurt me and was insensitive," she said, "You are an insensitive person." The label placed on the person usually describes the unacceptable behavior; the label serves to magnify the perceived negative intent.

10. *Personalizing.* Taking responsibility or blame for an event that is outside of one's control. For example, a couple went on their dream vacation. The husband acted depressed and angry throughout. His wife said, "I should have known what to do to cheer him up. I'm sure I did something to make this happen." She accepted responsibility for his moods although she had no control over them.

Dattilio (1998a) and Dattilio and Padesky (1990) identify additional common cognitive distortions:

1. *Arbitrary inference.* Individuals draw conclusions without substantiating evidence.
2. *Selective abstraction.* Information is taken out of context with certain details emphasized while others are ignored.
3. *Minimization.* Opposite of magnification, something is perceived to have less significance than appropriate.
4. *Tunnel vision.* An individual sees only what he or she wants to see or what fits his or her current state of mind.
5. *Biased explanation.* In times of distress, a polarized type of thinking develops with the automatic thoughts that the partner has a negative ulterior motive.
6. *Mind reading.* One partner "magically" knows what the other partner is thinking.

Schemas

Schemas are an individual's underlying core beliefs that they develop about the characteristics of the world and how it functions. Even though schemas are relatively stable cognitive structures, they may become unconditional and inflexible in character. Many of these schemas are learned early in life being influenced by family-of-origin interactions as well as outside sources. An individual's schema will influence how he or she reacts to new situations. Schemas are developed about individual family members and his or her relationship in the family unit (Dattilio, 1993; Dattilio et al., 1998). This schemata will be brought into any couple relationship along with other life experience schema. Although a partner's inferences and perceptions about current events in a relationship may be influenced by previous family-oriented schema, the old schema may also be modified by the current experiences (Epstein & Baucom, 1993). However, if strong feelings are associated with the pre-existing schema, modification may be difficult.

Members of a couple will also develop schema in relation to their identity as a couple which will be modified when children are born. A "family schema" is developed over time from the interactions of the individual family members that may include distorted cognitions leading to a dysfunctional family situation (Dattilio, 1994).

A typology of cognitions based largely on schema and automatic thoughts were defined by Baucom and Epstein (1990; Baucom, Epstein, Sayers, & Sher, 1989) and have been implicated in relationship distress and conflict.

1. *Standards*: Family members' beliefs about how relationships, in particular their own relationship, "should" be.
2. *Selective attention*: Each member of a relationship tends to notice only some aspects of events in the relationship while ignoring others.
3. *Assumptions*: Beliefs about the characteristics of and the workings of relationships.
4. *Expectancies*: Predictions about the probability of future events actually happening.
5. *Attributions*: Inferences individuals make on what caused events in their relationship.

These types of cognitions can create dissatisfaction in family relationships resulting in dysfunctional family interactions (Dattilio et al., 1998).

Cognitive Therapy and Systems Thinking

With the exception of Epstein (1982, 1986), none of the cognitive theorists comprehended the need to integrate their approach with systems thinking. Treating couples requires more than doing Cognitive Therapy with two individuals in a room who happen to be married. Beck's (1988) book, *Love is Never Enough*, is a classic example of how an individualistic approach to treatment is applied to a system without a systemic perspective. A couple must always be understood as an interactional system. The cognitions within that system need to be conceptualized as part of an interactional, not just an individual system. Couples marry, stay together, and experience happiness and difficulties as a result of their shared cognitions. Dattilio and Padesky (1990) were the first major cognitive theorists to recognize this shortcoming of cognitive therapy as applied to couples and families. He emphasizes that such issues as circularity and the multi-directional flow of how couples and family members influence each other's cognitions and behaviors is paramount in facilitating change (Dattilio, 1998a, 1998b).

It is our belief that there are two basic ways in which cognitions need to be conceptualized systemically. First, the couple may share many of the same, but irrational or unworkable ideas and cognitive distortions. These ideas may serve both to bind them together and to create dysfunctionality. For example, the couple may believe conflict should be avoided at all costs. The relationship serves to protect each of them from having to deal with anger and conflict. This idea binds the couple together, but it also creates a pathological condition in the relationship.

The second way in which cognitions can be understood systemically is in terms of their interlocking and complementary nature. The beliefs held by one may be complemented by the beliefs in the other. For example, one partner may think, "I must have my way," and the other may think, "I must be the perfect partner and let him or her do what she or he wants." Or a partner might think, "My partner is responsible for my moods," and the other partner may think, "I am responsible for my partner's happiness."

The cognitions must be processed within the context of the relationship as part of the interactional field. Each partner and the therapist can discuss the impact of symmetrical and complementary cognitions. If one partner changes a cognition, what will the impact be on the other? How must the other change his or her thinking? How will the relationship be different? These questions require careful consideration in order to shift the focus from individual therapy to systems or couples therapy.

Techniques

Using Socratic questioning, the hallmark of cognitive therapy (Beck, 1976; Beck, Rush, Shaw, & Emery, 1979), clinical interviews with couples (together or individually) can provide the opportunity to obtain information on idiosyncratic cognitions and to track inferential processes which cannot be obtained through standardized questionnaires (Dattilio et al.,

1998). The "downward arrow" technique developed by Beck et al. (1979) identifies the underlying schema (i.e., standards and assumptions) beneath an individual's automatic thoughts thereby becoming aware of how these chains of thought can lead into erroneous conclusions reinforcing long-standing assumptions (Dattilio et al., 1998). In 1996, Dattilio clearly demonstrated this technique on video. Baucom and Epstein (1990) recommend clients write about distressing events between sessions including their emotions, cognitions, and behavioral response to the event. This information would be used as a basis for discussion in the therapy sessions.

☐ Education

A significant part of a cognitive approach is teaching couples the basic principles of REBT and Cognitive Therapy. The clinician may review the theory in the office and answer questions. It is essential that the partners understand the relationship between their cognitions *and* their feelings and actions. Until they believe changing their thinking will result in other change, therapy with this approach should not proceed. Bibliotherapy can also be used to facilitate this learning process. The clinician may use handouts or recommend books that are easy to read such as *Feeling Good* by David Burns (1980/1997).

☐ Learning to Self-Monitor

The purpose of cognitive approaches is to help partners eventually identify their own individual and relational cognitive distortions and irrational thoughts. This process starts with education and is then worked on in the office. A technique to get the couple started is to ask them to answer the below questions at home and to bring their answers to the next session. Processing these answers may take several sessions.

As the process unfolds, the therapist carefully monitors the couple to help detect their distortions and negative statements. When a distortion is detected, it is fed back to the couple so they may begin to process it. As always, they should be asked to think the cognition through in accordance with the guidelines provided in the section on systems thinking. Specifically, does the other partner share the same or similar cognition or distortion or have one that is complementary? In other words, when a distortion or irrational thought is found for one partner, the therapist should work on developing a complete picture. The thought leads to a specific behavior. The behavior affects the other person, which means the other partner has a cognition about the behavior.

Once the thoughts of both partners are understood, it will then become clear what creates the problem. Both may then be asked to work on changing their thinking. After clearing up the irrational ideas and cognitive distortions, it is useful to obtain their thoughts about the relationship in general. The following questions may be asked to clarify this thinking:

1. What did you expect of marriage before you got married?
2. What did you expect of marriage just after you were married?
3. What do you expect of marriage now?

In addition, the couple may be asked to complete the following statements:

"A husband should _____." "A wife should _____."

The answers to these questions are then processed in the session. The couple would be asked to consider whether their thinking is realistic, productive, and workable. The clinician should not frame any of these thoughts as true or false or right or wrong. They can be framed as preferences, likes, or disbeliefs. This examination will help the partners to identify their distortions, enabling them to change their way of thinking. It is important to point out how the new thoughts will counter the old thoughts, but only with continued practice. Slips and regressions are to be expected.

The couple is reminded that old thoughts are deeply ingrained and automatic. By categorizing the commonly occurring distortions and irrational thoughts, the clients become more aware of when this type of thinking starts. Initially, it is useful to have clients do a daily review of what was discussed in the session in order to be more alert to the presence of problematic thinking.

This technique also involves becoming aware of all the negative cognitions associated with a specific problem. Once the negative cognitions have been made explicit, an attempt is made to change the cognition. The cognitions are either neutralized or changed in a positive direction. For example, if the problem is constant fighting, the underlying thought might be that the only way to preserve one's sense of self is to stay distant, with anger being used to create the needed distance.

Or a wife might complain that her husband doesn't tell her he loves her enough. The fact is that he rarely says anything. Her complaint is legitimate, but it is also escalated by her. She begins to think he does not love her and he is rejecting her by not saying something she has told him she would like. In this instance, it is important to change her cognition and, in turn, the behavior within the system. If she changes her thinking, then she might be nicer to him. He also needs to change his behavior by expressing more love and affection to her. His part of the problem could be that to tell his wife he loves her means he will be engulfed by her. His irrational thought might stem from a family of origin in which Mother was constantly manipulating the male partner for his approval and love. Once the husband can change his cognition, his attitude toward his wife will change and he will be freer to express his feelings.

☐ Other Techniques

There are several other techniques that may be taught to the couple. To help identify automatic thoughts, the couple may be instructed to individually record their automatic thoughts during a confrontational period in their relationship. The Dysfunctional Thought Record (Dattilio et al., 1998; Dattilio & Padesky, 1990), a version of the Daily Record of Dysfunctional Thoughts (Beck et al., 1979) may be utilized for this purpose. This record would include a description of the situation, the automatic thoughts, and the emotional responses produced. The therapist would use this information to demonstrate how thoughts are linked to emotional responses resulting in the negative framing of others. Once the couple understands the link between thoughts and emotional and behavioral responses, progress can be made to counteract the common tendency of disowning any responsibility of being able to influence their own feelings (Dattilio et al., 1998).

An individual's cognitions about an intimate relationship are often projections of his or her own conflicts, which need to be addressed in therapy sessions to help restructure any negative cognitive distortions. The therapist utilizes Socratic questioning and related procedures for that purpose. In relationship to potentially biased attributions and expectancies, Socratic questioning can also be utilized to aid clients in ascertaining possible determinants for his or her partner's behaviors or other possible unanticipated outcomes to particular situations (Dattilio et al., 1998).

Burns (1980) identified 10 techniques in his book, two of which are particularly applicable to couples. The first is what he calls the *alternative interpretation method*. An event (A) can be interpreted in a number of ways. Negative interpretations are harmful to the relationship, while positive interpretations are helpful. Couples need to master the art of positively reframing each other's behaviors. The reframe should be believable and consistent with the facts.

For example, a couple may share the belief that intimacy is sharing all their time together. When one violates this assumption, a negative judgment is made. A positive frame would be that separateness and individuality are as much a part of intimacy as togetherness. Traits, characteristics, and attributes may all be given a positive frame with a little effort. The therapist should model positive reframing and then encourage the partners to look for new ways of thinking about each other. The more they stress the positive, the more they feel good.

The second technique is to *examine the evidence* for a particular thought. Do the facts point in only one direction? Are the facts even known? Assumptions by their nature are often not checked out or verified. The interpretation of an event may be made in-and-of oneself without regard for the other's input. Partners must learn to identify when they are making assumptions and then to keep an open mind until these assumptions are confirmed or disconfirmed. Assumptions may be so entrenched that the partner is only able to hear the voice in his or her head and not the input from the other person. When conversations become monologues, such that each keeps saying the same thing over and over, it is time for the partners to recognize that they are each captives of their own thinking. They need to turn attention outward in order to find out what the other person said.

☐ Conclusion

Working with a couple means attending to their behavior, affect, and cognition. In the literature, emphasis on the cognitive aspect of the couple relationship has been lacking. This chapter stressed the usefulness of learning more about each partner's way of thinking and actual thoughts regarding the relationship. The essential point to remember from this chapter is that thoughts must be considered from a systemic frame of reference. The question is how the partners' thoughts form an interlocking system that leads to problems. Taken separately, the thoughts may seem acceptable. Considered together, the couple may be engaging in thoughts that put them at odds with or that place barriers to sharing greater intimacy. Just as with other issues, processing and changing the thoughts requires that the therapist go back and forth with the partners, thereby maintaining the balance. It is not a matter of a thought being right or wrong, but, rather, a question of whether the thinking is producing a workable relationship.

CHAPTER

Techniques of Marital Contracting

The purpose of this chapter is to discuss several techniques of marital contracting. A marital contract makes explicit those behaviors that are wanted in a marriage. The contract is usually written and identifies the behaviors to be exchanged in specific, concrete, and behavioral terms.

The use of contracts can be traced to the development of behavior therapy. According to L'Abate and McHenry (1983), five factors contributed to the development of contracting. First, as behavior therapy increased in use, behaviorists began to consider ways to use this approach with couples. The result was the development of behavioral marital therapy with the emergence of several contractual approaches. Second, some therapists were becoming disillusioned with intrapsychic approaches. These approaches were not active and directive enough to deal with couple difficulties. Third, as any field develops, it must produce reliable methods and demonstrate effectiveness. Contracting was a technique that could be scientifically replicated among clinicians. Fourth, the field of marital therapy needed to demonstrate that it produced the results claimed. Because contracting is replicable, it can be empirically evaluated for outcome. Finally, many couples coming for treatment were neither interested in or suitable for approaches that were cognitively or affectively oriented. These couples were primarily interested in changing the behaviors within the relationship. (The reader who would like to get a general overview of behavioral approaches to couple and family therapy should consult Horne and Sayger, 2000.)

The basic theory of marital contracts is that behavioral change leads to affective and cognitive change. It has been shown repeatedly that cog-

193

nition and affect do follow from behavior. The basic purpose of a marital contract is to increase the number of positive exchanges in the relationship. By increasing positive exchanges, the therapist is simultaneously decreasing punishing or coercive exchanges. Couples who are trapped in these negative exchanges are trying to get what they want and then retaliating when their needs are frustrated. Such a situation can create a power struggle in the relationship. Each partner attempts to "win" as a substitute for having his or her needs met.

Contracting is an ideal solution for obviating power struggles and creating positive exchanges. Because both partners contribute equally to the contract, they are creating a system of perceived equity and fairness. The contract or system they create diffuses the power struggle. With the power struggle being diffused, it is easier to begin making the positive changes specified in the contract.

The use of a contracting approach is more likely to work under certain conditions. First, both partners should be fully engaged in the therapeutic process. A contract cannot be developed by just one spouse. Both must be present and be working toward the same basic goal—to make the marriage fulfill their needs more effectively. Second, the partners must be relatively compliant, cooperative, and caring. If the couple are too angry, focused on externalizing or blaming each other, locked in a power struggle or impasse, this approach is not indicated. Third, each spouse must be willing to change his or her own behavior. They must both agree to try something different. Compromise is an important concept for the couple to comprehend. Each must know that by giving up something they value, they will gain other benefits.

Finally, the couple must be motivated to take control of their own relationship. A contract does not involve being told what to do, nor is it as mystical as just talking with a therapist who has charisma. The contract represents the couple's effort to take control of their own marriage in a way that appeals to common sense. Unconscious forces are not worked on directly. The personal commitment to change must be strong, and the therapist needs to reinforce each partner's individual change.

☐ General Principles of Contracting

Execute a Written Document

The term contract refers to a written agreement. A marital contract should also be placed in writing. Several reasons may be given to justify the need for a written contract. First, all important events in life are documented in writing. Birth certificates, death certificates, academic records, diplomas, all mark progress or events. The written word is permanent and has greater psychological import than the spoken word. It could be argued that the written word is more binding than the spoken word. Second, because the written word is permanent it is not easy to "forget" the agreement. Verbal statements may be ignored, repressed, confused, distorted, or otherwise minimized or sidetracked. A written record may be read and reread with the same meaning if it is clearly written. (Although written words can also have their meanings distorted until a mutually agreed upon interpretation of them is reached.)

Third, the fact that the message is permanent also allows the couple to use it as a constant reminder of their commitment. The contract may be displayed in some visible location or read daily as a reminder to help change the old habitual routine. Couples are usually asked to read the contract daily the first few weeks until it is committed to memory. Fourth, the contract should be carefully worded. Statements should be short, concise, and behavioral. The answer to the question of "who does what, when, and how" should be clear for each behavioral exchange. Finally, the contract should be presented as an evolving document. The couple may renegotiate or modify items over time. The key point is that the couple have an agreement to deviate from rather than constantly working toward something that is never clear and explicit.

Be Realistic

The behaviors to be exchanged must be perceived as being fair and equitable. A contract that is perceived as being one-sided will only serve to generate more resentment and anger. The contract is designed to create equity and justice in the relationship. In order to create this sense of equity, both partners must be willing to make a contribution. These contributions may sometimes be felt as sacrifices for the greater good of the relationship. In its simplest form, the contract represents each partner's needs for giving and getting. What one partner wants to receive should be what the other ideally wants to give or, realistically, what the other is willing to give for the sake of reciprocity and marital satisfaction.

The behaviors to be exchanged must be under conscious control. One should not ask for that which the other cannot or is unable to give. For example, in one case a husband demanded his wife have sex with him to meet his requirements of equity and justice in the marriage. He agreed to give her friendship, which is what she wanted and he, in turn, expected her to give him sex. However, his wife was experiencing inhibited sexual desire and her ability to simply give him sex was thus impossible. He had to be educated regarding her present limitations in order for therapy to proceed on the basis of an exchange other than the one which he originally wanted.

Be Positive

The contract should avoid the use of punishment. Punishment involves withholding, taking away, and coercive acts. In order to formulate a positive emotional environment in the relationship, the contract needs to be worded as positively as possible, for example, "I want to give you," "I will do _____ for you," and "I agree to _____."

Be Inclusive

Many contracts we have seen specify only one behavior exchange. These contracts fail to address the complexity of a relationship. A couple may focus on one particular problem area, but this may not be the only change they desire. Additionally, if they fail at their one item contract, their contract fails. While it is much easier to develop a one-item contract, it is not advisable.

Developing the contract will require several sessions. The couple should be told the contract is not complete until they have all the items they believe to be important. By being inclusive rather than overfocused, more aspects of the couple's relationship come under scrutiny and more change occurs after implementation. This approach is consistent with the concept of first-order versus second-order change. In second-order change, the relationship itself changes, not just elements of the relationship.

Discuss Problems with Implementation

After the contract has been developed and the couple are ready to implement it, the therapist should take time to discuss ways in which the contract might not work. The couple is then asked to reread the contract in the session and to discuss ways they might fail to live up to their part. The partners are asked to speak only for his or her self. The therapist may also add ideas that have emerged during previous discussions. The most common idea is that of the partner not living up to his or her side, which is viewed as making the contract null and void. Each partner needs to make a personal commitment to contribute 100 percent, irrespective of what the other partner does. The failure of a partner to fulfill his or her part will be addressed in the session following his or her failure to live up to the commitment.

Monitor Progress

An ingredient of contracting that is often underemphasized is that of monitoring progress. One interesting phenomenon that sometimes occurs with couples is that they begin to change, but do not "see" the change. In short, a lag may exist between the behavioral change and the perception of change. This phenomenon is consistent with evidence that suggests people are often more theory-driven than data-driven when monitoring events, that is, spouses may have a theory about how and why each one behaves. New data are often made to fit the theory or are discarded if they are not consistent with the theory. In one case a wife described her husband as incapable of having feelings. When he started to discuss his feelings in the couple's sessions, she dismissed his effort as an act designed to impress the therapist.

For systematic self-monitoring to occur, each spouse must do a daily review of his or her progress. The question the partners should ask themselves is, "How am I doing?" To answer this question, the items on the contract are used as behavioral criteria. Each item is reviewed in order to assess whether it was fulfilled, the frequency with which it was done, and the satisfaction derived from fulfilling the item. This assessment leads to the development of an ongoing log, which is brought to the session where the therapist can monitor and reinforce the progress with the couple.

In the previous paragraph, a nonbehavioral assessment or subjective assessment was recommended, namely, the satisfaction derived from fulfilling the item. The contract is seen as providing equity in the relationship and helping each partner receive what she or he wants. Thus, it is rewarding. However, these rewards are not the only compensations available. Partners should be asked to reinforce each other when agreements are fulfilled. When partners notice one of the agreements being enacted, they need to express their appreciation. The act of expressing appreciation may be discussed in the session. Once it is clear the couple share this attitude, then the phrases used to express appreciation may be discussed. Discussing the phrasing is important because partners sometimes feel their spouse is being patronizing. The statements of appreciation create a positive reinforcement loop in the couple, further reinforcing the utility of the contract.

☐ Techniques of Contracting

Four basic approaches to contracting may be found in the marital therapy literature. The first two to be discussed are derived from behavioral marital therapy; the third from a combination of therapeutic approaches; and the fourth is embedded within a cognitive-behavioral approach to marital therapy.

Quid Pro Quo Contracts

This type of contract is one in which the behavioral exchanges are cross-linked (O'Leary & Turkewitz, 1978). Quid pro quo literally means "something for something." The partners agree that if one partner fulfills his or her agreement, then the other fulfills his or her agreement. The behaviors are contingent on each other. In order for this agreement to work, the behavior offered must be reinforcing to the other spouse. For example, George wants Mary to stop working at 3:00 P.M. on the dot and then together they will go to do something they both find enjoyable. Mary wants George to help her for two hours or to do two hours of chores each day of the weekend. They agree that if George does two hours of work, Mary will stop at 3:00 P.M. and they will do something enjoyable.

The quid pro quo contract has major problems. First, there is the question of who goes first. This issue should be settled in the session. It is important to define a behavioral cycle, that is, the period of time in which the two behaviors are linked. Within that cycle one partner may have the first turn. It may be they can alternate turns or that no one needs to be specified as going first. If one person does not meet the terms of the agreement, the other is under no obligation within the specified behavioral cycle.

When such a failure occurs, the couple should not respond to the event with anger, but with disappointment. One partner may note his or her disappointment. In contracting, the partners are advised to acknowledge anger in the other, but then to ignore it until the next session. If the anger is allowed, the couple get trapped once again in their cycle of blaming and counterblaming. In the session the anger may be explored as a block to prevent change, as a hidden agenda, and so on (see Chapter 11, Conflict Resolution). The fact that a behavioral cycle has been defined allows the partners an opportunity to try to fulfill the agreement during the next cycle. If the cycle is day-by-day, then a new cycle and new opportunity would be available each day. Having short behavioral cycles enhances the chances for successful interaction during the week. Thus, the couple should be encouraged to think of daily exchanges.

Good Faith Contracts

Weiss, Hops, and Patterson (1973) introduced this type of contract. Unlike the quid pro quo contract, this technique does not tie together or make contingent the partner's behaviors. Each partner makes a commitment in good faith to provide the other with particular behaviors. If the discussed behavior is given, the person receives a reward that is independent of the partner's behavior. For example, if a husband wants his wife to go biking with him on Saturday and his wife goes with him, she chooses a reward she would like, such as going out one evening during the week with her friends. Good faith contracts are easy to formulate when the number of behaviors is small. However, as the contract grows, the number of reinforcements becomes more and more difficult to find.

A variation of the good faith contract is to ask the partners to help each other without any extrinsic reward. The reward would be the intrinsic satisfaction experienced from the improved and happier relationship. We employ this technique frequently because it is simple and agreeable to most couples. When using this technique it is very useful to have the partners verbally reward each other as was pointed out earlier.

Covenant Contracts

This method of contracting was developed by Clifford Sager (1976). It is different from behavioral contracts because of its much broader form. Emotions as well as behaviors are included in this contract. To use Sager's approach it is necessary to understand two components of his theory.

Sager (1976) stated that all couples have an implicit and explicit interactional contract which determines the behavior of each spouse within the relationship. The individual contracts may be conscious and verbalized, conscious and nonverbalized, or unconscious and nonverbalized. It is clear from this theory that much of what determines the behavior within a relationship is not known to the partners. The contract is implicit and unconscious. One of the purposes of covenant contracting is to make those nonverbalized and unconscious expectations known to oneself and one's partner.

As the couple becomes clearer about their unconscious contract, they may find three types of situations. Their contracts may be congruent. A congruent contract is based on healthy needs and emphasizes a trading off of needs, wants, and desires. A second possibility is the complementary contract. In this case the partners use the traits of the other to complete some missing part in self. For example, a shy person might use the extroversion of her or his mate to compensate for his or her deficiency. A third possibility is the conflictual contract. This contract makes effective and rewarding interactions impossible. Unfortunately, much of this conflicted material is unconscious and gradually emerges in the relationship. A couple might marry knowing some problems exist, but not the full extent of the problems.

The covenant contract involves making the implicit and unspoken expectations explicit. For example, a woman who feels her husband will leave her when he becomes angry because of her history of having partners who had actually done so, might need her husband to reassure her or affirm his commitment during or after a fight. Assessment and treatment are viewed as inseparable dialectic processes. The process of making the expectations explicit is diagnostic and also therapeutic in that the expectations may be changed or renegotiated.

In doing this type of contract each partner is asked to address four sets of issues: self, marriage, spouse, and children. For each issue, a want list is constructed. In addition to these four sets of issues, Sager (1976) has developed lists of questions that help to stimulate thinking about different aspects of the marriage. These questions are given to the couple early in the process so the partners may have time to consider their answers. Following each partner's reading of his or her list, the therapist helps the couple determine what is realistic and what can be negotiated. The process of doing the covenant contract may be fairly specific in format. Once the expectations are explicit, the therapist may choose to proceed in a less structured way.

Of the three types of contracts described, covenant contracting is the most complex and time consuming. The therapist assumes there are unconscious expectations. Time is needed to help the partners become aware that such expectations exist. Giving them the questions to consider helps to raise their unconscious expectations into awareness. Educating the partners that such expectations exist and giving them the questions to consider helps raise their awareness. The process of therapy itself promotes self-awareness allowing for the emergence of unconscious expectations.

However, not all of these expectations will become apparent to the partners. As the therapist gets to know how the couple relate, especially in conflictual ways, these expectations can be inferred by the therapist. Once an inference is made, the therapist may suggest to the couple that such an expectation exists. Additional inferences can be drawn from genogram information. Patterns, messages, and other key family-of-origin experiences tend to create specific expectations.

In one case a wife complained that she wanted her husband to be able to listen to and understand her, yet she said he had never been able to do so. The fact was that when he did understand her, it either did not register or did not count because she said it was about something trivial. Her behavior suggested she expected her husband would never have the qualities needed to listen to her. In her family of origin she felt the same way, that is, no one cared enough about her to listen. In spite of the fact that this woman said she wanted understanding, she was the one who could not allow it to occur and she was unconsciously sabotaging herself. When confronted about this pattern, she denied that such a thing was possible.

The problem for the therapist is that when some of these expectations are discovered, it can be difficult to get the client to accept them. Such a client would need gentle, yet persistent confrontation over time. This task is best accomplished through enactments in the office. In the case above, the wife would be asked to state what she needed, her husband encouraged and taught to respond, and her reaction noted. When she begins to discount his ability or sincerity, she should be confronted. Video playback in the session might be useful also to help her see the way she refuses to acknowledge her husband's attempts to communicate with her.

Behavioral Exchange

Jacobson and Christensen (1996) published a text entitled, *Integrative Couple Therapy: Promoting Acceptance and Change*. This book stressed the concepts of helping the couple to accept what was unlikely to change and to work from an integrative perspective and included a BE (behavioral exchange) intervention described as an adjunct to their integrative approach.

The authors suggested that "reinforcement erosion" is a natural rather than pathological phenomenon in all couples. In other words, as the couple moves forward the rate of positive behavioral exchange begins to erode. The purpose of behavioral exchange is to help increase the rate of positive interactions. Jacobson and Christensen (1996) offer an example of how behavioral exchange would look. They chose not to condense the intervention to a few steps. However, their description shows the intervention actually consists of just a few steps or behavioral assignments.

The first step consists of asking each partner to generate a list of items that if done more or less often would generate greater marital satisfaction. Each partner is to generate this list independently without any input from the other. They summarized the assignment by saying, "Ask not what your partner can do for you; ask what you can do for your partner" (p. 156).

The second step involves the therapist going over each list with each individual partner. The therapist wants to ensure the list is comprehensive and that the partner can actually do what appears on the list. As is true in all behavioral approaches, partners sometimes make comments that aren't behavioral and need to be operationalized. The therapist insists that the partner who is listening to this discussion remain absolutely silent, including non-verbal comments. At the conclusion of this session, the therapist asks each partner to pick one or two items to focus on during the next week, either increasing or decreasing a behavior. The person who provides the behavior is to monitor the effect it has on the relationship in order to see whether it increases satisfaction. Additionally, neither partner is to tell the other which items from the list were chosen to be worked on that week.

The third step involves evaluating how well the intervention worked with the task discussed from an interactional perspective. The therapist asks which items were chosen, which ones the recipient noticed, and which ones contributed to increased marital satisfaction. For the first time, the recipient is asked to comment or give input about the items. Further, the recipient is allowed to comment on all the behaviors on the list in terms of how important they are to them. This commentary gives the provider a better idea of what will help the most. The therapist also asks about the "costs" to the provider for each item. If an item costs too much to give, it is likely to become aversive and stop. The therapist encourages the provider to give only those behaviors which they enjoy giving.

The authors believe that if behavioral exchange is to work, it must involve the couple's compliance. In order to facilitate compliance, they state each partner must believe they are choosing to give freely and what they want to give. Otherwise, they would feel they were being coerced into giving some behavior and the result would be non-compliance.

☐ Conclusion

The four techniques of contracting described in this chapter represent varying types of behavioral approaches. There exists ample evidence to suggest changing behavior eventually leads to changes in affect and cognition. The therapist's choice is whether to focus on behavior, cognition, or affect from the outset. A behavioral approach utilizing a contract is useful with concrete, less verbal, and less psychologically sophisticated couples. There also must be sufficient motivation to change. In addition, the therapist should offer ample praise to help facilitate the changes and to stand as an all-important model for the couple.

When the partners see the therapist being positive and offering praise, they may begin to internalize that behavior as part of their own. Approaching one another positively further invites change from the other, which in turn creates even more positive behavior exchanges.

15

Feelings

In individual psychotherapy, there are approaches to treatment devoted solely to affect or emotion. Gestalt Therapy, for example, has been a major force in psychotherapy and deals exclusively with emotional awareness and expression. However, marital therapies have devoted little attention to the role of feelings in therapy. In fact, in some major approaches such as paradoxical, strategic, and behavioral, feelings are viewed as a hindrance to effective therapeutic work. Proponents of these approaches often speak of the need to avoid dealing with feelings because they are seen as a distraction. Greenberg and Safran (1987) identify three specific reasons for addressing emotion in psychotherapy: Processing information in an experiential manner produces productive client involvement in some forms of therapy; emotional arousal and expression are related to change in specific circumstances; and anxiety can be reduced by maintaining a high level of emotional arousal in specific circumstances. Of all the major approaches to systems/marital therapy, not one gives serious attention to the role of feelings (Gurman & Kniskern, 1981b), despite the fact that marriage is fundamentally an emotional attachment.

Although strong unconscious forces may exist, couples enter relationships on a voluntary basis and form the relationship on the basis of one overtly stated feeling—*love*. Close relationships such as marriage frequently evoke the strongest emotions an individual ever experiences. Rage, anger, and hatred may be felt in shocking intensity. Close relationships can also distort perceptions and feelings. During the idealization stage of courtship, partners may be "intoxicated" with feelings of love to the point of overlooking other feelings they have toward the partner and significant problems that might deter marriage. In an effort to sustain a close relationship, other feelings might be ignored, denied, suppressed, or repressed. For example, a partner who fears anger might suppress it in order to avoid harming or losing the other partner.

The role emotions play in a relationship is obviously complex and not predictable until the partners are understood. The nature of emotions themselves is not clear. Several theories are available to define and explain them and were reviewed by Greenberg and Johnson (1986a) in an article on the use of affect in marital therapy. In 1994, Johnson and Greenberg identified eight reasons why emotion is relevant in intimate relationships:

1. Emotional experience and expression is the primary building block of adult intimate relationships.
2. Emotions, such as love, are adaptive in human functioning.
3. Emotion is a primary signaling system.
4. Emotion primes and organizes people for action in general, and for interpersonal responses in particular.
5. Emotions play a powerful role in structuring interactional positions.
6. Experienced emotion provides access to needs and desires.
7. Emotions organize perceptions of self and other.
8. Emotion links self and system.

Emotion-focused therapy (EFT) uses nine steps in a synthesis of family systems and experiential approaches into psychotherapy (Johnson, 1996). EFT involves the identification and tracking of cycles of interaction with each partner's underlying emotional experience identified for each step of the cycle. Problems are reframed by the therapist with the partners accepting both his or her response as well as the partner's response. Through time, new requests and solutions are generated for the presenting problems. The old cycles are disrupted with more adaptive cycles developed (Greenberg & Johnson, 1988; Johnson, 1996). EFT's two main tasks are changing interactional positions by accessing emotional experience (Greenberg & Johnson, 1988). Studies have been conducted on the efficacy of EFT (Denton, Burleson, Clark, Rodriquez, & Hobbs, 2000).

Gordon (1993) developed the concept of the emotional jug to describe the multilayered effect of emotions. The cork in the emotional jug is indifference, the attitude that develops after years of repressing emotions. Gordon suggests that once anger, fear, and sadness are confided in a safe and validating relationship there is room in the emotional jug for love and tenderness.

The purpose of this chapter is to discuss some techniques that are helpful in facilitating the use of emotions with couples. We will avoid theoretical and academic explorations in favor of the practical.

☐ Expectations and Feelings

In Chapter 13 on cognitive therapy, the relationship between cognition and feeling was described. Basically, feelings are determined by the cognitions. In a close relationship, a number of strong and stable expectations come into play. When these expectations are met, partners feel satisfied, happy, fulfilled, gratified, contented, respected, cared for, and loved. On the other hand, when expectations are not met or are in conflict, other less pleasant emotions emerge. These feelings are an indication that expectations are not meshing. The therapist may wish to focus on a feeling to understand what is being felt and to validate the feeling and then move on to uncover expectation on which it is based. In some cases, the expectation is unknown to the partner. The only indication of its existence is its emotional effect. The feeling is much like the devastation resulting from a storm. One cannot see the wind, only its effects. Giving the feeling reality serves to give heretofore unknown expectations authenticity.

The therapist's use of empathic listening during the process of discovery not only can help the client become more aware of feelings but also provides a corrective emotional experience for the client. Often, repressed clients have experienced deprivation of appropriate emotional attunement early in their lives. The therapist also must be aware that a client may have difficulty accepting or dealing with "positive" emotional experiences. Corrective emotional experiences often are experienced as incongruent with previous relationship experiences. Most clients look to the therapist for reeducation and reframing of their emotional experience. This requires the therapist to move comfortably between cognitive and affective dimensions of emotion.

☐ Promoting Awareness of Feelings

Unfortunately, some marital therapists have dealt with the issues of feelings in an oversimplified way. The therapist has simply asked, "How do you feel?" The client responds and then the issue must be dropped until the therapist asks the question again. Apparently, the therapist believes that ventilation of the feeling alone is enough. Some people are more emotionally repressed than others, and these people need more help and support to become aware of the feelings. Gordon (1993) identified three levels of awareness of feelings: Level one: "I am aware of my feelings and I can share them with you"; Level two: "I am aware of my feelings but I choose not to share them with you"; and Level three: "I am not aware of my feelings, so I cannot share them with you."

Working with feelings always involves two steps. The first is to help the person to be aware of the feeling, and the second is to help the person express the feeling. One of our colleagues, Larry Hof (Hof & Miller, 1981), has developed a communications exercise for couples to help with both of these aspects. He calls this exercise "My World of Feelings."* The purpose of the exercise is *to help clients become more aware of the whole range of their feelings, to begin to express them appropriately, and to accept these feelings in themselves and in others.* This exercise is used with couples that are having some trouble getting in touch with their feelings and are not at the extremes of being suppressed or angry. The exercise is described below. The first part consists of instructions for the partners followed by a couple's exercise. This exercise was designed to be done at home in roughly one hour.

"My World of Feelings" Exercise

15 Minutes	1. Personal Reading: "The World of Feelings"
15 Minutes	2. Individuals complete statements on "My World of Feelings" form.
20 Minutes	3. Couple sits facing each other, knees touching, and decides who will start.
	4. The person starting says, "In our marriage, when we relate together, I am happiest when . . . " Having completed the statement, the person maintains eye contact as much as possible.
	5. Partner is to listen attentively to the feelings being expressed, and to accept them. The only comment acceptable is a question for clarification of what the person means. Statements are not to be discussed nor disagreed with. Hear them, accept them, and receive them as a gift of the one person to the other.
	6. After the first person has shared her/his response to item number 1, the partner then shares her/his response to the same item.
	7. Repeat the process until all the items have been completed.
10 Minutes	8. Talk together with your partner about what you experienced, thought, and felt as you went through this experience. Discuss the value of this experience for you and for your relationship.

---

* Note: This technique was developed by Larry Hof and appears in Hof and Miller's *Marriage Enrichment*, pp. 96–98. Copyright © 1981. Reprinted with permission.

Personal Reading: The World of Feelings

The world of feelings is the world of affection and sentiment, the world of emotion and passion. It is the world of happiness and sadness, of joy and anger, of excitement and boredom. My feelings are my spontaneous emotional responses to the events that occur in the world around me, the emotional responses associated with, and triggered by, my fulfilled or unfulfilled expectations, and my interpretations of events and behaviors. My feelings are expressed in and through my body; I may speak faster and louder when I am excited, and slower and softer when I am sad; my body may shake when I laugh, and my eyes may fill with tears when I am in pain. Even when I am not consciously aware of my feelings, my body is frequently giving off clues that I am feeling something, clues that other people may sense.

During any given day, I will feel a variety of feelings:

Happiness	Confusion	Relief	Satisfaction
Sadness	Loneliness	Hope	Boredom
Joy	Apathy	Fear	Love
Pain	Anger	Confidence	Suspense
Suspicion	Remorse	Silliness	Contentment
Pride	Irritation	Peacefulness	Tiredness
Hopelessness	Anticipation	Reverence	Surprise

The list could be expanded almost endlessly, with subtle variations and differing degrees of each feeling being present at different times. I can feel several feelings at once, and those feelings can conflict with each other.

My feelings are a very real and valuable part of me. They are just as important as my thoughts, my senses, and my behaviors. They can help me to deepen my understanding of life and the impact of people and events upon me. My joy helps me to celebrate and to identify things and people I like. My boredom gives me clues that I would rather be doing something else. My fears help me to protect myself. Without my feelings, I would live a greatly impoverished life.

Yet, for some reason, many of us have been taught to disregard our feelings-all of them, or a select few "bad" feelings. Some people have been taught to be "rational." Some have been taught to deny or avoid anger, pain, pride, or sexual feelings. Perhaps, each of us has a little list that we keep inside of "acceptable" and "unacceptable" feelings. Others feel them internally, but we don't permit ourselves to express them without words or actions. For example, we want to avoid conflict, so we don't express our anger. We don't want to be "soft," so we withhold our warmth. We don't want to appear "weak," so we don't disclose our fears.

If my feelings are to serve me and help me make sense of life, I must be aware of them and their heights and depths, and be able to express them appropriately in words and actions. If I deny or avoid them, I lose the ability to control them and they can gain control of me. Then, they may emerge when I don't want them to, perhaps inappropriately. Or, they may literally "eat a hole in my stomach" or "give me a pounding headache." In some way, I pay a great price when I refuse to let my feelings have an appropriate and natural place in my life.

When I accept the fact that it is normal to feel a whole range of feelings, I am freed from justifying my feelings or apologizing for them. I simply recognize that, "I am human; therefore, I feel. You are human; therefore, you feel, too." As I accept that fact, and increase my awareness of my feelings, I can express them in many ways. The choice of how I will express them is mine to make. I can change old ways of expressing them. The more I practice, the more I will become used to expressing my feelings.

In a marital relationship, the ability of two individuals to be aware of the whole range of feelings, to express them appropriately, and to accept them in themselves and in each other can pave the way for increased self-awareness and for stronger bonds of trust and deeper intimacy. It may make each partner more vulnerable, too. But, perhaps the potential for self-awareness and growth, and for increased trust and intimacy, is worth the risk!

Statement Completion: My World of Feelings Exercise

Please complete the following statements:

1. In our marriage, when we relate together, I am happiest when . . .
2. In our marriage, when we relate together, I am saddest when . . .
3. In our marriage, when we relate together, I am angriest when . . .
4. The best thing about our marriage is . . .
5. I feel most afraid when . . .
6. I feel loved when you . . .
7. My greatest concern/fear for our marriage is . . .
8. What I like most about myself is . . .
9. What I dislike most about myself is . . .
10. What I like most about you is . . .
11. My greatest concern/fear for you is . . .
12. The feelings that I have the most difficulty sharing with you are . . .
13. The feelings that I can share most easily with you are . . .
14. Right now I feel . . . towards you.
15. Right now I feel . . . towards myself.
16. I feel . . . sharing these feelings with you.

☐ Getting in Touch

As we indicated earlier, some partners are more emotionally repressed than others. For those partners, more work is needed. They are asked to define a feeling and to keep a feeling diary. Partners are first asked to define a feeling because they often confuse thoughts, judgments, and feelings. L'Abate presents an exercise in *Programmed Writing* (1992) that helps identify and define feelings and emotions and their importance. They must learn how to differentiate these by questioning themselves and by getting assistance from the therapist and, in many cases, from their partner. The type of confusion one commonly comes across is exemplified by the client who says, "I feel good (bad, okay, etc.)" Just because the word "feel" is used in the sentence, does not mean a feeling is being defined. This example involves value statements or judgments. The partner could have said, "I feel happy (unhappy, contented, etc.)" These terms represent feelings.

The daily diary is reviewed weekly. The partners are asked to note their feelings and the triggers for those feelings. Furthermore, they are asked to let the feelings "register" by staying with them for a few minutes. For some people, feelings are fleeting. As a consequence, the feeling is not registered or discussed later with one's partner.

The second half of this exercise involves the partner choosing one or two feelings to share with the other person. Time is to be set aside in the evening for this activity. The other partner should reflect back the feeling and discuss it with the partner who shared it. These exercises are simple homework for the couple that needs straightforward emotional assistance. Many couples need much more.

☐ Filtering Emotions

One of the most common problems in couples is that they filter all their emotions through one emotional channel—the most usual of which is anger. In other words, all the emotions experienced are either experienced and/or expressed in anger. A partner may experience guilt, fear, hurt, depression, insecurity, and so on, yet express any one of these emotions as anger. Anger becomes a defense to protect the partner from having to deal with an emotion she or he is ill-equipped to handle.

When the therapist observes one emotion being used to cover up others, it is time to explore the other underlying feelings. It is usually not difficult to guess what those feelings are likely to be. Continued explorations, with the client beginning to attend to and express the underlying feeling, are helpful.

The problem, of course, with revealing and expressing the underlying feeling is what the partner believes will happen if she or he does so. Once the unexpressed feelings have been identified, the partners may be asked what makes their expression so difficult. They may believe the partner will not hear them or will use the feelings against them. This belief can be processed objectively by the therapist, checked out with the partner, and then an enactment can take place in the session in which the couple deals with the feelings while being coached by the therapist.

☐ Genograms and Feelings

When a partner believes certain feelings should not be felt or expressed, genogram work may help to uncover the reason. The purpose of a Feelings Genogram is to trace the emotional history of the individual and the family system to help the client become more aware of patterns of emotional expression in the family in terms of both pleasure and pain so that effective and satisfying emotional experiences can take place in the present. The first school of emotional learning comes from family life. This emotional schooling is provided by the role model parents present to their children in not only how they handle their feelings with the children, but also the feelings shared by the husband and wife. The parents may be gifted emotional teachers or atrocious examples (Goleman, 1995). Emotional expressiveness in both nonverbal and verbal patterns appears to be socially shared within families (Berry & Pennebaker, 1993). To help promote therapeutic change, it is important to have a deeper understanding of the emotional connections in couples and families and how these connections can become disrupted (Greenberg & Marques, 1998).

Attitudes and decisions about expressing feelings usually are learned during childhood and adolescence. Feelings Genograms can help uncover the reasons for these attitudes and beliefs. Questions about how feelings were handled in the family, which feelings were acceptable or not acceptable, and how different feelings were expressed elucidate the historical basis of these attitudes. Attitudes that may have been functional and useful in growing up may not be functional in someone's life today. The partner can then begin to see how certain feelings were always blocked.

The Feelings Genogram

The Feelings Genogram may be used to collect considerable information about feelings in the family and may take several sessions to complete. Some questions the therapist may ask include the following:

1. What were the dominant feelings for each member of your family?
2. What was the predominant feeling in your family? Who set the mood?
3. Which feelings were expressed most often, most intensely?
4. Which feelings were not allowed? How were members punished when an unallowed feeling was expressed?
5. What happened to the unexpressed feelings in the family?
6. Who knew or did not know about how others felt?
7. What happened to you when you expressed the taboo feeling or feelings?

8. How did you learn how to deal with these so-called unacceptable feelings?
9. Did others try to tell you how you should feel?
10. Did you ever see anyone lose control over his or her feelings? What would happen? Did anyone get hurt? How?
11. If corporal punishment was used in your family, what feelings did parents express? What feelings were allowed for children?
12. Do you find yourself having feelings you cannot explain, but are close to feelings you have had in the past?

Additional information on genograms can be obtained from *Focused Genograms* (DeMaria, Weeks, & Hof, 1999).

In one case, a man was a "pseudospouse" to his mother. He learned that his mother desperately needed his love and admiration. He eventually discovered that by always being cheerful and loving, he could win his mother's approval. In his marriage, he gave the appearance of being emotionally well, but was seething with frustration, anger, and resentment. In this case, the emotions directed toward his mother were actually being displaced onto his wife.

When the emotions of the partners are not consistent with the situation, it is useful to think about emotional displacement from the family of origin. In one extreme case, a husband always found reason to be critical and angry toward his wife. Genogram exploration revealed he was carrying unresolved anger toward his parents. Conversely, his wife had felt guilt and depression for many years. She was the peacemaker in her own family, yet she was told she had failed in this role. She was unconsciously compelled to keep trying until everyone felt happy again.

Comfort with emotional intensity is an important part of working through the issues raised through the Feelings Genogram. When someone grows up in a family that is conflict avoidant, emotional intensity can be very uncomfortable. Likewise, those who grow up in volatile families are more likely to be volatile themselves.

☐ Emotional Congruence

Much of what has been discussed up to now assumes the feeling is what it appears to be. However, feelings may also be distorted or absent. The therapist's use of self is the only way to comprehend these two situations. As the therapist listens and resonates to the clients' situations emotionally, she or he may notice a lack of affect or an affect that does not quite fit. *Empathy between therapist and client is crucial. Emotional resonance fosters self-awareness and attunement as the self-other dialectic is processed through treat-*

ment. Empathic skills can aid the therapist in exploring feelings with the client.
Asking a question about feelings is most appropriate at this time. If the
partner does not identify the feeling, the therapist may give the client
time to safely explore the question, ask questions to guide the client, or
supply the missing affect. The therapist could say, "If I were in your
place . . . "or "I can't imagine you didn't feel . . . " If the client agrees with
the emotion, the therapist knows he or she is successfully tracking the
feeling or mood of the client. Once the feeling has been identified more
exploration can be done. The therapist may want to know what it means
to feel "_____," whether the person has felt that way before, what made it
so hard to identify the feeling, and what she or he fears about expressing
it. During this exploration, the partner is kept actively involved. Obviously, one partner is sharing this information with his or her mate, and
the other partner reflects the feeling back and may be asked to discuss
how she or he deals with the feelings in question, too.

In one case, a woman became very upset and started to cry when her
partner told her he did not want her to make love to him when she was
not interested. In the early part of this relationship, the woman had frequently had sex with him when she did not feel the desire. On the surface, his statement should have made her feel accepted and respected.
However, her response was actually a distortion, because she could not
allow herself to believe him. Her father and first husband were both narcissistic individuals who were only interested in meeting their own needs.
When she started to hear her partner take care of her, she was reminded
of the emotional betrayal and abandonment of the previous men in her
life, and this reminder provoked her tears.

☐ Managing Inappropriate and Intense Affect

Just as with all other issues that emerge during the therapy hour, the
therapist has a responsibility to provide an emotionally safe environment
for both partners. When anger is being expressed through inappropriate
behaviors such as snide remarks, critical remarks, shouting, or demanding, the therapist can intervene to establish some rules about what is
appropriate behavior. The partner would then be asked to discuss the
feelings behind those behaviors in a more constructive or assertive way.
Many partners will have no idea about alternative modes of expression.
The therapist may coach the partner through or model the expression of
the feeling. The partner who is helped to express the feeling assertively
allows the other partner to reflect back this feeling. The other partner
may have equal difficulty in reflecting the feeling. They may have prob-

lems in hearing certain feelings whether they are appropriately or inappropriately expressed.

When affect is too intense, the therapist needs to cool the session down. The therapist can accomplish this task by slowing down the pace. Usually the couple heat up emotionally when they talk directly to each other. The therapist can take a much more assertive role diffusing the couple's interaction by asking the couple to address the therapist, not each other. Additionally, the therapist can ask questions that are factually oriented. Asking about who does what, in what sequence, takes the partners away from their immediate feelings and directs them to take a more detached perspective.

☐ Intensifying Affect

Conversely, if the therapist wants to intensify affect, it is essential to promote talking and to focus on the partner's implicit or explicit feelings. This technique basically involves asking a couple to enact a problem. They are directed to discuss some problem that is known to be emotionally laden. As they discuss the problem, the therapist asks the partners to talk specifically about feelings. When feelings are not expressed directly, but are detected or inferred by the therapist, the process may be interrupted so the therapist can draw out the feeling. When the feeling(s) has been sufficiently amplified, the therapist directs the couple to continue their dialogue.

In one case, a wife felt her husband's parents were too intrusive. When she brought the issue up, she made a statement that they spent too much time at their house. The therapist had her talk about how she felt, and went back and forth with the partners. Fifteen minutes later, the wife took a strong stand realizing just how distressed and resentful she was about the situation. The therapist kept encouraging her to let herself feel those feelings, which her husband said were "not true." He did not like the fact that she was resentful, but he understood the consequences of her feelings in terms of the marriage.

☐ Conclusion

The therapist has the task of controlling feelings in the session. This task involves intensifying affect where necessary, changing the mode of expression when inappropriate, and facilitating a controlled release over time when the affect would otherwise run away.

Bringing feelings into marital therapy can add a dimension of humanness and connection among all parties not experienced in other approaches. At first, it may be frightening because the couple covertly communicate their fear of feelings. Once this fear has been challenged, the couple feel stronger and the therapist experiences a unique emotional bond with them.

16
CHAPTER

with Marian Brooks, M.S.

Extending Techniques
from the Office
to Home Using Homework

The value of out-of-session behavioral tasks in marital therapy has been recognized for several decades (Sheldon & Ackerman, 1974). Interpretation, analysis, and reflection, while integral parts of individual therapy, are insufficient in and of themselves as means of implementing solutions to the day-to-day problems faced by most couples and families. According to L'Abate (1986) and Andolfi (1980) the therapist must play an active and directive role both during the clinical hour and in the delegation of assignments at home. Clients learn by doing and so need the opportunity to repeatedly practice new behaviors and to process their results in order to develop alternative, more functional attitudes, cognitions, behaviors, and feelings.

Much that has been written on the subject of homework in psychotherapy is vague and confusing. Authors contradict each other and research results are variable and limited. Tasks are often geared to the theoretical framework of the many and varied models of marital and family therapy, rather than more generally applicable. Step-by-step, how-to directives on this subject are hard to come by.

Sheldon and Ackerman (1974) were pioneers in stressing the importance of homework assignments in enhancing desired behavior change through education and skill building. Their book was individually focused and the first to design tasks to match specific difficulties. The authors

215

discussed the importance of establishing rapport between client and therapist to promote compliance and emphasized the development of a clear understanding of problems and goals. Homework, they stated, must be clear and manageable, its logic explained, and the work reviewed in the next session. When tasks were not completed, the reasons for non-compliance must be explored carefully. Clients were told what and how often to do it, to record the results, and to bring them to the next session. Sometimes the scheduling of the next appointment was contingent upon completion of the assignment. However, these assignments and tasks were addressed to the individual and his or her problem area.

Warburton and Alexander (1985) focused on the establishment of the therapist's credibility, a detailed assessment process, clarity and specificity in assigning tasks, and the utilization of methods to deal with resistance. Once again strategies and assignments were individually designed.

According to Strong and Claiborn (1982), compliance is enhanced when clients understand the rationale in following the therapist's directives, when they perceive that there is a choice in carrying out the homework, and when instructions are implicit rather than explicit. Change occurs more readily when viewed as an emergence of what is already within the individual and as growth in his or her personal power and control. The complex needs and responses of couples and families were not taken into account.

More specific to families, Aponte and Van Deusen (1981) regarded task setting as a means of redirecting dysfunctional interactional patterns in families. Such tasks were used as vehicles for establishing appropriate boundaries, alliances, and hierarchies. Minuchin (1974) also suggested a variety of restructuring interventions along similar lines. Such interventions were the outgrowth of a school of thought rather than a reflection of the unique problems and goals of each couple or family.

Bowenian therapists (Bowen, 1978) use homework to teach or coach individuals in reconstructing relationships with members of their families of origin in a healthier way in order to develop a more differentiated self. Tasks outside of sessions are designed with this goal in mind rather than simultaneously addressing couple/family interaction directly (e.g., a wife might be instructed in how to resolve an old conflict with her father that was getting reenacted with her husband).

Social learning theorists like Jacobson (1981) and Stuart (1980) proposed that the utilization of positive reinforcement, behavioral exchange contracts, problem-solving, conflict resolution, and communication training are the foundations of successful marital relationships. The importance of pretreatment assessment in the office and at home, the development of a collaborative effort, and the explanation of the treatment and its relevance to mutually agreed-upon goals were highlighted. Resistance was seen as an expression of ambivalence and as a reaction to the difficulty of change, rather than as a desire to maintain the status quo. "Inducing" a collaborative set and "skillfully implementing" treatment strategies, however, were left to the therapist's ingenuity or trial-and-error efforts. The role of the symptom, the history of each individual, the couple, the family, and the impact of other stressors are, for the most part, ignored by the behavioral therapist in designing homework assignments that address significant problems on several levels at once.

Openshaw (1998) developed a method of introducing homework early in therapy, which is more amenable to compliance. The SEA Methodology (Summarization, Empowerment, and Active involvement) utilizes therapeutic techniques to enhance homework compliance. Summarization is utilized in the therapy session to clarify direction, demonstrate understanding and maintain focus. In relation to homework, it can be used to reiterate, in an abridged fashion, the foci and key patterns developed during the session. Empowerment is used to strengthen the clients' ego (self-esteem) reinforcing the couple's joint efforts to resolve problems in the relationship. The clients' active involvement in developing the homework further insures the assignments will be successfully completed.

In contrast, a strategic marital/family therapist will often delegate homework tasks without explanation, be indirect, reframe, restrain change, and even prescribe the symptom in order to "outwit the resistance" (Weeks & L'Abate, 1982). Here, although the function of the symptom is well understood, skill building and education are underplayed.

L'Abate (1986) described the use of systematic homework assignments (SHWAs), the vehicle through which his systematic family therapy approach is actually implemented. There are two basic issues in this approach—negotiation and intimacy. These two issues are broken down still further into specific elements that are systematically organized for the family to work through at home. Writing, whether structured (e.g., programmed) or personal journaling, can be utilized for this purpose (L'Abate, 1992, 1999; Pennebaker, 1997). But working through these issues is usually not discussed openly. This process facilitates treatment and should help to reduce the time spent in the office. The literature on tasks, assignments, and homework leaves the therapist with considerable confusion about what to do and how to do it. How does he or she have directives flow from the session and from the interaction between therapist and clients? How does the therapist create a customized fit between the partners' history, capacity, and commitment to work as a unit toward desired goals and the step-by-step process used to attain these goals? Exactly how does the therapist enhance compliance, deal with resistance, and learn from failure?

☐ Types of Homework

There are basically two types of homework assignments. The first type of homework is designed to provide information that promotes awareness, challenges attitudes, and supplies the tools necessary to establish new skills. This type of homework is known as *bibliotherapy*. A number of self-help books are currently available which may be prescribed. These books should be used exclusively with those clients who are motivated to read and to discuss the material.

The second type of homework is task-oriented and is designed to change behavior. These tasks may be paradoxical or linear (Weeks & L'Abate, 1982). Paradoxical tasks are those that seem contrary to common sense and produce quantum leaps in behavior change. Linear tasks are those that change behavior in a systematic, step-wise fashion. The assumption is that behavior may be shaped slowly over a period of time, given the proper conditions and appropriate experiences. In short, the client-system changes by doing.

Examples of linear homework have been widely discussed in family therapy (Nichols, 1984). The problem is that very little has been written on how to actually give homework. Assigning homework is a complex process involving knowing how and what to suggest, being able to facilitate compliance, and dealing with resistance. One of the most common errors new therapists make is to prescribe homework because it is "the thing to do" without actually understanding the process. In these cases, the homework is usually an idea gleaned from the professional literature, or perhaps a case study, and may not be appropriate or relevant to the couple or individual being treated.

☐ Creating Homework Assignments

The content of the homework assignment should emerge organically from the session. The homework should not simply be assigned to the client at the end of a session. Creating a homework assignment is best achieved through collaboration with the client. During the session the therapist and client-system are working toward a specific (behavioral) change. The question is how to bring about the change. When the clients have a clear definition of the desired change, they can then become participants in the collaborative process of creating homework to achieve that end. The therapist asks what type of change is wanted and how the client-system envisions this change being facilitated outside the session.

The change to be created should be approached systematically. Goals must be broken down into small steps from simple to complex, from less threatening to more threatening, and from more behavioral to more affective. The homework also should be congruent with the clients' style of learning. Some clients respond best when mechanical or highly structured assignments are developed. Others need experiences that are basically unstructured and promote creative engagement.

Whatever the homework is to be, under no circumstances should an assignment be prescribed that isn't first practiced in the session. In addition, the client-system should demonstrate that it possesses the motivation and fundamental skills to continue practicing it at home.

To ask clients to perform a homework task without having first demonstrated readiness is setting the client-system up for failure. One of the purposes of homework is to provide successful experiences, which in turn promote a greater sense of accomplishment, achievement, hope, and a spirit of cooperation for those involved. It also counters the emerging sense of learned helplessness, which begins to occur after a series of perceived failures in the client-system.

The issue of commitment and responsibility is important in starting the process of carrying out the homework. The therapist needs to ask each member of the client-system to make a commitment to carry out his or her part of the work. Commitment is a critical factor in whether homework is completed and in the success of therapy generally. By asking each partner to make a personal commitment, responsibility remains clearly within each individual for his or her failure or success. In many cases, a member of the system will wait for his or her partner to initiate the homework and then blame the other for noncompliance. When discussing commitment, the therapist should include how each person deals with his or her own resistance (e.g., How will you fail to get this done in spite of your good intentions now?) and with the resistance of his or her partner.

☐ Structural Elements

The homework itself has several structural elements. These elements are time, duration, frequency, and place (T, D, F, and P). The task should be carried out at a particular time of day, protected from interference. In the session the couple should discuss when they can schedule the task and what each/both need to do to avoid any intrusions. This discussion has the effect of giving the task, hence the relationship, priority.

The duration of the task refers to how long the client-system stays engaged around the assignment. A common error is to prescribe a task that is too long or too complicated. For example, many couples cannot tolerate more than a few minutes of talking with each other. Asking a couple to talk 30 minutes to one hour is impossible for most couples in the beginning phase of therapy.

The third element is frequency, "How many times during the day/week is the assignment to be done?" Again, the therapist needs to take a conservative approach at the beginning of treatment. For example, a couple might be able to manage three, 10-minute-long circumscribed talks during a week.

The final element is place. In order to change old habits, new associations are helpful. Couples who have argued intensely in the bedroom or living room need to change location for talking. A location that is comfortable and free of distraction and old destructive associations is preferable.

At some point in the session the therapist should discuss the importance of practice and the usefulness of even small changes. Clients often overestimate the gains to be made from homework, and underestimate the effort required to make such gains. One of this author's favorite sayings is "practice, practice, and more practice." Sometimes it helps to talk about how long and how much practice is involved in learning such things as tennis, golf, proper grammar, and so on.

The therapist should point out to the clients that homework is always a no-lose proposition. If the homework is done and the outcome is good, then the goal has been achieved. If the homework is not done or a good outcome is not achieved, then more data have been obtained. Because this information was generated in a context created during the therapeutic process, it is usually easier to understand the factors contributing to success or failure. In a sense, homework is an experiment. Regardless of the results, everyone learns something.

At the end of the session, the assignment should be repeated to make sure everyone is clear about what is to be done. Some clients benefit by taking notes. The therapist should also record the assignment in detail in order to follow up at the next session. The therapist will communicate disinterest in the homework by forgetting it altogether or by failing to follow up at the beginning of the next session. If the homework is done, whether successfully or unsuccessfully, the client-system should be praised. It is natural to praise clients who are successful. Clients who attempt but fail can still be commended for their effort and for taking responsibility (making sure that the therapist's comments are devoid of real or implied sarcasm). Then, the entire experience is evaluated in order to extract as much information as possible about the positive and negative outcome.

In the case of a successful experience, another assignment is then created which builds on the first. A failed assignment may be reassigned once obstacles have been examined and removed or a different assignment may be developed. The processing of resistance will be more fully addressed in the last section of this chapter.

☐ Examples of Homework Assignments

The tasks that follow, when properly selected and delivered to couples in treatment, can address problems on several different levels simultaneously.

1. Communication is one of the most common problems couples bring to therapists. Having each member of a couple talk for five minutes about himself or herself on a nonconflictual topic while his or her partner simply listens and reflects is an effective task for building the foundation of empathetic listening and constructive problem solving. The couple need to set aside ten minutes (five for each partner) free from distraction several times a week to practice this skill. They first perform this task during the therapy hour so that the clinician can coach the couple through the process. The clients decide how often, when, where, and how long they can realistically complete this assignment, and whether or not it addresses their target areas for change. They discuss what might interfere with task completion.

   The performance of the task requires some (albeit short) period of time when the relationship is a priority, promotes some level of intimacy, and decreases the amount of projection between the pair. It may realign hierarchies and detriangulate unhealthy alliances. Task performance can be diagnostic of the nature of the commitment between partners and to the therapeutic process. If the assignment is completed successfully, the therapist explores in detail feelings, thoughts, and behaviors and builds upon the earlier foundation with the clients' input. However, if the task has failed in some way, or has not even been attempted, the task may be repeated, perhaps in smaller steps or redesigned. The couple are asked what would enable them to carry out the assignment and what concerns they might have if the exercise, in fact, leads to the solution of the problem.

2. Having each member of a couple complete and share a genogram assists partners in learning how the patterns of the past are being acted out in their current struggles with each other in the present (DeMaria, Weeks, & Hof, 1999). Awareness of one's own and one's partner's history promotes greater empathy and less reactivity as well as the possibilities of alternative ways of perceiving, feeling, and acting in a given situation. For example, knowledge about a parent's lack of concern for a child, now an adult, can help that person and his or her spouse understand the confusing desire for and yet the rejection of affection

and approval. As a result, the ambivalent behavior feels somewhat less like a personal affront to the person on the receiving end of the anger and hurt.

Furthermore, discussion allows for less realistic expectations on the part of the person who unconsciously yearns for his or her partner to make up for all the wounds of the past. The task addresses the issues of expectations and communication on psychodynamic, cognitive, and affective levels. It brings the past into the present in a useful way. In sessions, the clinician guides the couple through the process, taking detours where necessary, but directing them back to the main highway. Between office visits, clients are instructed to gather information about parents, grandparents, aunts, uncles, and other relatives, setting in motion the process of change in perception, feelings, and patterns of behavior with individuals outside of but influencing the couple dyad.

3. Suggesting that couples spend the week noticing the positives in the relationship and in each other can reverse the negative momentum, which has probably been escalating for some time prior to treatment. Each partner is instructed not to discuss the findings but to bring a list to the next session. If the task has been completed, clients build on and process its success. If not, the assignment may be repeated or altered. Impediments to progress are removed and fears about success examined.

☐ Promoting Compliance to Homework

Strong and Claiborn (1982) discussed three principles that are useful in increasing spontaneous compliance. These principles should be particularly useful when resistance is high and the clients do not believe they have control over their behavior. The first principle is choice. It is important to give the prescription in such a way that the client perceives choice in how to respond. Common techniques include asking the client to think of alternatives, asking focused questions that lead the client in certain directions, and providing latitude for what the client does. The use of language is important in creating a sense of choice. The therapist should avoid terms that have a polarizing and/or pejorative effect. Absolutes such as right versus wrong, good versus bad, sane versus crazy, and truth versus fabrication need to be avoided. These terms imply that the client and therapist know the "facts" of a situation, facts that represent an immutable reality and demand certain consequences.

Language suggests choice by implying a sense that reality is something that happens interactionally and may be interpreted differently. The therapist can communicate this concept by talking about perceptions, opinions, beliefs, and appearances. The therapist can discuss what will "work," "be useful," "be productive," and "fit," rather than be the "right or perfect" solution, which implies no room for alternatives.

When labeling extrasession prescriptions, language is even more important. Consider what happens when the word "homework" is used with a school dropout or with someone who feels homework was a forced behavior in school. This term stimulates resistance immediately and thus suggests an attempt on the part of the therapist to force compliance. On the other hand, consider the person who believes that homework is an efficient way to learn. Many teachers and professionals, for example, may view the idea of homework as quite practical. They are anxious to comply with the task. Extrasession labeling and prescriptions must be congruent with the client's perception of how change occurs. These extrasession tasks may be called "prescriptions," "homework," "tasks," "assignments," "chores," "experiences," "exercises," "experiments," and so on. The prescriptions may be given with more or less structure, more or less input from the client, and more or less flexibility.

The second principle that can be used to increase compliance and attribution of change to self is called personalism. Personalism refers to the idea of not stating the homework in a way that makes the clients feel coerced. Clients are more likely to feel coerced when they believe they are being personally directed (i.e., commanded or demanded) by the therapist. The therapist can avoid this problem by talking about the action needed to respond to the situation. The therapist might say, "This problem requires that you . . . " or "Part of the treatment for this problem involves_____ doing _____ at home." The therapist can also avoid this problem by softening statements such as, "I know" to "I think," "You're wrong about that" to "Let's take a look at what was just said," and "You should do . . . " to "It seems one choice is . . . ."

When giving a prescription, the therapist can emphasize the need to do certain things as a function of the situation. For example, when a couple begin treatment with a power struggle in the relationship, each partner perceives that the other is trying to force him or her to be a certain way or to do certain things. If the therapist then says they "must" do certain homework tasks, the pattern will be replicated with the therapist attempting to take control. In order to avoid a power struggle with a client-system, the locus of power must be shifted away from individual members and the therapist.

Contracting approaches accomplish this goal by shifting the power to the contract. The contract diffuses this power struggle by placing control in the mutually developed contract. By giving control to a mutually agreed upon contract, the partners believe they created control for themselves.

An "external" system is now in control. Many systems of therapy rely on this principle. The therapist is seen as implementing a program, system, technique, and so on—not as imposing his or her own will on the client.

The degree of implicitness versus explicitness is the third principle. An implicit prescription produces greater compliance and self-attribution. An example of an implicit form of prescription is the Rogerian technique of reflective listening. Although it may appear that the therapist is exercising little control with this technique, the content of the material reflected back to the client and the way in which the material is reflected is indeed a form of control, albeit indirect.

In summary, the therapist does not want to increase the resistance of the client because this condition will be perceived as an attempt at forced compliance. The resistance of the client will be reduced if the client's sense of freedom is enhanced (e.g., the therapist offers several alternatives), and the degree of threat is reduced (e.g., the therapist accepts the client's pace).

☐ Resistance to Homework

Homework compliance is a good predictor of commitment to change. When homework is not performed or is not successful, three strategies may be employed. The first is to process the homework in order to make explicit the forces that sabotaged it. The reasons are often varied. In some cases, one partner does not believe the other will change so he or she does not follow through. In other cases, one partner will be feeling so resentful or angry that failure is certain. Explanations may reside in the individual, in the interactional system, or in the intergenerational system (Weeks, 1989b). The exploration of the meaning of change to the system may then free the client(s) to move forward. L'Abate (1975) has also developed a method of dealing with resistance that may be useful with many couples. This method is a structured program on confronting change, which focuses the system on the meaning of change for them and how this meaning prevents the change from occurring.

When attempts at homework have failed repeatedly and the in-office sessions are stalled, it might be an appropriate time to try some paradoxical techniques (Weeks & L'Abate, 1982). The first strategy to be used is what Weeks and L'Abate (1982) call negative consequences of change. This involves asking the client-system to describe what kinds of negative consequences would result from making the kinds of changes that have been stated as desirable. The therapist then poses each positive change from the clients' perspective in a negative light.

For example, conflict resolution homework might have been given to a couple. When their work fails, the couple would be asked to describe what would be negative about not fighting. The client(s) would probably say they would just "feel better," which is not really a response to the question. The therapist would challenge this statement with a rebuttal. For example, he or she might say, "It seems the only way to be close is to fight. Without it there might be nothing between you. Being really close might be too threatening for both of you at an unconscious level." The point of this strategy is to get the client(s) to resist not changing by pointing out the danger and in extreme cases the impossibility of change.

The second strategy is to shift to other paradoxical techniques, such as symptom prescription and restraint (Weeks & L'Abate, 1982). These strategies are specifically designed to turn resistance against itself and are beyond the scope of this book. They have been described extensively elsewhere (Weeks, 1991; Weeks & L'Abate, 1982).

☐ Conclusion

The change that is discussed and practiced in the session must extend beyond the therapist's office. In order to facilitate this change, the therapist may choose to assign homework. Homework involves doing something on a prescribed basis that is systematically laid out and designed to achieve a particular therapeutic goal. Homework assignments should grow from the sessions in an organic fashion. Many examples of homework can be found in the literature, but it works best to develop assignments that are tailored for each couple and developed collaboratively. Given this fact, standard assignments are usually not indicated. We may use other assignments as guides, but should not be limited by them. Giving homework is a therapeutic skill just like any other. Knowledge and experience combine to contribute to more effective, successful, and appropriately timed experiences for the couple.

17

Treating the Extramarital Affair

Very few issues in couples therapy are as vexing and as emotionally laden as treating affairs. When a couple presents this issue in therapy, it is almost always with considerable emotional turmoil. In fact, it is one of the most charged experiences in couples therapy and has the potential for tremendously destructive emotional, marital, familial, and financial consequences. On the other hand, if the couple is committed to working together, an affair can be a turning point for an individual and a couple, offering the prospect of new growth, understanding, and commitment.

While we are all aware of the feelings generated by the couple when an affair has taken place, we often overlook the feelings engendered in the therapist who is treating the couple. The senior author once conducted a week-long training in couples therapy. The fifth day contained the training unit on affairs. On the fourth day, he noticed the participants were becoming anxious and beginning to ask questions regarding the content of the fifth day. When the group was asked to discuss how they were feeling, almost all expressed concern that we would not have enough time to cover affairs and many expressed concern over how they had been dealing with this issue with their clients.

For clarification purposes, the following identifiers will be used in this chapter:

Affair partner – client having the affair
Betrayed partner – client not having the affair
Extramarital partner – individual with whom client is having the affair

226

☐ Dilemmas for the Therapist

For most therapeutic issues, the therapist is concerned about which technique or strategy will produce the best result. Treating extramarital affairs raises other concerns and anxieties in the therapist that are unique in treating this problem. Two of the most common issues raised are countertransference and ethical questions over confidentiality and effective management with so much at stake. In the references cited throughout this article, not one author mentioned countertransferential issues. Of course, this concept is anti-theoretical for many in the systems field anyway and it should be no surprise that it is absent in the extramarital literature. Unfortunately, no empirically based studies have been conducted regarding therapists' reactions and feelings in this area. Our experience in supervising hundreds of therapists over the years and in observing the attitudes of others has shown us that therapists bring a variety of attitudes about what affairs mean and how to treat clients. Attitudes range from permissive (even encouraging) to moralistic and judgmental.

In all likelihood, these attitudes do not have any professional grounding, but represent the life experiences of the therapist. For example, one seasoned therapist would encourage women to have an affair in order to test their commitment and feelings for their husbands. If this therapist's female client were already involved in an affair, she would presume it was because the extramarital partner was more suitable for the client than the spouse, thereby supporting the client's wish to leave the spouse to be with the extramarital partner. Obviously, this therapist is overlooking the numerous factors that can contribute to engaging in an extramarital affair such as conflicts arising within the individual client. Not incidentally, this therapist had divorced her first husband (an alcoholic) only after becoming involved in an affair. Clearly, in the therapeutic setting, the therapist unconsciously superimposed her experience on her clients. In effect, this therapist attempted to justify her personal choices through an over-identification with her clients. At the other extreme are those therapists who take a moralistic and judgmental stance toward the affair partner. They tend to assume these partners have done irreparable damage and should be punished by losing the relationship. They assume the marriage is beyond repair and their task is to help the betrayed partner leave. Through our supervisory experiences, we have noted that some of these therapists have strong religious convictions and others have experienced hurtful divorces in their own marriages and in those of their parents. In either example, the therapist reached a conclusion that circumvented the task of assessing the many factors that contributed to the affair. Also, working on the relationship was overlooked as a therapeutic option. We suggest that every therapist examine his or her attitudes about affairs in order to avoid getting caught in the emotional web of their own countertransferences. There are several common situations that evoke strong feelings in the therapist.

Affairs can "sneak up" on us. In many cases, the therapist has worked with a couple for several weeks or months before an affair is discovered or revealed. When such an event occurs, the therapist may also feel betrayed and foolish for not being able to see through the deception. When the clients keep this information from the therapist, strong negative feelings may develop toward the affair partner. The therapist will need to process these feelings with the clients, but also keep them under control and in perspective. The default assumption is that virtually everyone lies about having an affair initially, whether it is deception directed toward the betrayed partner or the therapist. The therapist must maintain a detached personal attitude about this deception and deal with it therapeutically. The therapist needs to be vigilant when assessing the relationship, looking for signs that might reveal the presence of a hidden affair. In addition, the therapist may be afforded an opportunity to model for the betrayed partner how to deal with the revelation of such information.

Affairs tend to place therapists in an emotional bind in more ways than one. First, the affair requires *immediate* confrontation. Many clients will try to minimize the impact an affair has had or is having on their relationship. The couple will argue that if the therapist can improve their marriage, the affair will stop. Unfortunately, the betrayed partner sometimes "goes along with" this idea hoping to save the marriage without confronting the fact that an affair has happened or is happening. Our experience has taught us that no real or lasting change can occur in a couple as long as an affair is occurring. Some couples will give the appearance of change, offering hope to the therapist, but will then relapse into the same patterns. Sometimes the couple will want to work on all kinds of other issues before approaching the affair. *The therapist cannot ignore the affair.* It takes priority over all other issues. We are asserting that the therapist may need to take control of the therapy and be clear about the need to deal with the affair first. This tactic may make the therapist uncomfortable because of the control taken and anxious over whether the clients might terminate treatment. Nonetheless, most clients will appreciate the forthrightness of the therapist's position and understand the need to talk about the affair before taking on other relationship issues. For those who reject the therapist's position, we believe that since no change can occur unless the affair is addressed, termination of therapy is an appropriate course of action. It is almost always the affair partner who rejects dealing with the affair first. In such cases, the betrayed partner might be offered individual treatment so that he or she can decide on their own course of action. The strategies for confronting the affair are covered later in this chapter.

The most ethically problematic and anxiety provoking aspect of dealing with affairs has to do with the problem of confidentiality. Information about affairs may be revealed in a myriad of ways. Ideally, the couple begins therapy with an admission of what has happened or is happening. However, in many cases, the affair is revealed or discovered during the course of therapy. What happens when just one partner reveals this information to the therapist? What happens if the therapist sees one of the partners on the street with someone other than his or her partner and it is clear they are acting physically inappropriate? What happens if a friend of the couple or another client reveals this information?

Karpel (1980) has offered some useful guidelines about establishing the rules of confidentiality. Before discussing his concepts, it is essential for the therapist to set up the guidelines for confidentiality in the first session. Without a clear understanding of the rules of confidentiality, the therapist may be placed in a position that interferes with effectiveness, thereby preventing the therapist from helping the couple. For instance, the therapist may find that he or she has information and does not know how to deal with it or feels uncomfortable with the information because of the assumption that *all* information revealed to the therapist must be kept confidential (the default position). This position renders the therapist innefective and powerless.

Karpel's (1980) work on therapeutic confidentiality suggests the therapist may take one of three positions. The first is the classic position of keeping *all* information confidential. In other words, any information gained outside the conjoint sessions is considered confidential. Thus, if partners are seen separately and one of the partners admits to an affair, the therapist would be obligated to maintain that client's confidence. The second, opposite, position is that all information received regarding the couple is open for discussion. Whatever one partner says in private is considered the same as if it were said to the other partner; this position assumes there are *no* secrets and ensures secrets will and should be revealed. The third position the therapist may take calls for both accountability and discretion. Our interpretation of this principle is that the therapist will agree to maintain information in confidence, but will, at the same time, require that each partner assume responsibility for any behavior which might impede the therapy such as an addiction, individual issues, affairs, etc. Accountability involves the partner in question being honest with the therapist and earnestly working on changing the behavior in question. Typically, when a partner is having an affair and is unable or unwilling to discuss it with his or her partner, he or she is encouraged to admit to being "unsure about commitment to the marriage" if he or she cannot admit to the affair. This kind of announcement to the partner enables the therapist to temporarily interrupt conjoint sessions while the individual client decides what to do about the affair. The couple will then continue via individual sessions with another therapist or the couple's therapist. In cases of extramarital affairs, we prefer that each partner work with the same couple's therapist in individual sessions. This strategy allows the therapist to stay fully informed. If the change in format creates suspicion in the partner who has not been told about the affair, the couple is encouraged to discuss their concerns together. This approach creates pressure for the person having the affair to assume responsibility rather than keep a secret from the partner. Furthermore, the therapist is not colluding with one partner in conjoint sessions by protecting the secret, thereby triangulating the unknowing partner. The onus of responsibility is on the affair partner to decide about his or her commitment to the relationship. This third approach will be discussed in greater detail later.

The position we take in working with couples is the third one mentioned above: discretion and accountability. The first two positions are simple and the therapist ostensibly does not get caught in any binds nor does the therapist have to experience any anxiety or dissonance over carrying a secret. Our experience has been that less experienced couples therapists prefer the first two positions because of their simplicity and the comfort level they afford the therapist. Unfortunately, when the first position is adopted, the therapist may have knowledge of an affair but his or her hands are tied. The therapist is without maneuvering room: She or he must pretend not to have this information or find some way to terminate therapy. With the second position, all information is shared. This has a chilling effect on revealing a secret affair. The therapist may operate in the dark not knowing what is actually happening. After several months of treatment, it sometimes becomes apparent that some secret must be in the system due to a lack of change without apparent reason. In the third approach, accountability and discretion, rules of confidentiality give the therapist access to the most information and create some room for the therapist to maneuver. The therapist has an opportunity to intervene with the affair partner in order to try to stop the affair or at the very least expose what is happening indirectly.

The third option is the most complex and produces the most discomfort in the therapist. As we stated, the rules of confidentiality must be stated in the first session and clearly defined. The couple should be allowed to process this idea so they fully understand the concept. Suppose this rule is in place and one member (or both members) of the couple reveal a past or present affair to the therapist. In either case, the therapist would want to spend time with that partner(s) discussing the affair. When there is an ongoing affair, the affair partner should be given the following information:

1. The therapist will not divulge this information, but expects accountability.
2. Accountability means taking responsibility for the affair by understanding why it is occurring and by stopping it.
3. The affair partner should be told quite clearly than an active affair will impede any progress being made in the couples therapy and if it is their intension to work on the marriage, the affair must stop quickly.
4, The affair partner is told that he or she is not expected to stop the affair immediately, but should be prepared to do so within no more than four weeks from the session.
5. If the affair partner is unwilling to stop the affair, then the therapist suggests that he or she is not really motivated to work on the marriage. The affair partner is given the options of informing the betrayed partner about the affair and/or discussing divorce, or informing the betrayed partner that he or she has a personal issue which will not permit couples therapy to move forward at that time. The affair partner is informed that if he or she does not choose one of these options, the therapist will tell the betrayed partner that couples therapy cannot proceed because of a personal issue the affair partner revealed in the individual session. In our experience, it is rare for a client to be unwilling to stop the affair. However, Humphrey (1985) found that 24% of husbands and 23% of wives were still involved in an affair at the end of a course of brief therapy. He does not mention what type of treatment was provided nor does he suggest any individual sessions were held to help the affair partner break the bond with the extramarital partner. The therapist tells the couple that due to the rules of confidentiality, this information will be kept in confidence, and that it is their responsibility to arrive at some understanding as to why termination of couples therapy occurred. At this point, the betrayed partner will be thinking about all the possible reasons the other partner cannot proceed with couples therapy. He or she knows there is a secret and begins to investigate more vigorously the nature of this secret. Although this situation has been rare in our experience, partners have no trouble ascertaining a third party must be involved. This suspicion leads to a confrontation and in all but one case we can recall, an admission of the truth.
6. The therapist recommends that each partner seek individual therapy in the hope that some individual movement can be made that will enable them to return to couples therapy.

This rule of confidentiality has worked in all of our cases. The fear that many therapists have expressed is that the betrayed partner will be angry with the therapist for keeping the secret. In fact, it is our experience that the betrayed partner typically understands the agreement and is appropriately angry with the affair partner, not the therapist for keeping the secret. Oftentimes, the client has felt bad that the therapist was caught in the middle or caught up in the affair partner's deception. Fortunately, most couples that come to therapy do want to improve the marriage or save it. Because they are motivated by this goal, each partner is usually willing to do what is required to make the couples therapy work for them. The affair partner is then seen for several sessions in order to help him or her understand why the affair began and learn how to stop it. In addition, the betrayed partner might require some individual work in order to deal with the intense emotions he or she experiences when the affair is revealed. Treating the individual partner is a therapeutic issue that will be described later in this chapter in the treatment section.

☐ Definition and Prevalence

One of the earliest writers to grapple with the definition of an extramarital affair was Thompson (1983). According to him, "extramarital sex is defined as genital sexual involvement outside the marriage without express knowledge or consent of one's partner . . . An extramarital crisis occurs for many married couples when the uninformed partner becomes aware of the extramarital involvement" (p. 240). The advantage of this definition is that it is fairly easy to behaviorally ascertain whether an affair has occurred or not. Of course, there are those who believe that certain acts such as oral-genital sex are functionally the same as a handshake and do not count as extramarital involvement. Unfortunately, a definition as simple as Thompson's still presents many problems for the clinician and the couple in treatment. As we just mentioned, one partner may try to redefine what genital involvement means stating that if there was no intercourse, oral-genital sex, mutual masturbation, or fondling, then there was no affair.

Another issue is whether the betrayed partner really knew about the affair. Charny and Parnass (1995) surveyed therapists who had extensive experience in treating affairs and found that most therapists believed the spouse knew the "secret" affair was occurring and was in collusion with it's continuation. They stated, "even the majority of the betrayed spouses who claimed consciously that they opposed their spouses' behavior were unconsciously in collusion with them" (p. 100). The respondents believed that only 10% of the spouses were genuinely and actively opposed to their mate's affair. Many partners wish to deny the existence of an affair because of the emotional, marital, familial, and economic consequence that might follow if the issue was confronted. Those partners who "know but choose not to know" represent an interesting problem as far as the definition goes. If a partner has given implicit approval for the affair, does it invalidate the concept that an affair has actually occurred?

Another problem obviously has to do with what have been called emotional affairs. Glass and Wright (1992) attempted to correct the shortcomings of Thompson's (1983) definition by offering three categories of affairs: primarily sexual, primarily emotional, and a combined-type (emotional and sexual). These categories make sense from an intuitive and clinical perspective, but again it is difficult to operationalize the types. The most difficult type of affair to define would be the emotional affair characterized by a great deal of emotional intimacy and a strong sense of commitment. In our practice, these affairs are characterized by: 1) considerable emotional sharing; 2) sharing thoughts and feelings which are not revealed to one's partner; 3) a strong urge to spend time with the extramarital partner; 4) maintaining secrecy around the relationship; and 5) a sense in the betrayed partner that a line or boundary has been crossed in which matters that are private to the couple are discussed with the extramarital partner. Couples do draw different lines regarding these criteria that are sometimes quite different from the lines the therapist might draw. For example, if a man has a close female friend with whom he spends time and shares feelings, does that automatically mean that relationship is an affair? Some wives would feel this kind of friendship is inappropriate and would demonstrate considerable jealousy. At the extreme are exceptionally jealous partners who believe that if their partner looks at or has a brief conversation with an opposite sex individual it is the same as an affair. At the other end of the spectrum from Thompson (1983) is a definition offered by Don-David Lusterman (1998). He states, "once a committed relationship is established, if there is a secret sexual and/or romantic involvement outside of the relationship, it is experienced as an infidelity" (p. 186). This definition stresses commitment and secrecy rather than passion and intimacy.

Having a definition that can be operationalized is more important to researchers than clinicians. As clinicians, we must deal with ambiguity on a daily basis. In most cases, it is not difficult to tell when a relationship has become inappropriate. In fact, once the discussion begins most couples do not quibble over definition, but agree that something was inappropriate. This is not to suggest partners do not deceive or deny that an affair has or is occurring. Once the admission has been made that "something happened," it is usually with the idea that it was inappropriate.

Finally, the term *extramarital sex* fails to capture the problems encountered by those partners who are in a committed dating relationship. Many unmarried couples present for treatment with the same issue. One partner had assumed there would be fidelity only to discover the other partner had gone outside the relationship.

The prevalence of extramarital affairs is difficult to determine because affairs are almost always concealed. Even though researchers promise confidentiality, some subjects are reluctant to reveal their affairs. Some studies have utilized methodologies that would suppress reporting of such data. Kinsey, Pomeroy, and Martin (1948) and Kinsey, Pomeroy, Martin, and Gebhard (1953) reported that an estimated 50% of husbands and 26% of wives had had an extramarital relationship during the course of their marriage. Many other researchers have examined the frequency of affairs and found the following:

- 40% for men and 36% for women (Athanasious, Shaver, & Travis, 1970)
- 20% for men and 10% for women (Johnson, 1970)
- 41% for men and 18% for women (Hunt, 1974)
- 47% for men (Yablonsky, 1979)
- 32% for women (Maykovich, 1976)

Two recent large-scale studies utilizing sophisticated sampling techniques and data collection deserve special attention. The 1993 National Opinion Research Center conducted a study with approximately 1,200 respondents. On average, about 15% of married or ever married individuals reported having had an extramarital affair. When broken down by sex, the percentages were 21% for men and 12% for women. Wiederman (1997) analyzed data from the General Social Survey conducted in 1994. This sample consisted of over 2,000 respondents. He found that 22.7% of men reported an affair compared to 11.6% for women. Additionally, he found that for the members of the sample under 40 years of age, there was no difference in the incidence of affairs. The incidence for affairs tended to increase for men as they age (at least up to age 70), whereas for women the highest incidence was between 30-50. For example, 34% of men in the 60–69 year age group reported having had an affair compared to 7.6% for women.

In addition to the statistics mentioned above, a few other studies help us understand the frequency and nature of affairs. Thompson (1984) found 43% of the subjects in his study had been involved in one of the three types of affairs mentioned earlier. Primarily sexual affairs were reported by 21% of the subjects, with men being more likely to be involved in sexual affairs and women more likely to be involved in emotional affairs. One item of information that is missing from all these studies is the duration of the affairs, particularly protracted affairs.

Finally, it is important to have some understanding of the prevalence of extramarital affairs in those couples seeking treatment. Humphrey and

Strong (1976) did a survey of clinical members of the American Association of Marriage and Family Therapy. The therapists reported that 46% of the couples coming for help reported an affair in their marriage. A replication of this study in 1984 showed higher rates with some therapists reporting that the majority of their caseload has experienced an affair (Humphrey, 1985).

☐ Dimensions of Extramarital Affairs

Defining the term extramarital affair has been shown to be a difficult matter. Not all affairs are alike and are presented in many different variations. Assessing an affair presupposes an understanding of the various dimensions in which an affair may be presented. Several authors have attempted to identify these various dimensions and their ideas have considerable overlap (Westfall, 1989, 1995; Humphrey, 1987). The therapist should consider the following dimensions of affairs and assess these during the evaluation phase of treatment.

1. *The frequency, duration, and location of the affair.* Some affairs are one-night stands only. Many of the clients we have seen have had just one sexual encounter, sometimes with a prostitute, and became frightened by what they had done. Other individuals have had sex frequently or have had frequent contacts with the extramarital partner. Duration is an extremely important factor. Just how long did the affair last? Was it a week or two decades? The dynamics involved in these situations would be very different. Long-term affairs tend to stabilize a relationship that is not working and are very difficult to stop. The attachment between the affair partners has grown strong to the point the affair partner cannot choose between partners. The third element is the location of the affair. If an affair occurred in a person's home (i.e., in the bedroom), the symbolic meaning for the betrayed partner is quite significant. Partners will sometimes comment angrily, "How could you have sex in our bed with him/her?" Sometimes affairs occur in a motel/hotel or in a person's office. In one recent and unusual case, the affair was primarily emotional with a lot of sexual talk and was conducted almost entirely by voice-mail. Each person had such a busy schedule that they would exchange up to 60 short messages a day between meeting with their clients. They were also reluctant to enter into a sexual affair, fearing people would find out and their careers would suffer. The Internet is another place where more and more people are meeting for emotional and "cybersex" affairs.

2. *Number of past and present sexual partners.* The day the author was writing this particular section of the chapter, it was reported that a recently deceased basketball player claimed to have had several thousand sexual partners. One client of this author reported he had 150 partners prior to marriage and 150 after his marriage. Partners who report large numbers of sexual partners should be evaluated for a sexual or love addiction. For the non-addicted individuals who report only a few extramarital partners, their need for other partners should be explored. This need will be discussed further in the section on treatment.

3. *The gender of the affair partner.* We usually think of an affair as involving a person of the opposite sex. Sometimes affairs are with members of the same sex. In some cases, this fact indicates that the partner is gay but living in a heterosexual relationship. In other cases, it represents having explored a curiosity. One case involved a man who had an affair with another man because they both shared an interest in cross-dressing. The affair provided validation for his transvestism, a particular type of fetishistic behavior.

4. *The level of the sexual activity.* Sexual activity can occur along a continuum from verbal or written exchanges to intercourse for the purpose of impregnation. The therapist will want some idea about the actual behaviors that were experienced. It could range from a lap dance in a public bar to sexual intercourse in the back seat of one's car behind a nightclub.

5. *Whether the affair(s) were unilateral or bilateral.* For most couples, the affair has involved just one partner. In other couples, both partners have had affairs. It is uncommon to find that when couples present for treatment they are both in an affair. However, the history may reveal that each one has had one or more affairs. It is also important to determine whether an affair may have been retaliation against the other partner's affair. One client, for example, discovered her husband was once again having an affair with one of his secretaries and it had become common knowledge at the office. She responded by having an affair of her own which involved a public tour through Europe with a man. On another occasion, she responded to one of his affairs by flagging a ride with a truck driver on an interstate highway and having sex with him. This particular couple happened to consist of a narcissistic husband and a histrionic wife.

6. *The degree of emotional involvement and attachment.* This is a critical factor. Glass and Wright (1992) found that men tend to have affairs more for sexual reasons and women more for reasons of emotional involvement. Women are more likely to link sex and love while men are better able to keep the two separate. Therefore, it is useful to

explore the level of emotional sharing which has occurred and how attached the partners feel toward each other. A one-night stand at a convention or sex with a prostitute does not usually represent much emotional involvement when compared to a long-term affair with frequent contacts.

7. *Each partner's relationship to the extramarital partner.* This relationship affects the affair's impact on the couple. Generally speaking, it is easier for a couple to handle an affair when the extramarital partner is someone the betrayed partner does not know. Unfortunately, many affairs involve persons who are close to both partners such as a friend, family member, or fellow church members. When the extramarital partner falls into one of these categories, the other partner's sense of betrayal is much greater—it is a double betrayal. One husband, for example, came home early from work one day to find another man in his bedroom with his wife. It turned out he was the cantor in his synagogue. The husband was a deeply religious man who attended services on a regular basis and considered this man a friend and religious mentor. The affair shook his trust in both his wife and marriage and in his faith.

8. *The degree of secrecy, lies, and deception around the affair.* A continuum of secrecy, lies, and deception may surround the affair and impact the ability to restore trust. Some partners will admit to having had or even thinking about an affair. For the most part, partners will deny it until they are confronted. Those affairs which have a long history (several weeks to months) usually involved considerable deception. The person having the affair must keep compounding his or her lies in order to maintain the secrecy. This pattern of deception creates an overlay on the affair. The betrayed partner is upset about the affair and also upset over the fact that his or her partner deliberately and consistently lied to them in order to protect the affair. Such behavior is severely and catastrophically related to a loss of trust that may be impossible to rebuild.

9. *The degree of implicit approval or consent by the betrayed partner.* Without question, most partners strongly disapprove of affairs when asked or confronted with the reality that it is happening. However, the research of Charny and Parnass (1995) mentioned earlier, suggests there are situations when spouses often collude in allowing this behavior to continue without confrontation. There are also some couples that clearly know about the affair and state that it is acceptable. There are usually conditions to these affairs such as being told about an affair before it happens, being assured that it is for sex only, and keeping the affair discrete. Many years ago when open marriage was popular, couples would swing with other couples provided everything was

out in the open. In a sense, the partners gave each other permission to have sex with others and sometimes participated in a group sex experience. In today's culture, this activity is much less popular and has gone underground. An Internet search will show that some cities still have clubs devoted to swinging as the movement lives on. These couples may come to therapy when one partner is consistently breaking the rules they have agreed to or when one feels threatened that an emotional involvement is taking place. We suspect that a small percentage of couples tolerate each other's affairs in order to preserve the appearance of a marriage and for financial reasons. One woman who was married to a famous and wealthy man said she did not mind his affairs as long as he was discreet. They came to therapy because he broke the rule and had an affair with an employee that became public knowledge. His relationship resulted in her losing face in the community and she was insisting he terminate the relationship immediately. She admitted that her marriage had been dead for many years, but she liked the wealth and the social position she received from being married to such a well-known person.

10. *The tolerance for an extramarital affair within the couple's social group, community, ethnic/cultural group, and religious affiliation.* Each one of these factors plays a role in how the partners perceive and deal with the affair. Some couples, for example, belong to sexually permissive social groups such as swinging clubs. Affairs are tolerated and even accepted to the extent they conform to the norms of the group. The group may operate autonomously in terms of the greater community or culture. While all religious communities sanction marriage and disapprove of affairs, some groups exhibit less tolerance than other. Fundamentalists tend to take a firm position equating the act with sin and shunning the sinner. Penn, Hernandez, and Bermudez (1997) are some of just a few researchers to describe infidelity from a religious (specifically Catholicism, Eastern Philosophy, Islam, and Protestantism) and ethnic (African-American, Hispanic, and Asian-American) perspective. The clinicians need to assess the affair within each of these contexts keeping in mind that partners will sometimes have different interpretations of their cultural norms. One couple who had immigrated to the United States from the Middle East presented for therapy due to the husband's affair. The husband claimed it was his right to have an affair and that it was extremely common in his culture. His wife strongly disagreed. The therapist suggested they both seek help from a senior family member or clergy person for help in understanding whether this behavior was acceptable in their culture. They did in fact seek out an elder in the family who explained that such behavior did occur, but was neither common nor acceptable.

Apparently, the husband was trying to use his culture to justify his behavior and hoped the therapist might be uninformed enough to accept this claim.

☐ Marital and Emotional Consequences of an Affair

An affair is a very serious event in the life of a marriage. The consequences generally fall into two categories. The first is the potential the affair has for dissolving the marriage and the second is the emotional impact on the marriage. Divorce is one of the most common outcomes of an affair. Betzig (1989) conducted an ethnographic study of 160 cultures and found that infidelity was the most common reason for divorce given across cultures. Divorce studies in Western culture have shown that between 25–50% of couples that divorce state infidelity was the primary reason (Hunt, 1974; E. Kelly & Conley, 1987; Levinger, 1976). Humphrey (1987) examined the divorce and separation rates for couples during and after therapy. He found that when the husband had the affair the divorce rate was 10% and when the wife had the affair the rate was 17%. Additionally, when the husband had the affair 45% of couples separated and when the wife had the affair 31% separated. It would appear that many of those who separated would eventually divorce. Unfortunately, Humphrey was not able to track these clients long enough to determine the eventual outcome. He conducted the same study in 1976 and found the divorce rates were higher, which suggests more tolerance of affairs in the mid-1980s.

A survey of couples therapists also showed that affairs are one of the most damaging events in the life of a marriage. Affairs ranked second in negative impact after physical abuse (Whisman, Dixon, & Johnson, 1997). The same researchers asked therapists to rank couples' problems in terms of the difficulty of treatment. Ranked first in the level of treatment difficulty was a lack of loving feelings with alcoholism second and affairs third.

Charny and Parnass (1995) surveyed 62 therapists who had an intimate knowledge of at least one affair in their caseload. In those couples presenting with an affair, 34% of these marriages ended in divorce primarily due to the affair. The researchers were also interested in those marriages that were preserved following an affair. Of the 43.5% of marriages that continued, the overall atmosphere was dysphoric or negative. Another 6% reported the marriages appeared empty and the couple was not hopeful about the future.

Only a small fraction of the couples (9%), were characterized by improvement and growth and many of those in this category had experienced a one-time affair. Humphrey (1987) reported that 26% of husbands and 21% of wives were improved at the end of treatment even though treatment only averaged about 10 sessions. As grim as these statistics appear to be, the researchers did not address the issue of treatment longevity or type of treatment provided. Thus, we do not know whether treatment lasted only a few sessions, as is common in these studies or what type of therapy was provided.

The emotional impact of an affair can be devastating. The therapists in Charny and Parnass' (1995) study observed injuries to self-esteem and confidence, feelings of abandonment, a betrayal of trust, feelings of exclusion and rejection, rage, and a sense of justification in leaving the spouse. Humphrey (1987) found that shock, anger, and denial were common initial reactions. When the husband had the affair, shock was ranked first (45%) followed by anger (35%). When it was the wife who had the affair, husbands ranked anger first (38%) followed by shock (19%). About 7–8% of spouses initially responded with denial. Charny & Parness (1995) identified a long list of negative consequences flowing from an affair including, "breaking of religious teaching; the breaking of trust; guilt; dishonesty; lies; anger; humiliation; depression; suicide; homicide; marital conflict; separation; divorce; anxiety; regret; lost respect and love; disruption of careers, marriage, and families. . . . " (pp. 161–162). Furthermore, he also mentions that many marriages continue to suffer for years and some eventually end in divorce.

☐ The Typological Approach

Several writers have tried to develop typologies of affairs. All the typologies are based on clinical observation rather than research and are loosely constructed. Generally speaking, they either attempt to simply describe the nature of the affair or suggest the motivation for the affair. These typologies are clinically useful in that they give us some clues as to the motivations partners have for violating their relationship. Emily Brown (1991) developed one of the earliest and best known of these typologies. Brown describes five types of affairs. These are:

1. *Conflict-avoidant affairs.* These affairs are designed to help the couple avoid having to deal with their conflict. Emotional energy is drained from the marriage and invested elsewhere. The fights that might occur are distracted by the affair. Unfortunately, attempts to resolve disagreements are also circumvented.
2. *Intimacy avoidant affairs.* Many couples can only tolerate so much closeness. When they begin to get too close, someone must do something to create more distance. An affair is just one of many strategies which serves the purpose of creating distance, thereby maintaining an equilibrium that is safe but lacking in intimacy.

3. *Sexual addiction.* Sometimes a partner is a sex or love addict (Turner, 1995). These partners have a compulsion to seek love or sexual experiences. Their sexual acting-out has little to do with the quality of the marriage and is related first and foremost to their addiction.
4. *Empty nest affairs.* This type of affair is similar to intimacy avoidance. As long as children are in the house, they may be used to avoid closeness. Once gone, the couple must face the emptiness in the marriage. The affair serves to fill the void within the marriage by becoming the new distraction. The marital intimacy equilibrium, therefore, remains undisturbed.
5. *Out the door affair.* Sometimes one partner wants to leave the marriage, but cannot leave without having another partner. They cannot tolerate being alone or thinking that they may never find anyone else. Thus, they must have an extramarital partner in order to transition from the marriage.

Pittman (1989) identified four common patterns. These are:

1. *The accidental encounter.* A one-time encounter which usually occurs while drinking, being with friends at a bachelor party, strip club, massage parlor, etc., or being propositioned by someone.
2. *Habitual philandering.* These partners show a consistent pattern of changing sexual partners and being disloyal to a primary partner. He also agrees that such a pattern is addictive.
3. *Romantic affairs.* These affairs are about being in love with love. The person wants to recapture the intense feeling of being in love in order to escape from life's difficulties.
4. *Marital arrangements.* The partners implicitly agree they need to create distance and avoid the problems of their marriage. One or both partners engage in an affair to accomplish this goal.

Don-David Lusterman's (1998) typology deals primarily with the *motivations* for having affairs. Much of what Lusterman has to offer has been described in the other typologies. He identifies affairs that result from mid-life events, entitlement, sexual identity (homosexual orientation), sexual addiction, exploratory affairs, tripod affairs, retaliatory affairs, and exit affairs. Three of his terms may be unfamiliar to the reader. An entitlement affair simply means the person having the affair feels entitled to engage in this type of behavior. Men, for example, are sometimes able to compartmentalize affairs by believing that they are entitled to have sexual relationships in which there is no emotional attachment. The tripod affair refers to the phenomena of using the affair to stabilize a marriage that is not working. Finally, the exploratory affair is used to explore another relationship when the marriage is not working, but the affair partner has not decided whether to stay or leave the marriage.

Israel Charny (1992) has one of the most extensive clinical classifications for extramarital affairs. He lists 18 types of affairs. We will list them using his headings and provide a brief description:

1. *Corruption, Including Sadism/Masochism.* The affair is carried out with hostile intent often serving narcissistic needs in the person having the affair.
2. *Superficiality and Apathy.* The affair itself is devoid of emotional connection. These types of affairs are usually repetitive and sexual.
3. *Escapism.* The affair allows the partner to escape from the tensions of the marriage.
4. *"A matter of no importance."* The affair is for sexual release alone and the person claims it is of no emotional significance.
5. *"Search Committee."* The purpose of this type of affair is to find a replacement partner.
6. *Falling in Love to Threaten Spouse.* The purpose of this affair is to force some change in the mate.
7. *Falling in Love to Complete Missing Qualities in Oneself.* The extramarital partner is supposed to fill in the missing parts perceived in oneself.
8. *Enable Continuation of the Marriage.* The affair compensates for what is missing in the marriage and thereby stabilizes it.
9. *Challenge to Improvement and Recreation of the Marriage.* The affair is designed to create a crisis in the marriage that may help to save it.
10. *Renewal of Excitement and Adventure.* The affair partner hopes to bring home some of the excitement of the affair.
11. *Desire-Daring-Survival.* This type of affair is experienced as a test of courage and power.
12. *Sexual Excitement Plus "Safe" Opportunity.* These affairs take place under "safe" conditions where the possibility of discovery *is minimal.*
13. *Fun and Variety, Anti-Boredom, Social Contagion.* The purpose of the affair is to introduce variety into one's life.
14. *Release of Nonmarital Tensions.* The purpose of this type of affair is to flee from the problems of everyday life.
15. *Hope at Difficult Moments.* The affair is an escape from some intolerable life situation such as a death or illness in the family.
16. *Freedom and Independence.* The mate who has the affair feels a lack of freedom and independence in the marriage. The affair is a way to assert one's freedom.
17. *Open Marriage.* These partners both agree to have affairs under specified conditions.
18. *Hedonism—An Insistence on the Pleasure Principle.* The partner who has this type of affair subscribes to hedonism as a basic life principle.

☐ Intersystemic Assessment

Weeks (1977, 1994) developed an intersystemic model for marital and family therapy. In this comprehensive model, every client system is evaluated and possibly treated from multiple perspectives, including the individual, the interactional, and the intergenerational. Westfall (1995), a colleague and author in the field of affairs, utilized this model when describing the assessment of affairs in one of Weeks' earlier books. This section will provide a brief overview of her writings. Of course, there is overlap between the factors and some factors could be listed under two or more headings.

Individual Factors

At the individual level, some of the more common factors are: 1) developmental crises; 2) psychiatric problems; 3) sexual orientation; and 4) major medical illness. A developmental crisis occurs when the couple or family is having difficulty moving from one lifecycle stage to another. For example, most couples experience a "honeymoon stage" in their relationship. When the relationship has matured some, this phase comes to an end and the partners are no longer idealizing each other or being driven by their initial fantasies about the other person. They may experience an intense feeling of disappointment to the point they feel the need to dissolve the relationship.

Psychiatric problems such as drug, alcohol, and sexual addictions, depression, anxiety, bipolar illness, and many of the personality disorders may interfere with the functioning of the relationship. The untreated bipolar partner is unpredictable and it is difficult to stay emotionally connected to someone who is so labile. The addict is essentially married to the drug or behavior of their choice. They are incapable of having an adult-adult relationship, but form addict–co-addict relationships. Many couples have partners with personality disorders such as narcissistic-borderline or passive aggressive that predispose them to conflicts.

The third factor that may appear is that of sexual orientation. One partner may have conflicts about his or her sexual orientation that may interfere with the relationship. A person may marry in order to "look normal" and deny his or her homosexuality. Eventually such relationships lose their passion (assuming any was there from the beginning) and the secret may be revealed to the partner or discovered. When the extramarital partner is of the same sex, the betrayed partner knows he or she cannot compete because the affair partner's interest is based on gender and not on the qualities of the mate.

The final individual factor is that of medical illness in one of the partners. A partner may develop a chronic and potentially life-threatening or life-shortening illness. The mate may not know how to cope with this illness and turn elsewhere as an escape. Sometimes it is the ill mate who has the affair in order to feel young and healthy again. Also, it is a way of affirming life, starting over, and serves to bolster their denial. Sometimes partners just think they are going to die and they want to experience as much from life as possible.

Interactional Factors

Interactional or dyadic factors are those that have to do with the dynamics of the relationship. Westfall (1995) identified three sets of factors:

1. infertility problems;
2. problems in establishing a loving relationship; and
3. gender role conflict.

Infertility is a problem that affects a sizeable number of couples, especially those who have waited until their 30s to have children. Sexual problems may grow from the regime of having to engage in sex on schedule. Moreover, sex acquires a singular meaning, procreation instead of recreation. Month after month of disappointment creates a sense of personal and relationship failure as well as grief over the anticipated loss of having a biological child of one's own.

Weeks (1995) published a more extensive theory about intimacy and love than what was originally published in the first edition of this volume in 1992. Using Sternberg's (1986a, b, 1999) model of love, the implications of having insufficient commitment, intimacy, and passion were discussed. Problems in any one or several of these areas will predispose a partner towards having an affair. The couples that share little emotional intimacy are at risk when one partner desires more affective sharing than the other can provide. Sometimes, the affair partner will comment on the friendship part of the affair and how they can tell the extramarital partner things they cannot share with the husband or wife. Often times the affair partner will describe a yearning or quest for sexual passion that is typical of the early stages of a relationship. Failing to appreciate the less intense yet completely fulfilling value of a long-term stable relationship, he or she fears that he or she has fallen "out of love."

A major part of marital satisfaction depends upon having one's expectations meet. Many of our marital expectations are gender based, men do one thing, and women do another. Conflicts, anger, and disappointment emerge when the couple cannot agree on these expectations. In traditional couples, men work and women stay at home to take care of the family. If one partner does not want this system and the other does, major conflict will arise.

Intergeneratonal Factors

This set of factors deals with events that have occurred or are occurring within the family of origin. They include, but are not limited to:

1. Family life cycle issues;
2. Death in the family;
3. Issues of individuation and enmeshment; and
4. Incest.

Family life cycle issues are similar to the developmental issues discussed earlier. With family life cycle issues, the problems are usually related to the age(s) of the children. For many couples, the birth of the first child and departure of the last child are crisis points in a marriage. The couple must now restructure the relationship or confront the lack of relationship that exists. When this confrontation begins to take place, some partners will avoid it and start an affair in order to find what they feel is missing to stabilize a relationship devoid of feeling.

A death in the family can also contribute to an affair. When a family member, such as a parent, dies, the adult child is confronted with his or her own mortality. In an effort to recapture a feeling of youthfulness and vitality, some will have an affair. A parent who was a pivotal or all-important figure will need to be replaced with a fantasy figure that can supply what the parent had to offer.

The level of differentiation of the mates is also crucial to marital functioning in many ways. Differentiation can be defined in many ways, but one simple way to describe it is related to the degree of individuation or enmeshment in the family. In one of our cases, a man was highly enmeshed with his mother. When this man married, he immediately began having affairs and did so for over 20 years of his marriage. His affairs were one way to avoid enmeshment with his wife. He feared that should he truly commit himself to his marriage, he would repeat the same pattern and become enmeshed in two relationships. The affairs allowed him to maintain emotional distance from all women except his mother.

Incest in the family is a final factor that can lead to an affair. The experience of incest can have long-lasting consequences. Some incest survivors become sexually disinterested. While the partner may tolerate this lack of interest for some period of time and hope that it will change, continued lack of interest may lead the other partner to seek sexual satisfaction elsewhere. Sometimes the survivors are sexually limited; they will only allow "patterned" or sexual expression within a limited range that becomes frustrating to the partner. On the other hand, some survivors become sexually compulsive and driven to act-out. They are searching for sexual validation, but, in fact, re-creating their original sexual trauma in that they are being used simply for sexual satisfaction. This type of relationship is based on what Turner (1995) has described as a trauma bond. A number of these individuals also become love or sex addicts and are mistaken for being immoral and bad.

At the beginning of this chapter, we stated that we would be focusing more on treatment than etiology because etiology has been covered extensively in a prior volume (Weeks & Hof, 1995). The reader desiring a more in-depth analysis should consult Westfall's (1995) chapter.

☐ Intersystemic Treatment

As we stated earlier, few events in the life of a marriage stir up as much emotional turmoil as an extramarital affair. In this section, we will deal with various treatment issues and offer strategies that encourage recovery from the trauma of the affair. Couples present for treatment with a variety of issues. For some couples the affair is a secret, in others it has just been revealed, for others it is revealed or discovered during therapy, and for some it is suspected, but never revealed nor discovered. The therapist must be prepared to deal with all kinds of contingencies when affairs are involved. Additionally, the emotional climate of a relationship in which an affair has occurred can be emotionally volatile. One of the most common presentations is when the couple enters therapy shortly after an affair has been revealed or discovered and the affair partner has not actually severed the relationship or is unsure about whether he or she wants to end the extramarital relationship.

The first issue to explore is whether the partners want to preserve the marriage. They may be enraged and unhappy with each other at this point and making threats about leaving the marriage. A great deal of emotional reactivity may stand in the way of being able to rationally work through the affair. The question is really one of whether they want to maintain their commitment to each other and to a process (therapy) which will help them sort out whether they will be able to preserve and build a satisfying marriage. The therapist might say, "As hurt, unhappy, and angry as you may be right now, would you like to be able to save this marriage?" The therapist must listen carefully to whether there is sufficient commitment to continue working with the couple toward recovery. Gaining some statement of commitment is important at the outset, even if it is only to the process of therapy. Many couples yo-yo between being in the relationship and out of the relationship. In other words, they go back and forth between wanting to stay and wanting to leave. Such a pattern can go on endlessly until one partner is exhausted. At a minimum, the therapist can argue that at the conclusion of therapy the couple will have made a rational decision about what they want to do. Some couples will proclaim immediately that they want the marriage to work. In fact, some will initially report that the marriage has been the best ever since the affair because they have both been trying so hard. Unfortunately, these couples have taken a flight into health and have not yet confronted the underlying unhappiness and problems between them. If both are committed, the therapist can move quickly to the next issue. If one or both are not committed, then the therapist may need to spend time helping them decide what they want to do. This might include staying with the therapy long enough to come to some self-understanding about why they might want to flee the situation immediately or feel ambivalent about staying. Sometimes individual sessions help the uncommitted or ambivalent partner sort out his or her feelings without worrying about the implications of what they say in front of their partner. It will be necessary to allow time and opportunity for the expression of intense feelings of guilt, pain, and betrayal. Such intense feelings can become overwhelming in and of themselves. The partners need to be reminded that the decision to remain committed to each other can be influenced by these intense emotions, but should not be made solely on the basis of the *reactions to* the affair. Factors that predisposed the betrayal also need to be considered when deciding to stay with or to exit the relationship.

Individual Sessions

In individual sessions, the betrayed partner might focus on how deeply he or she was hurt, but does not wish to risk being this vulnerable in the presence of the affair partner. Vulnerability involves trust and in this situation, the trust between partners has been violated. Also, the betrayed partner might talk about how he or she had a parent who had an affair that ended the parents' marriage. Exploring these strongly held fears and feelings about leaving can often help the partner see he or she is running from a situation rather than dealing with it. The betrayed partner must be encouraged to *stay with* the intense feelings in order to understand and ultimately control them.

When the emotional reactivity is less intense, the affair can be reframed as a *marital* problem. That is, the affair may have been a symptom of a *marriage* that was not working rather than a symptom of a *partner* who is impaired. It takes two to make a marriage work or not work. Framing the affair in this way suggests the problem is in the marriage, not just one partner. Further, it suggests that the same thing can happen to any marriage that is not working and that *both* parties changing could help the marriage. Eventually, the betrayed partner will be helped to see that the affair is partly of his or her own making although it is crucial that a he or she never be blamed for another partner having an affair. Moreover, the therapist *must* say that nothing excuses the affair. More attention will be devoted to reframing the affair later in this section. The partner who received the individual session(s) will eventually return to the couple sessions to either stop the relationship or to proceed to see what the next step will be.

The affair partner may have stopped the affair or be in the process of trying to stop it. We believe the therapist must take a firm stance regarding the continuation of the affair. The therapist must inform the couple that the affair must stop and stay stopped if they are serious about working on the marriage. In fact, we will guarantee that as long as the affair continues, even if intermittently, no real progress can be make in the couple's relationship. Stopping the affair means that all contact, albeit incidental, must cease—including brief discussions, e-mail, voice mail, and signals such as "hang-ups," etc. Should the affair partner affirm the affair is over, some individual work still needs be done to assess the reasons that partner had for becoming involved in the extramarital relationship. The reason the work is done individually is so that affair partner does not have to hold back any information that he or she thinks might be hurtful to the betrayed partner. Also, the discussion partly revolves around the attraction of the extramarital partner. Should the betrayed partner hear some of the descriptions and graphic details such as "she gave me the best blow jobs" of my life, these pieces of information would compound the sense of anger and competition with the extramarital partner. Moreover, if the affair partner truly gives up all contact with the lover, the loss of this relationship predictably results in profound sadness and sometimes depression. The betrayed partner often has little empathy for this experience of sadness and in fact may be wounded by the recognition of the importance of the affair to his or her significant other.

The Secret Affair

In some couples, the affair is a secret at the beginning of therapy. Two situations are likely to occur. The first is that the partner(s) ask for an individual session or the therapist asks for individual sessions to gain more information. Sometimes, the therapist has a sense that an affair is occurring. These individual sessions are usually held at the beginning of treatment after a few conjoint sessions to get some sense about how the partners operate as a couple.

The second situation is when therapy has proceeded for a number of sessions and the change expected by the therapist has not occurred. An unexplained lack of change is an indicator of a secret—most commonly an affair. The therapist may suggest an individual session or two in order to gain background information that might have been missed and which is important in getting the couple unstuck.

In the individual session, the therapist should state that something appears to be missing that might explain the lack of change. If a partner has expressed concerns about an affair, this should be stated emphasizing the importance of honesty in the therapy sessions. Recall the therapist has already defined the rules of confidentiality, but it might be useful at the beginning of the individual sessions to repeat the rules so that the partner feels free to divulge information. The client might then reveal that he or she has been and still is involved in an affair. The therapist needs to take a nonjudgmental stance toward this behavior, otherwise, the client will reveal very little more and will write the therapist off as taking a moral rather than helpful psychological stance. The therapist should also remind the affair partner that no lasting change would occur as long as there is an affair. Because the affair is still continuing and the client is coming in for couples therapy, the client is either ambivalent about stopping the affair or has tried to end it but found this cannot be easily accomplished. The client is asked to talk about what he or she really wants for the marriage. Again, the therapist is trying to establish, without the betrayed partner's presence, how much commitment there is to the marriage.

Assuming the betrayed partner is still in love with the affair partner and states he or she wants the marriage to work, but is uncertain as to its outcome, the therapist must proceed by suggesting that therapy can only be accomplished if the affair partner is working toward severing the affair in a timely manner. We usually give a client 3–4 weeks to stop the affair before ending the therapy due to a lack of change by stating that one partner has individual issues which are preventing change from occurring. Of course, if the therapist has to end therapy, this is also an indication to the betrayed partner that things are not going to improve and they should plan accordingly. It is perceived by the betrayed partner that a secret is the cause for termination of treatment.

The relationship the therapist has to the affair partner is isomorphic with the relationship between the affair partner and the extramarital partner—both are secret relationships. Partners who are in denial must at this point confront the reality of the situation. In many cases, the betrayed partner confronts the affair partner with the ultimatum that he or she must know what is going on or they will leave. When the affair partner is confronted in this manner, he or she may then admit to the affair and will either wish to end the marriage by default or say he or she wants to stop the affair, but has been unable to terminate it.

Hopefully, the affair partner will want to work on the marriage realizing he or she must stop the affair. The therapist will then need to explore the motivations for the affair with the client. One aspect of this exploration is to ask about the dimensions of the affair described at the beginning of the chapter such as how long it has been occurring, with whom, what is the extramarital partner's relationship with the betrayed partner, etc. In short, the therapist will want to gather a good deal of factual information about the affair. The other focus of the individual sessions is on being able to stop the affair and help the client understand why it began. The therapist can ask questions such as the following:

1. How did you meet this person?
2. What was the attraction?
3. Who initiated the relationship?
4. How were you feeling about yourself when this relationship started?
5. How were you feeling about your marriage when this relationship started?
6. What was going on in your life about the time this relationship started?
7. How attached have you become to this person? Do you think you love this person?
8. What has this relationship meant to you?
9. How has this relationship helped/hurt your marriage?
10. How has this relationship helped/hurt you?
11. Did you ever imagine that you would have an affair?
12. How has this relationship challenged your ethical, moral, or value system?
13. What do you like most about this person/relationship?
14. What do you like least about this person/relationship?
15. How do you feel about ending this relationship?
16. How do you think your extramarital partner will feel about this relationship ending?
17. Do you think he/she will be able to let go of this relationship if you end it or do you think they will continue to pursue you?
18. Who else knows about this relationship?
19. Have you thought of ending this relationship or tried to end it unsuccessfully?
20. Has your partner thought of ending this relationship or tried unsuccessfully to end it?
21. How much mental energy does it take to keep both of your relationships going? Are you feeling worn down by this situation?
22. How do you think you will feel when it is over?

23. Do you think you might resent your husband/wife for having to end this relationship?
24. Have you ever had to end a relationship?
25. What has it been like when relationships have ended for you in the past?
26. Are you prepared to grieve over the loss of this person?

These questions will provide the therapist with the information needed to process the motivations for the affair as well as help the client end the affair. The therapist may need to validate that the client has developed a strong sense of attachment for the extramarital partner and that to lose this partner will mean to grieve. Most affair partners do not want their partner to know how strongly attached he or she has become to the extramarital partner nor do they want the betrayed partner to see them grieve over the loss of the extramarital partner. Hence, most affair partners will minimize the emotional involvement when the betrayed partner is in the room.

Part of the therapist's task in the individual sessions is to help the affair partner grieve over the loss of the relationship and to ensure that the relationship does not start again. The affair partner will need to be encouraged and coached about what to say to the extramarital partner. The affair partner might say that they are working on their marriage and need to be fully committed. This necessitates ending the relationship and having no further contact with the extramarital partner. Sometimes affairs partners are unwilling to sever the affair immediately and permanently. In those cases, we suggest putting the relationship on hold for six months in order to give the marriage a chance. During that time, no contact is allowed. The rationale we provide the client is that by putting the affair on hold and making a commitment to work on the marriage for six months, he or she will either experience the marriage as working or beginning to work. If after six months (in some cases sooner) the marriage is not working, the affair partner can leave the marriage with a clear conscience that he or she tried their best. The affair partner can leave the marriage with less guilt knowing the affair did not cloud the decision to stay or go. Removing the affair as an issue helps the client move in one direction or another with more conviction that the decision was properly made.

The motivations for an affair may vary according to the assessment criteria mentioned in the earlier section and the type of affair. Due to the secret nature of most affairs, the two parties have relatively little time to spend together. In fact, it is much like dating. When they do get together it is for a meal, to talk, or to have sex in finite periods of time. The relationship is not challenged by the normal day-to-day events that most couples face such as children and having to solve problems as they come along. It is also a new relationship. One of the greatest sources of sexual desire is that of novelty of a new partner. We often point out that the established relationship does not have a chance compared to a new relationship because the brain is awash in "feel-good" chemicals. These chemicals are so powerful they are like addictive drugs—we crave more and more. Information such as this puts the intensity of feelings in perspective for the client.

Finally, the time-limited and artificial nature of an affair relationship plus the fact that most clients will not see any flaws or shortcomings in the extramarital partner suggests a considerable amount of projection. In many of the cases we have treated, the extramarital partner was a projection of a parental figure or an idealized figure. The parental figure projection involves seeing qualities in the extramarital partner, which were loved and admired in a parent, but perceived, as missing in the partner. Obviously, some of the characteristics perceived are that of being taken care of, cared about, and accepted. The idealized figure projection means seeing the extramarital partner in idealized terms. They are the embodiment of goodness and kindness. Moreover, the idealized figure often has traits that the other person would like to have but feels he or she is missing. For example, affair partners are sometimes attracted to extramarital partners because they are seen as outgoing and socially skillful. They have friends and are good listeners. The affair partner will sometimes comment about how the extramarital partner has "brought them out." They may be referring to bringing out their feelings or bringing them out socially with his or her closest friends who know about the affair. The projective aspects of the relationship require exploration and the affair partner must be helped to see these qualities in the betrayed partner, if they exist. When the idealized projection is a search for that which is missing in oneself, then the therapist needs to help the client develop that aspect of self. A client who is emotionally repressed could be assisted in exploring his or her feelings and discovering the reasons for his or her repressions. A client who has never felt he or she could expose his or her real self may be aided in self-exploration and acceptance.

☐ The Affective Phase of Treatment

Beginning the Couple Work

In addition to the couple affirming their commitment to work on the relationship or to the therapy, there are a few other issues that require immediate attention. If the partner knows about the affair, the first task is to deal with the affair.

One of the tasks is to deal with the feelings generated by the affair. In most partners, there are intense feelings of anger, shock, betrayal, and so on. The intensity of these feelings may be frightening to both partners because the feelings seem endless and irrational. The betrayed partner must be given an opportunity to discuss these feelings in the couple session and the affair partner must be willing to acknowledge and validate these feelings. For most couples, the betrayed partner's feelings have not been adequately acknowledged. The affair partner may have offered an apology or stated he or she could understand how the betrayed partner felt but not sufficiently discussed the feelings. A great deal of time is spent in-session just talking about the feelings. First, the betrayed partner has an opportunity to talk about his or her feelings and then the other affair partner has an opportunity to talk about how he or she feels. The couple also needs to agree that when they have a need to express some of these feelings at home they should set aside time to talk about them. When these feelings are discussed at home, they should be contained and not the topic of continuous conversation.

Because most couples have avoided this painful emotional conversation, the focus has shifted to an endless search for facts. Facts have been substituted for feelings. The betrayed partner will want to know every detail of the affair—with whom, how long, when did they meet, how many times, what did the extramarital partner look like, what did they talk about, where did they go, what gifts were given, and what happened sexually. We strongly believe this endless search for facts is a substitute for discussion about feelings. Some facts are useful for the betrayed partner to know. We generally think the betrayed partner should know:

- Who the extramarital partner was;
- How long the affair lasted;
- How often they meet; and
- Where they meet.

The search for sexual details represents a voyeuristic interest providing memories and images of what the affair partner did which are difficult for the betrayed partner to overcome.

Beyond these basic facts, we suggest that every time the betrayed partner wants to start asking questions, he or she should express these feelings and needs. We often say, "Talk about the feelings and needs, not the facts. You already know what happened; hearing it again will not help you." The need that many betrayed partners have is that of emotional reassurance that the affair has ended. They should think about how they are *feeling* and what they *need*. They usually desire to be reassured that the affair partner wants to work on the marriage and still finds them attractive and lovable. We encourage affair partners to become more vocal in expressing how they feel about their partner on an ongoing basis. The more that feelings are discussed, the less the need for facts.

The emotional turmoil surrounding an affair can last from several weeks to several months. A significant amount of time may be spent in session discussing feelings as they emerge and change. The couple needs to be forewarned that feelings will be quite changeable, and just when they think one feeling has subsided it may reappear. This phase of therapy cannot be accelerated. Trying to go around rather than through the feelings will just keep the therapy stuck at the level of searching for facts and accusations. Two additional points may be mentioned here. First, the betrayed partner may have feelings that do not subside which appear to have another or deeper source. Part of the discussion around the betrayed partner's feelings is to discover past betrayal in that person's life, including experiences in the family of origin. For example, Christine reported that when she was growing up her father had had multiple affairs she knew about but which apparently her mother did not. She was determined that she would never experience an affair in her own marriage, but was told by her husband that he had been having an affair. Her feelings about her situation resonated to her old feelings toward her father and exacerbated her reaction. In another case, Jonathan had been married three times. All three of his marriages ended due to his wives' affairs. Of course, he was in a state of disbelief that such an occurrence could happen again and assumed his current marriage would end.

Second, sometimes the betrayed partner has an obsessive-compulsive personality disorder or obsessive-compulsive personality traits. The affair will become an obsession for them. The therapist should assess the premorbid functioning in this area and if the feelings about the affair persist beyond what seems reasonable, concurrent treatment, including medication, should commence for that client.

The grief reaction may also include depression and anxiety. In some cases, these symptoms predated the affair and have not been treated. A psychiatric referral may be useful. The SSRIs can be very useful in lifting the depression as well as reducing the obsessional thinking when prescribed at higher doses.

Accountability and Trust

An affair is highly disruptive to the feelings of trust in a relationship. Not only is the betrayed partner injured by the affair, but also by the lies and deception that accompany most affairs. Rebuilding trust is not an easy matter. An affair partner cannot simply apologize and say he or she is trustworthy again. We emphasize that trust will be rebuilt slowly, and through experience and communication. The betrayed partner will be wondering what is really going on in the life of his or her partner. Communication can give the betrayed insight regarding the inner-life of their partner, which is essential for trust to be reformed. Affair partners must also recognize and take responsibility for the rejection sensitivity they have created by having the affair. Their actions destroyed the trust and lead to the ongoing hypervigilance and suspicions of their betrayed partner. In order to alleviate these suspicions and demonstrate accountability, affair partners must be careful to explain their comings and goings. When traveling, they need to make calls home and be reachable by telephone. The information previously provided about the extramarital partner (i.e., where and when they met) helps the betrayed partner know that the affair has not re-started. For example, one man met his extramarital partner for lunch almost every day. He would always have an excuse for being out of the office for a long lunch and could not be reached, even by cellular telephone. Part of his accountability to his wife was to either eat lunch in or be reachable by telephone around lunch. He was also told it would be helpful if he could go home for lunch since home was nearby or to call his wife during lunch for a little chat.

The basic information provided by the affair partner is actually for the purpose of helping the betrayed partner know whether he or she has reason to suspect the affair has begun again. Additionally, we tell the couple that absolute honesty is important. Any communication with the extramarital partner should be reported. In many cases, the extramarital partner will call, send a letter, or just be seen in the office or neighborhood. An innocent meeting on the street could be reported back to the betrayed partner and cause alarm if the meeting is not reported. In other cases, the affair partner will violate the agreement and call the extramarital partner. This information should also be reported in the couple session since the therapist needs to know in order to help the affair partner who is struggling with stopping the affair and the betrayed partner needs to know where he or she stands in the process. Restoring trust and a sense of loyalty can only be accomplished through honesty, even if the news is not always what the couple would like to hear.

☐ The Cognitive Phase of Treatment

Once the feelings about the affair have been discussed and the affair is not such an emotionally charged event, the second phase of therapy can be integrated with the couple agreeing to work on the relationship with openness and honesty. The phases may overlap, but for conceptual clarity they are separated. The couple needs to find:

1. Some way of making sense of what happened;
2. What the affair meant and means to the couple; and
3. What they can learn from the affair to prevent it from happening again.

In the assessment section of the chapter, we reviewed a number of individual reasons a partner might have an affair such as mid-life, psychiatric disorders, chronic illness, etc. For some couples, the explanation is as simple as identifying the factors in the individual which lead to the affair. Then it is a matter of helping that person remedy those factors and restoring the trust in the relationship.

In our experience, the vast majority of affairs have resulted from marital dysfunction or dissatisfaction. As such, it takes two to create marital dysfunction. While we say quite clearly to the couple that nothing justifies the affair, we also believe the couple needs an explanation which helps them make sense of the situation and gives them a sense that if those problems are rectified another affair will not occur. Thus, the therapist has the task of systemically reframing the affair.

Reframing is a generic strategy in marital and family therapy. It involves helping the couple find another way of viewing their problem, which has the effect of putting everyone on the same level. In other words, both members are defined as having some part in creating the problem. Based on the study mentioned earlier in this chapter, which stated that couples collude in allowing the affair to continue, it is clear that the partners can be told they both were unwilling to confront the unhappiness or dissatisfaction contributing to problems appearing elsewhere. In order to reframe the affair, the therapist needs to elicit information about the couple's relationship. As bits and pieces of information are gathered, a picture begins to emerge which points to their dissatisfaction or dysfunction. These pieces of information can be given emphasis by the therapist to help the couple have "insight" as to why the affair happened. If the couple is unable to draw some conclusion from the facts emphasized by the therapist, the therapist may need to state the reframe and ask the couple to react to it.

The reframe needs to focus on some dysfunctional dynamic in the relationship or on each partner's problems that lead to an interlocking dysfunctional pattern of behavior. In the first case, the therapist might reframe their dynamic as one in which both partners failed to engage in effective communication or conflict resolution. A pattern such as this is likely to erode the quality of marital satisfaction until one partner decides to have an affair. In the second case, the therapist might reframe each partner's problems. For example, in one case the wife was chronically depressed and refused treatment. Her husband was resigned to her depression having grown up with a depressed mother. He felt powerless to effect any change or get what he needed from his wife. He began to withdraw from her and overwork. Interestingly, it was the wife who had the affair thinking it might help her depression because she felt so alone. In another case, the partners colluded in forming a parent–child relationship. Over time, this pattern created conflict and marital dissatisfaction that contributed to the affair.

Intergenerational factors may also play into the affair. The most common pattern we have observed is a partner having an affair in order to create distance in the marriage due to parental enmeshment. Mark, for example, was 45 when he entered therapy. At this time, the truth was revealed that he had had affairs since the beginning of his marriage at the age of 23. Mark was from an Italian family and extremely enmeshed. He would see his mother every day. The cover story was that his mother needed help in the house with repairs and so forth that justified his daily visits. When Mark married, he was unable to extricate himself emotionally from his family. Knowing that he needed some emotional and relationship space of his own, he began having a sequence of two-year affairs. The affairs helped him maintain stability in the marriage by allowing him to stay emotionally disengaged. His wife had never suspected an affair, but was certainly aware of the fact that he was close to his family and not emotionally engaged with her. She had been reared in an abusive family. The only time family members became close was to be angry and violent. Thus, she feared that closeness might bring more of the same and unconsciously needed the distance in the marriage. Family-of-origin work was indicated for this couple.

An effective reframe allows the couple to find *meaning* in the affair. They can both see a connection between their behavior and the affair as a symptom. Once this connection has been established, they can begin the final phase of therapy. The cognitive or reframing phase of therapy is usually brief lasting only a few sessions. This phase lays the groundwork for the final phase. Both partners can now participate in the therapy, often with them sharing responsibility for allowing problems to continue in their relationship.

☐ Reconciliation, Recovery, and Restructuring

Having worked through the first two phases of treatment allows the partners to gain some understanding of each other's dynamics, vulnerabilities, and humanness. In order to reconcile with each other, they must grasp the complexity of their relationship and each other in such a way as to see the struggle that every marriage endures. The partners need to feel they are working together toward a common goal of building the relationship out of liking and loving each other. This phase of treatment may take anywhere from a few months to a couple of years. The research cited earlier suggested that brief treatment of affairs is ineffective. No research has been conducted on longer-term treatment. Our experience in treating affairs over many years has taught us that a quick fix is not possible. Couples must be willing to make a long-term commitment to the therapeutic process if they are to achieve a satisfactory relationship.

Worthington and Drinkard (2000) have published one of the most comprehensive models for facilitating reconciliations. The purpose of reconciliation is to restore harmony in the relationship while acknowledging that differences may continue to persist. Reconciliation is similar to forgiveness, but not the same. McCullough, Worthington, and Rachal (1997) suggest that a person experiences forgiveness from within when the person (a) no longer desires to avoid or withdraw from the individual that offended him or her; (b) releases a sense of revenge or just anger; and (c) desires a conciliation if it is prudent, possible, and safe to do so.

Worthington and Drinkard's (2000) model of reconciliation consists of six "planks" which consist of the following:

1. *Decide whether to reconcile.* Reconciliation may not be possible or desirable, especially if a person's safety or health may be threatened by such action. Safeguards must first be established. The likelihood of successful reconciliation should be assessed by the therapist.
2. *Softness.* An attitude of mutual softness must be created between the partners or reconciliation will not occur. The therapist must stress that both parties must drop his or her wall of defense that was erected as protection from further injury by the other partner. Two-way concessions will be needed for a successful reconciliation.
3. *Forgiveness.* After a soft environment is created, forgiveness is promoted. Worthington (1998) presents a five-step pyramid model of forgiveness.
   a. *Recall the hurt.* Recall the specific hurtful and offensive events. In freeflowing conversation, the couple discuss the events utilizing the therapist to prevent escalation of anger.
   b. *Empathize with the offending partner.* Empathy is expressed for the other's situation by having the partner's describing the events from the other partner's point of view. Each partner's empathetic under standing of the event is discussed.
   c. *Altruistic gift of forgiveness.* Partners recall when he or she offended or hurt someone other than his or her partner and were subsequently forgiven. The resulting feelings of gratitude and freedom from being forgiven are discussed.
   d. *Commit to forgive.* A verbal commitment to forgive the partner is nec-

essary. The therapist invites the partners to forgive each other when they are ready.

   e. *Holding onto forgiveness.* The therapist informs the partners that offenses and hurts will not be totally forgotten, but it does not mean forgiveness has not been granted if a forgiven hurt is recalled.

4. *Reverse the negative cascade.* Marriages deteriorate, usually in steps— criticism, defensiveness, contempt, and stonewalling (Gottman, 1994). Partners seek and find new negative interactions as the nonlinear change in perception of the relationship becomes negative, global, and stable (Fincham & Bradbury, 1993) negating any possible interactions. For successful reconciliation, good times must be recalled to reinforce the positive aspects of the relationship.

5. *Deal with failures in trustworthiness.* Partners must be made aware that failures in trustworthiness are inevitable, but it does not mean the reconciliation program has failed. Failures can be positively reframed by the therapist as opportunities to practice forgiveness and a positive maintenance of reconciliation behaviors.

6. *Actively build love.* Reconciliation is more than just resolving conflicts, but also involves the rebuilding of love that has been damaged by hurtful acts that offended and devalued a partner. Devaluing behavior must be avoided and behavior communicating value of the partners must be increased to rebuild love.

An affair is a traumatic event for both partners. They have both experienced intensely painful emotions, felt threatened over losing the relationship, and have in fact lost a great deal of trust and certainty that they had previously enjoyed or taken for granted. A hidden loss is that of losing the image and dreams that each one carried at the beginning of the marriage. Many couples begin the relationship with the idea that their partner is almost perfect and they will have the storybook marriage. An affair shatters this fantasy with an ugly reality that does not pass. Occasionally in session, the couple benefits from talking about this trauma aspect of the affair. Debriefing and feeling heard and supported are crucial elements to trauma recovery.

An important aspect of recovery is that of forgiveness. Forgiveness is a topic that has eluded most writers in the field of marital and family therapy even though it is a basic human need and needed nowhere more that in the violation of a marriage through infidelity. During the first few sessions, the affair partner usually asks for some understanding and forgiveness and it is often granted. At that stage of treatment, not enough work has been done to create a foundation for a deeper level of forgiveness. The insights gained into each partner helps provide this foundation. As the couple begins to comprehend and appreciate how they failed to address various issues in their marriage, they begin to see how they created vulnerability for the couple to experience an affair. A deeper level of forgiveness is possible once a deeper level of understanding has been achieved. In those cases where one partner clearly has a problem such as alcoholism or bipolar illness, the other partner may come to see how they served as a co-addict or an enabler by allowing the illness to continue through their care-taking or over-responsibility rather than confrontation and constructive action.

As we pointed out earlier, trust and accountability are important from the beginning of therapy. The therapist should expect that it would be difficult for the affair partner to stop the affair with finality. Telephone calls, visits, and encounters in the office or community are commonplace even though the intent is to stop the affair. These are to be reported to the betrayed partner and processed in the session with the appropriate reassurance that the encounter was not at the affair partner's initiation. If it were, he or she would accept responsibility for it and work with the therapist individually to stop the relationship.

The restructuring of the relationships may involve work on the individual partners, the dyadic relationship, and some family-of-origin work. Restructuring refers to the changes that need to be made in order for the relationship to thrive. In the Intersystemic Model described earlier, a treatment plan (Weeks & Hof, 1995) is developed which allows for the systematic integration of whatever treatment issues need to be addressed. Unless there is severe pathology or addiction in one partner, we generally prefer to do most of the work with the couple together with occasional individual sessions. The exception to this rule is when the affair partner needs help at the beginning of therapy to stop the affair. The couple work allows each partner to learn about the issues of the other, how some of these patterns are interlocking, and how they must work jointly to create a working relationship. Each partner's perspective is also useful in working on individual issues. Sometimes one partner will be unaware of some of his or her symptoms, particularly the severity of their symptoms. In one recent case, the husband pointed out that he believed his wife had been depressed for years. She initially disagreed with his assessment, but as she learned more about depression and her symptoms began to understand that she was in fact depressed.

The following case illustrates the initial phase of treatment:

> Marta Jo and Henry had been married 24 years. Marta Jo learned that Henry had been having an affair for about the last 12 years of their marriage with a woman in his office. The affair was discrete in that they would travel on business and they worked on various projects together. Only one or two people in his office suspected what was happening. The affair started just after the birth of Marta Jo and Henry's second and last child. Henry

only wanted one child, not two, because he was an only son. The couple had meet when they were in their mid-twenties. Henry had established himself as a successful businessman, and she was also in a career path headed for success. Each one had had several failed relationships prior to meeting and each partner was beginning to wonder if he or she would ever find the right person.

This case was filled with a variety of issues. Henry had suffered depression for many years, but had never been prescribed medication, in spite of analytic treatment with a psychiatrist. He was also an undiagnosed adult with ADD that made it difficult for him to stay in conversations with his wife. Marta Jo did not have any diagnosable conditions.

The relationship had been a difficult one from the beginning. Henry worked long hours and Marta Jo became pregnant right after marriage and stopped her career. It was obvious that he was over-involved in work and she was over-involved with the child. They did not communicate much and what communication they had was superficial. They both tried to avoid anger, which allowed resentments to build. A major resentment on Henry's part was Marta Jo's insistence on a second child.

Henry's major complaint was that his wife always got her way and needed to be the center of attention. Interestingly, Henry could not conceive the fact that for many years in his marriage he was so passive he could not ask for the smallest thing. He took every wish of his wife to be a demand and virtually every comment about her dissatisfaction was perceived as a criticism. How could such a relationship have survived for so many years?

Henry grew up in a Christian Science family with two very critical parents. He was constantly told he was selfish and that his unhappiness was his own doing. He was trained to be passive and responsible for all "bad" feelings from his earliest years. A father and stepmother reared Marta Jo. Her father was an extremely narcissistic man who demanded that she do and be everything he wished. If she did not conform to his wishes, he would withdraw his love from her. Neither Marta Jo nor Henry had experienced intimacy in their respective families. They needed a relationship that was emotionally safe and distanced. Unfortunately, Marta Jo violated the unconscious dictum that she not want anything from Henry. The more she wanted for herself, the smaller and more inadequate he felt. This would have been a rich case to treat because it involved individual, interactional, and intergenerational issues. Although Marta Jo was interested in continuing the marriage, Henry decided he wanted no part of marital therapy once his secret was learned. He externalized full responsibility for the problem onto his wife and stated she would never change. It seemed he only had two choices, either he was fully responsible or she was fully responsible. Either way would have been doomed to failure. The couple proceeded to divorce, with the husband moving quickly to solidify the affair relationship. This case is an exception in our experience.

Another case illustrates a couple that successfully moved through the initial phases of treatment and was committed to staying together.

Jeff and Susan had been married 17 years and had two teenage children. They came to therapy because Jeff learned Susan had been having an affair with a married man for a period of about two years. This couple had what is typically called a parent–child relationship. They were traditionally oriented in terms of gender roles and Susan had always been a passive partner. She worked part-time, but was primarily a mother and homemaker. She felt under-appreciated by Jeff and stated that he had always had the control in their relationship. She also talked about not knowing what she wanted in life and having a poor sense of self-worth. In addition, she had become depressed over the years, but did not recognize her depression. The couple accepted the reframe that what contributed to the affair was their dissatisfaction over having created a parent–child relationship. The therapy focused on helping each partner understand their individual issues and how they feed into each other's dysfunctional individual need to being taken care of or to taking care of another. As they began to understand their pattern, they could see they were eventually headed for disaster. The mental template for their relationship was established in their families of origin, that necessitated an analysis of these early patterns. This couple needed about a year of work in the restructuring phase in order to change their dynamic and feel secure that another affair would not happen. Susan was also referred to a psychiatrist and began taking an antidepressant.

Most couples who come for help with an affair, whether the affair is known at the beginning or not, do commit to working on the relationship for an extended period of time. While we have not collected hard data on the percentage of couples that stay together, it is our impression that over 80% of couples complete the therapy successfully and stay together. Clearly, this model of treatment needs to be subjected to empirical scrutiny.

☐ Conclusion

The first edition of this volume did not contain a chapter on the treatment of extramarital affairs. The focus of the text has been on general treatment issues such as the process of therapy and the application of specific techniques and treatment methods to couples. Since the publication of the first edition, we realized that affairs were a common dilemma presented by couples coming for treatment. We also realized that the treatment of affairs provoked uncertainties in therapists about what to do, as well as anxiety over strategic, ethical, and personal issues.

Although this chapter is the longest in the book, we have only offered essential information about the definition, prevalence, countertransference issues, ethical and etiological factors, and basic treatment issues. Understanding and treating extramarital affairs is one of the most complex issues confronting the couples therapist. We did not touch on the fact that significant gender differences exist in the motivations for affairs and in their impact, nor did we fully explore some of the theoretical issues underlying treatment or the newly evolving literature that would support our approach to treatment. We hope to elaborate on these issues in our subsequent writing. What we have been able to provide is a basic blueprint for the treatment of affairs based on the Intersystem approach that the senior author has been developing over the last twenty years. We have tried to impart some clarity to the issues of confidentiality and ethical concerns and the motivations for affairs, and we have tried to lend a sense of direction, purpose, and focus to the process of treatment. Material found in previous chapters in the text will be useful in treating affairs, especially as it relates to the issue of commitment and the techniques used in the recovery and restructuring phase of treatment. Additionally, the enhancement or intimacy work can help to prevent the occurrence and reoccurrence of an extramarital affair.

AFTERWORD

This revised edition of *Couples in Treatment* includes new developments that have taken place since the publication of the first edition and two new chapters on treating narcissistic vulnerability in couples and extramarital affairs. Our goal from the outset was to maintain the integrity of the first edition because it proved to be such a successful and well-received volume. The goal was to provide the reader with an easy to use guidebook for working with couples without presenting too much theory, supporting research, or jargon. We wanted to provide clinicians at all levels who are learning to work with couples easily digested principles and techniques that would be effective. Among our colleagues, there is consensus that working with couples, as opposed to individuals or families, is the most challenging therapeutic modality. There are many pitfalls in getting started and finding a position of strategic neutrality, as we reviewed early in the text.

Throughout the text, we have referred to five other texts published by the senior author on couples therapy. These texts cover the spectrum of issues related to couples including theory, research, technique, case studies, and treatment of common problems presented by couples. No single text on couple therapy could cover all the areas needing in-depth attention. The present text is the core text of the series. After reading this text, the reader may refer to one or more of the other volumes to fill the gaps that exist in this basic book.

Before concluding, we should also note how the field has changed in the past several years. Managed care has penetrated the market much more than it had when the first edition appeared. Of course, managed care providers are under pressure to do the therapy as quickly as possible and to solve the presenting problems. The material in this text can be used in a brief problem-focused format. It can also be used over a much longer course of therapy that initially focuses on problem remediation and later on helping the couple achieve optimal health and intimacy. In addition, couple therapy is a unique niche in the field of psychotherapy.

Many of the couple therapists we know have escaped the bounds and confines of managed care by specializing in couple work. We believe both the therapist and the couple benefit when the therapy is provided outside the managed care context. Couples we treat often comment that they leave couple therapy having received much more than they had initially expected. They enter therapy simply wanting to repair a broken relationship, and they leave with a renewed sense of love. This is love in the sense of understanding what it means to have a healthy loving relationship, having the skills to remove the barriers and problems that had prevented them from being able to be loved and to express love before. What could be more gratifying for a therapist than to be a part of helping a couple achieve this level of understanding and fulfillment?

REFERENCES

Abramson, L. Y., & Alloy, L. B. (1981). Depression, nondepression, and cognitive illusions: Reply to Schwartz. *Journal of Experimental Psychology: General, 110,* 436–447.

Abroms, M. (1981). Family therapy in a biomedical context. *Journal of Marital and Family Therapy, 7,* 385–390.

Akillas, E., & Efran, J. (1995). Symptom prescription and reframing: Should they be combined? *Cognitive Therapy and Research, 19,* 263–279.

Alberti, R. E., & Emmons, M. L. (1983). *Your perfect right: A guide to assertive living.* San Luis Obispo, CA: Impact Publishers.

Alexander, J., & Parsons, B. (1982). *Functional family therapy.* Monterey, CA: Brooks, Cole.

Alloy, L. B., & Abramson, L. Y. (1979). Judgment of contingency in depressed and nondepressed students: Sadder but wiser? *Journal of Experimental Psychology: General, 108,* 441–485.

American Psychiatric Association. (1987). *Diagnostic and statistical manual of mental disorders, third edition, revised.* Washington, DC: Author.

Andolfi, M. (1979). Redefinition in family therapy. *American Journal of Family Therapy, 7,* 5–15.

Andolfi, M. (1980). *Family therapy: An interactional approach.* New York: Plenum Press.

Aponte, H., & Van Deusen, J. (1981). Structural family therapy. In A. Gurman & D. Kniskern (Eds.), *Handbook of family therapy,* Vol. I. New York: Brunner/Mazel.

Ascher, L., Bowers, M., & Schotte, M. (1985). A review of data from controlled case studies and experiments evaluating the clinical efficacy of paradoxical intention. In G. Weeks (Ed.), *Promoting change through paradoxical therapy.* Homewood, IL: Dow-Jones & Erwin.

Athanasion, R., Shaver, P., & Travis, C. (1970). Sex. *Psychology Today, 4*(2), 37–52.

Bach, G., & Wyden, P. (1968). *The intimate enemy: How to fight fair in love and marriage.* New York: Morrow.

Bagwell-Reese, M., & Brack, G. (1997). The therapeutic use of reframing and worldview in mental health counseling. *Journal of Mental Health Counseling, 19,* 78–86.

Bandler, R., & Grinder, J. (1990). *The structure of magic.* Palo Alto, CA: Science & Behavior Books.

Bandler, R., & Grinder, J. (1982). *Reframing: Neuro-linguistic programming and the transformation of meaning.* Moab, UT: Real People Press.

Bandura, A. (1977). *Social learning theory.* Englewood Cliffs, NJ: Prentice-Hall.

Bateson, G. (1979). *Mind and nature. A necessary unity.* New York: Bantam.

Baucom, D., & Epstein, N. (1990). *Cognitive-behavioral marital therapy.* New York: Brunner/Mazel.

Baucom, D., Epstein, N., & Rankin, L. (1995). Cognitive aspects of cognitive-behavioral marital therapy. In N. S. Jacobsen & A. S. Gurman (Eds.), *Clinical handbook of couple therapy* (pp. 65-90). New York: Guilford.

266

Baucom, D., Epstein, N., Sayers, S., & Sher, T. G. (1989). The role of cognitions in marital relationships: Definitional, methodological, and conceptual issues. *Journal of Consulting and Clinical Psychology, 57,* 31–38.

Beck, A. (1976). *Cognitive therapy and the emotional disorder.* New York: International Universities Press.

Beck, A. (1988). *Love is never enough.* New York: Harper & Row.

Beck, A. T., Rush, A. J., Shaw, B. F., & Emery, G. (1979). *Cognitive therapy of depression.* New York: Guilford.

Beck, J., & Strong, S. (1982). Stimulating therapeutic change with interpretations: A comparison of positive and negative connotation. *Journal of Counseling Psychology, 29,* 551–559.

Becvar, D., & Becvar, R. (1993). *Family therapy: A systemic integration.* Boston: Allyn & Bacon.

Beisser, A. (1979). The paradoxical theory of change. In J. Fagan & I. Shepherd (Eds.), *Gestalt therapy now* (pp. 110–116). New York: Harper & Row.

Berkowitz, L. (1993). *Aggression: Its causes, consequences, and control.* New York: McGraw-Hill.

Berman, E. (1982). The individual interview as a treatment technique in conjoint therapy. *The American Journal of Family Therapy, 10,* 27–37.

Berman, E., Lief, H., & Williams, A. (1981). A model of marital interaction. In M. Scholevar (Ed.), *The handbook of marriage and marital therapy* (pp. 3–34). New York: S. P. Medical and Scientific Books.

Berman, E., & Hof, L. (1987). The sexual genogram—missing family-of-orgin perform in treatment of sexual function. In G. Weeks & L. Hof (Eds.), *Projection, sex & marriage in therapy.* New York: Brunner/Mazel.

Bernal, G., & Barker, J. (1979). Toward a metacommunication framework of couples intervention. *Family Process, 18,* 293–302.

Berry, D. S., & Pennebaker, J. W. (1993) Nonverbal and verbal emotional expression and health. *Psychotherapy Psychosomatics, 59*(1), 11-19.

Betzig, L. (1989). Causes of conjugal dissolution: A cross-cultural study. *Current Anthropology, 30,* 654-676.

Bowen, M. (1972). The use of theory in clinical practice. In J. Haley (Ed.), *Changing families* (pp. 159–192). New York: Grune & Stratton.

Bowen, M. (1976). Theory and practice in psychotherapy. In P. Muerin (Ed.), *Family Therapy: Theory and practice* (pp. 42–90). New York: Gardner Press.

Bowen, M. (1978). *Family theory in clinical practice.* New York: Jason Aronson.

Brown, E. (1991). *Patterns of infidelity and their treatment.* New York: Brunner/Mazel.

Bugental, J. (1987). *The art of psychotherapy.* New York: Norton.

Bulman, R. J., & Wortman, C. B. (1977). Attributions of blame and coping in the "real world": Severe accident victims react to their lot. *Journal of Personality and Social Psychology, 35,* 351–363.

Burns, D. (1980/1997). *Feeling good: The new mood therapy.* New York: Signet.

Burton, A. (Ed.). (1976). *What makes behavioral change possible.* New York: Brunner/Mazel.

Carnes, P. (1983). *Out of the shadows: Understanding sexual addiction.* Minneapolis, MN: Compcare Publications.

Charny, I. W. (1992). Catering and not catering affairs: The proper and improper pursuit of extramarital relationships. In I. W. Charny (Ed.), *Existential/dialectical marital therapy* (pp. 220-244). New York: Brunner/Mazel.

Charny, I. W., & Parnass, S. (1995). The impact of extramarital relationships on the continuation of marriages. *Journal of Sex & Martial Therapy, 21*(2), 110–115.

Christensen, A., Jacobson, N., & Babcock, J. (1995). Integrating behavioral couple therapy. In N. Jacobson & A. Gurman (Eds.), *Clinical handbook of couple therapy* (pp.31–64). New York: Guilford.

Clark-Stager, W. (1999). Using solution-focused therapy within an integrative framework: An integrative model. *Journal of Family Psychotherapy, 10*, 27–47.

Conoley, C., & Garber, R. (1985). Effects of reframing and self-control directives on loneliness, depression, and controllability. *Journal of Counseling Psychology, 32*, 139–142.

Crowe, M., & Ridley, J. (1990). *Therapy with couples: A behavioural-systems approach.* Oxford: Blackwell Scientific.

Dattilio, F. M. (1993). Cognitive techniques with couples and families. *The Family Journal, 1*(1), 51–65.

Dattilio, F. M. (1994). Families in crisis. In F. M. Dattilio & A. Freeman (Eds.), *Cognitive-behavioral strategies in crisis management* (pp. 278–301). New York: Guilford.

Dattilio, F. M. (1996). *Cognitive therapy with couples: The initial phase of treatment* [Videotape]. Sarasota, FL: Professional Resource Exchange.

Dattilio, F. M. (1998a). Cognitive-behavioral family therapy. In F. M. Dattilio (Ed.), *Case studies in couple and family therapy. Systemic and cognitive perspectives* (pp. 62–84). New York: Guilford.

Dattilio, F. M. (1998b). Finding the fit between cognitive-behavioral and family therapy. *The Family Therapy Networker, 22*(4), 63–73.

Dattilio, F. (1998). *Case studies in couple and family therapy. Systemic and cognitive perspectives.* New York: Guilford.

Dattilio, F. M., Epstein, N. B., & Baucom, D. H. (1998). An introduction to cognitive-behavioral therapy with couples and families. In F. M. Dattilio (Ed.), *Case studies in couple and family therapy. Systemic and cognitive perspectives* (pp. 1–36). New York: Guilford.

Dattilio, F. M., & Padesky, C. A. (1990). *Cognitive therapy with couples.* Sarasota, FL: Professional Resource Exchange.

Davidson, G., & Horvath, A. (1997). Three sessions of brief couples therapy: A clinical trial. *Journal of Family Psychology, 11*, 422–435.

Dayringer, R. (1976). Fair-fight for change: A therapeutic use of aggressiveness in couple counseling. *Journal of Marriage and Family Counseling, 2*, 115–130.

DeMaria, R., Weeks, G., & Hof, L. (1999). *Focused genograms: Intergenerational assessment of individuals, couples, and families.* New York: Brunner/Mazel.

Denton, W. H., Burleson, B. R., Clark, T. E., Rodriguez, C. P., & Hobbs, B. V. (2000). A randomized trial of emotion-focused therapy for couples in a treatment clinic. *Journal of Marital and Family Therapy, 26*(1), 65–78.

Doherty, W. J. (1981a). Cognitive processes in intimate conflict: I. Extending attribution theory. *American Journal of Family Therapy, 9*(1), 3–13.

Doherty, W. J. (1981b). Cognitive processes in intimate conflict: II. Efficacy and learned helplessness. *American Journal of Family Therapy, 9*(2), 35–44.

Doherty, W., Colangelo, N., Green, A., & Hoffman, G. (1985). Emphases of the major family therapy models: A family FIRO analysis. *Journal of Marital and Family Therapy, 11*, 299–303.

Dryden, W. (1990). *Dealing with anger problems: Rational-emotive therapeutic interventions.* Sarasota, FL: Practitioner's Resource Exchange.

Duhl, J., & Duhl, P. (1981). Integrative family therapy. In A. Gurman & D. Kniskern (Eds.), *Handbook of family therapy,* Vol. I (pp. 483–516). New York: Brunner/Mazel.

Ellis, A. (1962). *Reason and emotion in psychotherapy.* New York: Lyle Stuart.

Ellis, A. (1973). *Humanistic Psychotherapy.* New York: McGraw-Hill.

Ellis, A. (1976). Techniques of handling anger in marriage. *Journal of Marriage and Family Counseling, 2*, 305–315.

Ellis, A. (1977). *Anger: How to live with it and without it.* New York: Citadel.

Ellis, A. (1987). The impossibility of achieving consistently good mental health. *American Psychologist, 42*, 364–375.

Ellis, A. (1995). Rational-emotive behavior therapy. In R. J. Corsini & D. Wedding (Eds.), *Current psychotherapies* (5th ed.), (pp. 162-196). Itasca, IL: F. E. Peacock.

Ellis, A., & Harper, R. (1961a). *A guide to rational living.* North Hollywood, CA: Wilshire Books.

Ellis, A., & Harper, R. (1961b). *A guide to successful marriage.* North Hollywood, CA: Wilshire Books.

Ellis, A., Sichel, J. L., Yeager, R. J., DiMattia, D. J., & DiGiuseppe, R. (1989). *Rational emotive couples therapy: Psychology practitioner guidebook.* New York: Pergamon.

Epstein, N. (1982). Cognitive therapy with couples. *The American Journal of Family Therapy, 10,* 5–16.

Epstein, N. (1986). Cognitive marital therapy: A multilevel assessment & intervention. *Journal of Rational Emotive Therapy, 4,* 68–81.

Epstein, N. B., & Baucom, D. H. (1993). Cognitive factors in marital disturbance. In K. S. Dobson & P. C. Kendall (Eds.), *Psychopathology and cognition* (pp. 351–385). San Diego: Academic Press.

Epstein, N., & Baucom, D. (1998). Cognitive-behavioral couple therapy. In F. M. Dattilio (Ed.), *Case studies in couple and family therapy. Systemic and cognitive perspectives* (pp. 37–61). New York: Guilford.

Feldman, L. (1982). Dysfunctional marital conflict: An integrative interpersonal-intrapsychic model. *Journal of Marital and Family Therapy, 8,* 417–428.

Feldman, D., Strong, S., & Danser. D. (1982). A comparison of paradoxical and nonparadoxical interpretations and directives. *Journal of Counseling Psychology, 29,* 572–579.

Fincham, F. D., & Bradbury, T. N. (1993). Marital satisfaction, depression, and attributions: A longitudinal analysis. *Journal of Personality and Social Psychology, 64,* 442–452.

Fincham, F. D., Bradbury, T. N., & Scott, C. K. (1990). Cognition in marriage. In F. D. Fincham & T. N. Bradbury (Eds.), *The psychology of marriage* (pp. 118–149). New York: Guilford.

Firestone. R. W., & Catlett, J. (1999). *Fear of intimacy.* Washington, DC: American Psychological Association.

Fisher, R., & Ury, W. (1981). *Getting to yes: Negotiation agreement without giving in.* New York: Penguin.

Fleuridas, C., Nelson, S., & Rosenthal, D. (1986). The evolution of circular questions: Training family therapists. *Journal of Marital and Family Therapy, 12,* 113–128.

Fraser, J. (Ed.). (1984). Special issue on integration/disintegration (special issue). *Journal of Strategic and Systemic Therapies, 3.*

Friedlander, M. L., & Heatherington, L. (1998). Assessing clients' constructions of their problems in family therapy discourse. *Journal of Marital and Family Therapy, 24*(3), 289–304.

Glass, S., & Wright, T. (1992). Justifications for extramarital relationships: The association between attitudes, behaviors, and gender. *The Journal of Sex Research, 29,* 361–387.

Glass, S. P., & Wright, T. L. (1997). Reconstructing marriages after the trauma of infidelity. In K. Hartford & H. Markman (Eds.), *Clinical handbook of marriage and couples interventions* (pp. 471–507). New York: Wiley.

Goleman, D. (1995). *Emotional intelligence: Why it can matter more than IQ.* New York: Bantam Books.

Gordon, L. (1993). *Passage to intimacy.* New York: Simon & Schuster.

Gottman, J. M. (1993/1994). *What predicts divorce?: The relationship between marital processes and marital outcomes.* Hillsdale, NJ: Erlbaum.

Gottman, J. M. (1994). *What predicts divorce? The relationship between marital process and marital outcomes.* Hillsdale, NJ: Erlbaum.

Gottman, J. M., Coan, J., Carrere, S., & Swanson, C. (1998). Predicting marital happiness and stability from newlywed interaction, *Journal of Marriage and Family, 60*(1), 5–22.

Gottman, J. M., & Gottman, J. S. (1999). The marriage survival kit: A research-based marital therapy. In R. Berger & M. T. Hannah (Eds.), *Preventive approaches in couples therapy* (pp. 304–330). New York: Brunner/Mazel.

Green, R., & Kolevzon, M. (1982). Three approaches to family therapy: A study of convergence and divergence. *Journal of Marital and Family Therapy, 8,* 39–50.

Greenberg, L., & Johnson, S. (1986a). Affect in marital therapy. *Journal of Marital and Family Therapy, 12,* 1–10.

Greenberg, L., & Johnson, S. (1986b). When to evoke emotion and why: Process diagnosis in couples therapy. *Journal of Marital and Family Therapy, 12,* 19–23.

Greenberg, L. S., & Johnson, S. M. (1988). *Emotionally focused therapy for couples.* New York: Guilford.

Greenberg, L. S., & Marques, C. M. (1998). Emotions in couples systems. *Journal of Systemic Therapies, 17*(2), 93–107.

Greenberg, L., & Safran, J. (1987). *Emotion in psychotherapy.* New York: Guilford.

Greenwald, A. G. (1980). The totalitarian ego: Fabrication and revision of personal history. *American Psychologist, 35,* 603–618.

Grunbaum, H., & Chasin, R. (1978). Reframing reconsidered: The beneficial effects of a pathological label. *Family Process, 17,* 449–456.

Guerin, P. J., Jr., Fay, L. F., Burden, S. L., & Kautto, J. (1987). *The evaluation and treatment of marital conflict: A four-stage approach.* New York: Basic Books.

Gurman, A. (1992). Integrative marital therapy: A time sensitive model for working with couples. In S. Budman & M. Hoyt (Eds.), *The first session in brief therapy* (pp. 186–203). New York: Guilford.

Gurman, A., & Kniskern, D. (Eds.). (1981a). *Handbook of family therapy,* Vol. 1. New York: Brunner/Mazel.

Gurman, A., & Kniskern, D. (1981b). Family therapy outcome research: Knowns and unknowns. In A. Gurman & D. Kniskern (Eds.), *Handbook of family therapy,* Vol. 1 (pp. 742–776). New York: Brunner/Mazel.

Gurman, A. S., & Kniskern, D. P. (Eds.). (1991). *Handbook of family therapy,* Vol. 2. New York: Brunner/Mazel.

Haley, J. (1973). *Uncommon therapy: The psychiatric techniques of Milton H. Erickson.* New York: Ballantine.

Haley, J. (1976). *Problem-solving therapy.* San Francisco: Jossey-Bass.

Hatcher, C. (1978). Intrapersonal and interpersonal models: Blending gestalt and family therapies. *Journal of Marriage and Family Counseling, 4,* 63–68.

Hatfield, E. (1988). Passionate and companionate and love. In R. J. Sternberg, & M. L. Barnes (Eds.), *The psychology of love* (pp. 191–217). New Haven, CT: Yale University Press.

Heller, J. (1987). A beginner's guide to the first family interview. *American Journal of Family Therapy, 15,* 291–304.

Hendrix, H. (1988). *Getting the love you want.* New York: Holt.

Hickman, W. A., Jr., Protinsky, H. O., & Singh, K. (1997). Increasing marital intimacy: Lessons from marital enrichment. *Contemporary Family Therapy, 19*(4), 581–589.

Hof, L., & Miller, W. R. (1981). *Marriage enrichment: Philosophy, process, program.* Bowie, MD: Robert & Brady Co.

Hoffman, L. (1981). *Foundations of family therapy.* New York: Basic Books.

Humphrey, F. G. (1985, October). *Extramarital affairs and their treatment by AAMFT therapists.* Paper presented at the meeting of the American Association of Marriage and Family Therapy, New York, NY.

Humphrey, F. (1987). Treating extramarital sexual relationships in sex and couples therapy. In G. Weeks & L. Hof (Eds.), *Integrating sex and marital therapy: A clinical guide* (pp. 149–170). New York: Brunner/Mazel.

Humphrey, F. G., & Strong, F. (1976, May). *Treatment of extramarital sexual relationships as reported by clinical members of AAMFC*. Paper presented at the meeting of the Northeastern American Association of Marriage and Family Counselors, Hartford, CT.

Hunt, M. (1974). *Sexual behavior in the 1970's*. Chicago: Playboy Press.

Jacobson, N. (1981). Behavioral marital therapy. In A. Gurman & D Kniskern (Eds.), *Handbook of family therapy*, Vol. I. New York: Brunner/Mazel.

Jacobson, N., & Christensen, A. (1996). *Integrative couple therapy: Promoting acceptance and change*. New York: Norton.

James, M., & Jongeward, J. (1971). *Born to win: Transactional analysis with gestalt experiments*. Reading, MA: Addison-Wesley.

James, W. (1907). *Pragmatism*. New York: World Publishing.

Jessee, E., & L'Abate, L. (1985). Paradoxical treatment of depression in married couples. In L. L'Abate (Ed.), *The handbook of family psychology and therapy* (pp. 1128–1151). Homewood, IL: Dorsey.

Johnson, R. (1970). Extramarital sexual intercourse: A methodological note. *Journal of Sex Research, 19*, 279–282.

Johnson, S. M. (1996). *The practice of emotionally focused marital therapy: Creating connection*. New York: Brunner/Mazel.

Johnson, S. M., & Greenberg, L. S. (1994). Emotion in intimate relationships: Theory and implications for therapy. In S. M. Johnson & L. S. Greenberg (Eds.), *The Heart of the Matter: perspectives on emotion in marital therapy* (pp. 3–26). New York: Brunner/Mazel.

Johnson, S. M., & Greenberg, L. S. (1995). The emotionally focused approach to problems in adult attachment. In N. S. Jacobson & A. S. Gurman (Eds.), *Clinical handbook of couple therapy* (pp. 121–141). New York: Guilford.

Johnson, S., & Lebow, J. (2000). The "coming of age" of couple therapy: A decade review. *Journal of Marital and Family Research, 26*, 23–38.

Jones, W. (1986). Frame cultivation: Helping new meanings take root in families. *American Journal of Family Therapy, 14*, 57–68.

Karpel, M. A. (1980). Family secrets: I. Conceptual and ethical issues in the relational context II. Ethical and practical considerations in therapeutic management. *Family Process, 19*, 295–306.

Kaslow, F. (1981). A diaclectic approach to family therapy and practice: Selectivity and synthesis. *Journal of Marital and Family Therapy, 7*, 345–351.

Kassinove, H. (1995). *Anger disorders: Definition, diagnosis, and treatment*. Washington, DC: Taylor & Francis.

Kelly, E. L., & Conley, J. J. (1987). Personality and compatibility: A prospective analysis of marital stability and marital satisfaction. *Journal of Personality and Social Psychology, 52*, 27–40.

Kelly, G. (1955). *The psychology of personal constructs, Vol. I, A history of personality*. New York: Norton.

Kelly, H. (1973). Commitment. In H. Kelley et al. (Eds.), *Close relationships* (pp. 287–311). New York: Freeman.

Kelley, H. (1983). Love & commitment. In H. Kelley et al. (Eds.), *Close relationships*. New York: Freeman.

Kerr, M. (1981). Family systems: Theory and practice. In A. Gurman & D. Kniskern (Eds.), *Handbook of family therapy*, vol. l. (pp. 226–266). New York: Brunner/Mazel.

Kinsey, A. C., Pomeroy, W. B., & Martin, C. E. (1948). *Sexual behavior in the human male*. Philadelphia: W. B. Saunders.

Kinsey, A. C., Pomeroy, W. B., Martin, C. E., & Gebhard, P. H. (1953). *Sexual behavior in the human female*. Philadelphia: W. B. Saunders.

Kraft, R., Claiborn, C., & Dowd, E. (1995). Effects of positive reframing and paradoxical directives in counseling for negative emotions. *Journal of Counseling Psychology, 32*, 617–621.

L'Abate, L. (1975). A positive approach to marital and family intervention. In L. Wolberg & M. Aronson (Eds.), *Group therapy 1975—An overview*. New York: Stratton.

L'Abate, L. (1977). *Enrichment: Structural interventions with couples, families and groups*. Washington, DC: University Press of America.

L'Abate, L. (1986). *Systematic family therapy*. New York: Brunner/Mazel.

L'Abate, L. (1992). *Programmed writing. A self-administered approach for interventions with individuals, couples, and families*. Pacific Grove, CA: Brooks/Cole.

L'Abate, L. (1999). Taking the bull by the horns: Beyond talk in psychological interventions. *The Family Journal: Counseling and Therapy for Couples and Families, 7*(3), 206–220.

L'Abate, L. (1999). Increasing intimacy in couples through distance writing and face-to-face approaches. In J. Carlson & L. Sperry (Eds.), *The intimate couple* (pp. 328–340). Philadelphia: Brunner/Mazel.

L'Abate, L., (Ed.). (1975). *Enrichment programs for the family life cycle*. Atlanta, GA: Social Research Laboratories.

L'Abate, L., Ganahl, G., & Hansen, J. (1986). *Methods of family therapy*. Englewood Cliffs, NJ: Prentice Hall.

L'Abate, L., & L'Abate, B. (1977). *Help for troubled marriages*. Atlanta, GA: John Knox.

L'Abate, L., & McHenry, S. (1983). *Handbook of marital interventions*. New York: Grune & Stratton.

L'Abate, L., & Samples, G. (1983). Intimacy letters: Invariable prescriptions for closeness-avoidant couples. *Family Therapy, 10*, 37–45.

Lawrence, E., Eldridge, K., Christensen, A., & Jacobson, N. (1999). Integrative couple therapy: The dyadic relationship of acceptance and change. In J. Donovan (Ed.), *Short-term couple therapy. The Guilford family therapy series* (pp. 226–261). New York: Guilford.

Lazarus, R. (1991). *Emotion and adaptation*. New York: Oxford.

Lazarus, R. S. (1983). The costs and benefits of denial. In S. Breznitz (Ed.), *Denial of stress*. New York: International Universities Press.

Lebow, J. (1984). On the nature of integrating approaches to family therapy. *Journal of Marital and Family Therapy, 10*, 127–138.

Lerner, H. G. (1989). *The dance of anger*. New York: Harper/Collins.

Lerner, H. (1997). *The dance of anger: A woman's guide to changing the patterns of intimate relationships* (Rev. ed.). New York: Harper/Collins.

Levant, R. (1984). *Family therapy: A comprehensive overview*. Englewood Cliffs, NJ: Prentice Hall.

Lewinsohn, P. M., Mischel, W., Chaplin, W., & Barton, R. (1980). Social competence and depression: The role of illusory self-perceptions. *Journal of Abnormal Psychology, 89*, 203–212.

Levinger, G. (1976). A social psychological perspective on marital dissolution. *Journal of Social Issues, 32*, 21–47.

Lusterman, D. (1998). *Infidelity: A survival guide*. Oakland, CA: New Harbinger.

Mack, R. (1989). Spouse abuse—A dyadic approach. In G. Weeks (Ed.), *Treating couples: The intersystem model of the Marriage Council of Philadelphia* (pp.191–214). New York: Brunner/Mazel.

Maykovich, M. D. (1976). Attitudes versus behavior in extramarital sexual relations. *Journal of Marriage and the Family, 38*, 633–699.

McCullough, M. E., Worthington, E. L., Jr., & Rachal, K. C. (1997). Interpersonal forgiving in close relationships. *Journal of Personality and Social Psychology, 73*, 321–336.

McGoldrick, M., & Gerson, R. (1985). *Genograms in family assessment*. New York: Norton.

Miller, D. T., & Ross, M. (1975). Self-serving biases in the attribution of causality: Fact or fiction? *Psychological Bulletin, 82*, 213–225.

Millon, T. (1981). *Disorders of personality: DSM-III, Axis II*. New York: Wiley.

Millon, T. (1999). *Personality-guided therapy*. New York: Wiley.

Milliner, C. B., Grinder, J., & Bretto, D. C. (2000). *Leaves before the wind: Leading edge applications of NLP*. Portland, OR: Metamorphosis Press.

Minuchin, S. (1974). *Families and family therapy*. Cambridge, MA: Harvard University Press.

Minuchin, S., & Fishman, H. (1981). *Family therapy techniques*. Cambridge, MA: Harvard University Press.

Minuchin, S. L., & Lee, W., & Simon, G. M. (1996). *Mastering family therapy: Journeys of growth and transformation*. New York: Wiley.

Morris, S., Alexander, J., & Turner, C. (1991). Do reattributions of delinquent behavior reduce blame? *Journal of Family Psychology, 5*, 192–203.

Napier, A. (1978). The rejection-intrusion pattern: A central family dynamic. *Journal of Marriage & Family Counseling, 4*, 5–12.

Napier, A. (1990). *The fragile bond*. New York: Harper & Row.

Nichols, M. (1984). *Family therapy: Concepts and methods*. New York: Marber Press.

Nichols, M. (1998). *Family therapy*. New York: Gardner Press.

Nichols, W. C., & Napier, A. Y. (1996). *Treating people in families: An integrative framework (Guilford Family Therapy Series)*. New York: Guilford Press.

Nichols, M., & Schwartz, R. (1998). *Family therapy: Concepts and methods*. Boston: Allyn & Bacon.

Odell, M., & Quinn, W. H. (1998). Therapist and client behaviors in the first interview: Effects on session impact and treatment duration. *Journal of Marital and Family Therapy, 24*(3), 369–388.

O'Leary, K., & Turkewitz, H. (1978). Marital therapy from a behavioral perspective. In T. Paolino & B. McCrady (Eds.), *Marriage & marital therapy* (pp. 260–297). New York: Brunner/Mazel.

Openshaw, D. K. (1998). Increasing homework compliance. *Journal of Family Psychotherapy, 9*(3), 21–29.

Palazzoli, M., Boscolo, L., Cecchin, M., & Prata, G. (1978). *Paradox and counterparadox*. New York: Aronson.

Paolino, Jr., T., & McCrady, B. (Eds.). (1978). *Marriage and marital therapy*. New York: Brunner/Mazel.

Penn, P. (1982). Circular questioning. *Family Process, 12*, 267–279.

Penn, C. D., Hernandez, S. L., & Bermudez, J. M. (1997). Using a cross-cultural perspective to understand infidelity in couples therapy. *The American Journal of Family Therapy, 25*(2), 169–185.

Pennebaker, J. W. (1997). Writing about emotional experiences as a therapeutic process. *Psychological Science, 8*(3), 162–166.

Pierce, R., Nichols, M., & DuBrin, J. (1983). *Emotional expression in psychotherapy*. New York: Gardner Press.

Pittman, F. (1987). *Private lies*. New York: Norton.

Prager, K. J. (1995). *The psychology of intimacy*. New York: Guilford.

Praser, K. (1995). *The psychology of intimacy*. New York: Guilford.

Prochaska, J., & DiClemente, C. (1988). *The transtheoretical approach to therapy*. Chicago: Dorsey.

Prochaska, J., DiClemente, C., & Norcross, J. (1992). In search of how people change: Application to addictive behaviors. *American Psychologist, 47*(9), 1102–1115.

Protinsky, H., & Quinn, W. (1981). Paradoxical marital therapy with symptom triangulation. *Family Therapy, 8*, 136–140.

Rubin, Z. (1973). *Liking and loving.* New York: Holt, Rhinehart, & Winston.

Sager, C. (1976). *Marriage contracts and couples therapy.* New York: Brunner/Mazel.

Sager, C., & Hunt, B. (1979). *Intimate partners.* New York: McGraw-Hill.

Satir, V. (1967). *Conjoint family therapy.* Palo Alto, CA: Science & Behavioral Books.

Schachter, S., & Singer, J. E. (1962). Cognitive, social and physiological determinants of emotional state. *Psychological Review, 69,* 379–399.

Schaefer, M., & Olson, D. (1981). Assessment of intimacy: The PAIR inventory. *Journal of Marital and Family Therapy, 7,* 47–60.

Scharff, D., & Scharff, J. (1987). *Object relations family therapy.* New York: Aronson.

Scharff, D. E., & Scharff, J. S. (1991). *Object relations family therapy.* New York: Aronson.

Scharff, D., & Scharff, J. (1995). *Object relations couple therapy.* New York: Aronson.

Sheldon, J., & Ackerman, J. (1974). *Homework in counseling and psychotherapy.* Springfield, IL: Charles C. Thomas.

Sherwood, J. J., & Scherer, J. J. (1975). A model for couples: How two can grow together. *Small Group Behavior, 6*(1), 11–29.

Sloan, S., & L'Abate, L. (1985). Intimacy. In L. L'Abate (Ed.), *Handbook of family psychology therapy* (pp. 405–431). Homewood, IL: Dorsey.

Stanley, S. M., Blumberg, S. L., & Markman, H. J. (1999). Helping couples fight for their marriages: The PREP approach. In R. Berger & M. T. Hannah (Eds.), *Preventive approaches in couples therapy* (pp. 279–303). New York: Brunner/Mazel.

Stanton, M. (1981). An integrative structural/strategic approach to family therapy. *Journal of Marital and Family Therapy, 7,* 427–439.

Stanton, M., Todd, T., & Associates. (1982). *The family therapy of drug addiction.* New York: Guilford.

Sternberg, R. (1986a). A triangular theory of love. *Psychological Review, 93*(2), 119-135.

Sternberg, R. (1986b). Love, sex, & intimacy. *Psychological Review, 93,* 119-135.

Sternberg, R. J. (1988). Triangulating love. In R. J. Sternberg & M. L. Barnes (Eds.), *The psychology of love* (pp. 119–138). New Haven, CT: Yale University Press.

Sternberg, R. (1997). Construct validation of a triangular love scale. *European Journal of Social Psychology, 27,* 313–335.

Steinberg, R. (1999). *Love is a story: A new theory of relationships.* Oxford: Oxford University Press.

Strong, S., & Claiborn, C. (1982). *Change through interaction: Social psychological processes of counseling and psychotherapy.* New York: Wiley.

Stuart, R. (1980). *Helping couples change.* New York: Guilford.

Swoboda, J., Dowd, E., & Wise, S. (1990). Reframing and restraining directives in the treatment of clinical depression. *Journal of Counseling Psychology, 37,* 254–260.

Taylor, S. E. (1983). Adjustment to threatening events. *American Psychologist, 38,* 1161–1173.

Tennen, H., Affleck, G., Allen, D. A., McGrade, B. J., & Ratzan, S. (in press). Causal attributions and coping with insulin-dependent diabetes. *Basic and Applied Social Psychology.*

Tennen, H., Eron, J., & Rohrbaugh, M. (1985). Paradox in context. In G. Weeks (Ed.), *Promoting change through paradoxical therapy* (pp. 187–215). Homewood, IL: Dow Jones-Irwin.

Tennen, H., Eron, J., & Rohrbaugh, M. (1991). Paradox in context. In G. Weeks (Rev. ed.), *Promoting change through paradoxical therapy* (pp. 187–214). New York: Brunner/Mazel.

Tennen, H., & Herzberger, S. (2000). *Depression, self-esteem, and the absence of self-protective attributional biases.* Manuscript submitted for publication.

Thompson, A. P. (1983). Extramarital sex: A review of the research literature. *The Journal of Sex Research, 19,* 1–22.

Thompson, A. P. (1984). Emotional and sexual components of extramarital relations. *Journal of Marriage and the Family, 46,* 35–42.

Tiger, L. (1979). *Optimism: The biology of hope*. New York: Simon & Schuster.

Turner, M. (1995). Addictions in marital relationship therapy. In G. Weeks & L. Hof (Eds.), *Interpretive solutions* (pp. 124–147). New York: Brunner/Mazel.

Turner, N. W. (1982). Conflict utilization in marital-dyadic therapy. *Psychiatric Clinics of North American, 5*(3), 503–518.

Ury, W. (1991). *Getting past no: Negotiating your way from confrontation to cooperation*. New York: Bantam.

Viaro, M. (1980). Case report: Smuggling family therapy through. *Family Process, 19,* 35–44.

Wachtel, E., & Wachtel, P. (1986). *Family dynamics in individual psychotherapy*. New York: Guilford.

Warburton, J., & Alexander, J. (1985). The family therapist: What does one do? In L. L'Abate (Ed.), *The handbook of family psychology and therapy,* Vol. II (pp. 1318–1343). Homewood, IL: Dorsey.

Watzlawick, P., Beavin, J., & Jackson, D. (1967). *Pragmatics of human communication*. New York: Norton.

Watzlawick, P, Weakland, J., & Fisch, R. (1974). *Change: Principles of problem formation and problem resolution*. New York: Norton.

Watzlawick, P, Weakland, J., & Fisch, R. (1988). *Change: Principles of problem formation and problem resolution* (Rev. ed.). New York: Norton.

Weber, T., McKeever, J., & McDaniel, S. (1985). A beginner's guide to the problem-oriented first family interview. *Family Process, 24,* 357–364.

Weeks, G. (1977). Toward a dialectical approach to intervention. *Human Development, 20,* 277–292.

Weeks, G. (1986). Individual-system dialectic. *American Journal of Family Therapy, 14,* 5–12.

Weeks, G. (1989b). An intersystem approach to treatment. In G. Weeks (Ed.), *Treating couples: The intersystem model of the Marriage Council of Philadelphia* (pp. 317–340). New York: Brunner/Mazel.

Weeks, G. R. (Ed.). (1989a). *Treating couples: The intersystem model of The Marriage Council of Philadelphia*. New York: Brunner/Mazel.

Weeks, G. (1989b). An intersystem approach to treatment. In G. Weeks (Ed.), *Treating couples: The intersystem model of the Marriage Council of Philadelphia* (pp. 317–340). New York: Brunner/Mazel.

Weeks, G. (1990). Paradox. In J. Zeig & W Munion (Eds.), *What is psychotherapy?* (pp. 262–265). San Francisco: Jossey-Bass.

Weeks, G. (1991). (Ed.). *Promoting change through paradoxical therapy*. New York: Brunner/Mazel.

Weeks, G. R. (1994). The intersystem model: An integrative approach to treatment. In G. R. Weeks & L. Hof (Eds.), *The marital relationship therapy casebook: Theory and application of the intersystem model* (pp. 3–34). New York: Brunner/Mazel.

Weeks, G. R. (1995). Commitment and intimacy. In G. R. Weeks & L. Hof (Eds.), *Integrative solutions: Treating common problems in couples therapy* (pp. 21–54). New York: Brunner/Mazel.

Weeks, G., & Hof, L. (Eds.). (1987). *Integrating sex and marital therapy*. New York: Brunner/Mazel.

Weeks, G., & Hof, L. (Eds.). (1994) *The marital-relationship therapy casebook: Theory and application of the intersystem model*. New York: Brunner/Mazel.

Weeks, G. R., & Hof, L. (1995). *Integrative solutions: Treating common problems in couples therapy*. New York: Brunner/Mazel.

Weeks, G., & L'Abate, L. (1982). *Paradoxical psychotherapy: Theory and practice with individuals, couples, and families*. New York: Brunner/Mazel.

Weiss, R., & Heyman, R. (1990). Observation of marriage interaction. In F. D. Fincham & R. Bradbury (Eds.), *Psychology of marriage* (pp. 87–117). New York: Guilford.

Weiss, R., Hops, H., & Patterson, G. (1973). A framework for conceptualizing marital conflict: A technology for altering it, some data for evaluating it. In L. Hamerlynck, L. Handy, & E. Mash (Eds.), *Behavior change: Methodology, concepts, and practice.* Champaign, IL: Research Press.

Westfall, A. (1989). Extramarital sex: The treatment of the couple. In G. R. Weeks (Ed.), *Treating couples: The intersystem model of The Marriage Council of Philadelphia* (pp. 163–190). New York: Brunner/Mazel.

Westfall, A. (1995). Working through the extramarital trauma: An exploration of common themes. In G. R. Weeks & L. Hof (Eds.), *Integrative solutions: Treating common problems in couples therapy* (pp. 148–194). New York: Brunner/Mazel.

Whisman, M. A., Dixon, A. E., & Johnson, B. (1997). Therapist's perspectives of couple problems and treatment issues in couple therapy. *Journal of Family Psychology, 11*(3), 361–366.

Wiederman, M. W. (1997). Extramarital sex: Prevalence and correlates in a national survey. *The Journal of Sex Research, 34*(2), 167–174.

Worthington, E. L., Jr. (1998). The pyramid model of forgiveness: Some interdisciplinary speculations about unforgiveness and the promotion of forgiveness. In E. L. Worthington, Jr. (Ed.), *Dimensions of forgiveness: Psychological research and theological perspectives* (pp. 107–137). Philadelphia: Templeton Foundation.

Worthington, E. L., Jr., & Drinkard, D. T. (2000). Promoting reconciliation through psychoeducation and therapeutic interventions. *Journal of Marital and Family Therapy, 26*(1), 93–101.

Yablonsky, L. (1979). *The extra-sex factor: Why over half of America's married men play around.* New York: Times Books.

Young, M., & Long, L. (1998). *Counseling and therapy for couples.* Pacific Grove, CA: Brooks/Cole.

INDEX

Note: Page numbers in italics refer to charts.

ABOUT THE AUTHORS

Gerald R. Weeks, Ph.D., APBB, is Chair of the Department of Counseling at the University of Nevada, Las Vegas, where he is also Professor. He is the former Director of Training at the Penn Council for Relationships/Division of Family Study at the University of Pennsylvania. Dr. Weeks is a Fellow and Approved Supervisor of the American Association of Marriage and Family Therapy and holds Diplomates from the American Board of Professional Psychology and the American Board of Sexology. He is the author of numerous articles and more than a dozen professional books, including *Focused Genograms* and *Erectile Dysfunction*. Dr. Weeks lectures nationally and internationally with some of his books appearing in several languages.

Stephen R. Treat, D. Min., is Director and CEO of the PennCouncil for Relationships and an Instructor in Psychiatry and Human Behavior at Jefferson Medical College, both in Philadelphia, Pennsylvania. Author of two books and numerous chapters and articles on marital and family therapy, Dr. Treat has also been the keynote speaker at many conferences on topics including fathers and sons, marital therapy, and spirituality. He is a Clinical Member and Approved Supervisor in the American Association for Marriage and Family Therapy, a member of the American Association of Pastoral Counseling and the American Family Therapy Association.